D0819647

WESTERN PHILOSOPHY

AN ILLUSTRATED GUIDE

WESTERN PHILOSOPHY

AN ILLUSTRATED GUIDE

GENERAL EDITOR: DAVID PAPINEAU

DUNCAN BAIRD PUBLISHERS
LONDON

Contents

Western Philosophy
General Editor: Professor David Papineau

First published in the United Kingdom and Ireland
in 2004 by
Duncan Baird Publishers Ltd
Sixth Floor
Castle House
75–76 Wells Street
London W1T 3QH

Conceived, created and designed by
Duncan Baird Publishers

Managing Editors: Susan Watt and Christopher Westhorp
Senior Text Editors: Peter Bently and Susan Watt
Editorial assistance: James Hodgson
Picture Editor: Julia Ruxton
Designer: Paul Reid at Cobalt id

British Library Cataloguing-in-Publication Data:
A CIP record for this book is available from the
British Library

ISBN-13: 978-1-84483-697-0 ISBN-10: 1-84483-697-5

10 9 8 7 6 5 4 3 2 1

Typeset in Ehrhardt 11/14.5pt
Colour reproduction by Colourscan, Singapore
Printed in China by Imago

NOTES
The abbreviations CE and BCE are used throughout this book:
CE Common Era (the equivalent of AD)
BCE Before the Common Era (the equivalent of BC)
Captions to pages 1–3 appear on page 224

Introduction

When he was on trial for his life, charged with corrupting the youth of Athens, Socrates explained why it would be impossible for him to give up philosophy. As Socrates put it, "the unexamined life is not worth living" – from his point of view, a life that was not enriched by philosophical reflection was no better than death. Few people are called to sacrifice everything for philosophy, but even so there are deep reasons why it remains of fundamental importance to everyone. Most obviously, we all need to think about the right way to live. Conventional practices are not automatically the best practices, whether they concern parents and children, rulers and ruled or rich and poor nations. All responsible people need to pause, at least sometimes during their life, to reflect on whether they are really doing the right thing.

However, philosophy is not only important to questions of how we should conduct our lives. Human beings are thinking creatures, for whom pure understanding is an end in itself. Finding out about the origin of the universe, or about the nature of consciousness, may make no difference to the way we behave, but it would run counter to human nature not to pursue such questions. A society in which humans never asked about the fundamental nature of reality would be the poorer for it.

What exactly is the subject matter of philosophy? What makes something a philosophical question, rather than a scientific or political issue? It is doubtful whether there is any definite subject matter that is particular to philosophy. Rather, philosophy is needed whenever we are faced by questions that are not only important but also intellectually perplexing. It is this last requirement that distinguishes philosophy. There are plenty of big unanswered questions in science: Is there life elsewhere in the universe? How many fundamental forces are there? However, these questions lack answers only because we haven't yet amassed enough empirical evidence to reach a conclusion. Philosophical questions raise a different kind of difficulty. When we ask whether humans have free will, or whether animals have moral rights, our puzzlement is not just due to a lack of information. Rather the questions themselves are confusing. To make progress we need to scrutinize the very terms – "free will", "moral rights"– that are used to pose the issues.

Philosophizing can quickly become abstruse. In the pages that follow, there are plenty of familiar issues, such as the justifiability of capital punishment or the existence of a divinity. But there are also more esoteric topics, such as the reality of properties, or the definition of knowledge. Such abstraction is inevitable in philosophy. Once we start to query the terms in which everyday issues are posed, we quickly find ourselves forced to think about the categories we use to make sense of the world.

Philosophy has six chapters, each written by a leading academic expert in the relevant field. The subject ranges too widely for coverage of every possible topic, but this volume discusses all the most important issues in the history of philosophy, and what the great philosophers have said about them. Among the questions addressed are: space, time and the possibility of inifinity; consciousness and its relation to the physical world; whether it is possible to gain objective knowledge; the possibility of an afterlife; the morality of sex and friendship; and concepts of democracy, equality and freedom.

As well as describing theories, this book also seeks to equip the reader with intellectual tools. The chapters that follow will introduce you to distinctive styles of philosophical thinking, and to intellectual techniques that have proved fruitful in the history of philosophy. If this book succeeds, it will not only tell you about what other philosophers have said, but will also enable you to start thinking philosophically yourself.

David Papineau
Professor of Philosophy
King's College, University of London, United Kingdom

A series of frescos based on Platonic and alchemical theories adorn the crypt of Anagni Cathedral in Italy. The frescoes include this macrocosmos that represents various correspondences with the four different ages of man – a work that suggests man questioning the religious orthodoxies of the day and thinking deeply about the world around him.

WORLD

What is reality?

The question of the nature of reality, or being, is one of the most ancient in Western philosophy. But what does it really mean to call something real? And which things should we credit with the most fundamental reality?

In Woody Allen's film *The Purple Rose of Cairo*, the heroine has to choose between two lovers: the actor who plays her favourite character in a romantic movie and the "character" himself – who has jumped out of the screen because of his fascination with the heroine, who goes to see this movie every day. Pleading his case, the character points out that he is handsome, rich, charming and intelligent. The actor counters: "But I'm real!"

> *'Being' is obviously not a real predicate; that is, it is not a concept of something which could be added to the concept of a thing.*
>
> Immanuel Kant, *Critique of Pure Reason*

The joke plays on the absurdity of the idea of choosing between two things, only one of which is real. But why is this idea absurd? Surely the answer is because reality is not a property of things, as being yellow or being heavy is. It makes no sense to say that reality is a property that some things have and some things lack, since the idea of being something carries with it the idea of being real. Likewise, to say something is, or has being, surely implies that it is real. Nothing could have being, unless it were real.

So certainly everything that exists is real – but do all real things exist? Some philosophers have said no to this question, and argued that there are real things that do not exist. For example, there are many characters in Shakespeare who do not exist, never did and never will (for example Othello), as opposed to others who did exist (such as Julius Caesar). But even to say that there "are" such non-existent characters, as we just have, seems to acknowledge that they have some kind of being or reality. Yet if they do, how does Othello's kind of reality differ from Julius Caesar's?

It is tempting to answer that existent things have being in space and time, while non-existent things do not. But this is just another way of saying that some things are "spatio-temporal things", and some are not – just as some things are green and some are not. Real things are of many kinds, and all we have done here is to distinguish between two groups of things; we have not said what it is about some of them that makes them "existent". So the question of what property of existence that Julius Caesar is supposed to have had, and Othello is supposed to lack, remains.

Faced with this difficulty, many philosophers follow Bertrand Russell (1872–1970) and W.V.O. Quine (see p.89) and deny that there is any distinction at all between reality, being and existence. Beings are what exist, or what are, or what is real, or what things are. The three words – being, existence, reality – all express fundamentally the same idea. By this account, there are no things that do not exist, since this is really the same as saying that there are things that there are not, and this is a contradiction.

So Othello does not exist in any sense. Of course the idea of Othello exists – we know what people are talking about when they mention Othello – but this must not be confused with the existence of Othello himself. (Similarly, the question of whether God exists should not be confused with the question of whether the idea of God exists, as theists and atheists can agree that such an idea exists, but differ on whether it corresponds to anything in reality. See also p.108.)

According to Plato, individual things – such as a particular horse – are merely rather poor copies of the abstract, idealized "forms" existing beyond the world of experience.

Substances and attributes

These questions about being and existence belong to the area of philosophy known as ontology, which is the study or theory of being (from the Greek root *ont-*, from *ontos* or "being"). Supposing we agree with Russell and Quine that being and existence are the same thing, then the next ontological question is: are some kinds of beings or existing things more fundamental than others? Ever since Plato and Aristotle, it has been customary in philosophy to distinguish between individual things and their properties or attributes. We can distinguish, for example, between an individual man and his weight, height, hair colour and so on. But which are most fundamentally real: individual things, their attributes – or neither? Plato (see pp.76–79) took the "neither" view. He argued that the fundamentally real things are what he called the "forms": ideal, eternal, unchanging types of things that exist outside the world of experience. Everyday things in the world of experience have a lesser degree of reality: they are real only in so far as they "participate" in the forms.

Aristotle (see pp.13–15) rejected this whole picture, and argued that individual things – which he called "substances" – are the fundamental realities. While Plato's view was that an individual horse depends for its existence and nature on the form of horse, Aristotle held that individuals are basic entities. In his view, substances do not depend on attributes; rather, attributes depend on being possessed by substances – so colours, shapes and sizes cannot exist independently of the things whose colours, shapes and sizes they are. The colour of a particular horse, for example, cannot exist independently of being possessed by the horse or some other substance.

Fundamental reality

This notion of a substance, of something that is the most fundamental kind of being or entity, has dominated philosophy since Aristotle. On this basis, the next ontological question is whether substances are all of the same kind, or if there are fundamentally different kinds of substance. Monists argue that there is only one kind of substance, while dualists argue that there are two (while pluralists argue that there are many kinds.) Among monists we can distinguish between materialists, who believe that all substances are material, or made of matter, and idealists, who believe that all substances are mental (see pp.26–27). Leibniz, Berkeley, Kant and Hegel were all idealists, although in very different ways. Dualists typically hold that the two kinds of substance are the mental and the material. Among

Ontological categories

Ontology, or the theory of being, attempts to impose a fundamental order upon everything that is real or existent. It does this by distinguishing between the most general categories of reality that there are. Of course, there are philosophers who will reject some entities of these kinds (for example, some deny the existence of abstract entities) – but the diagram shows what it is that they are rejecting.

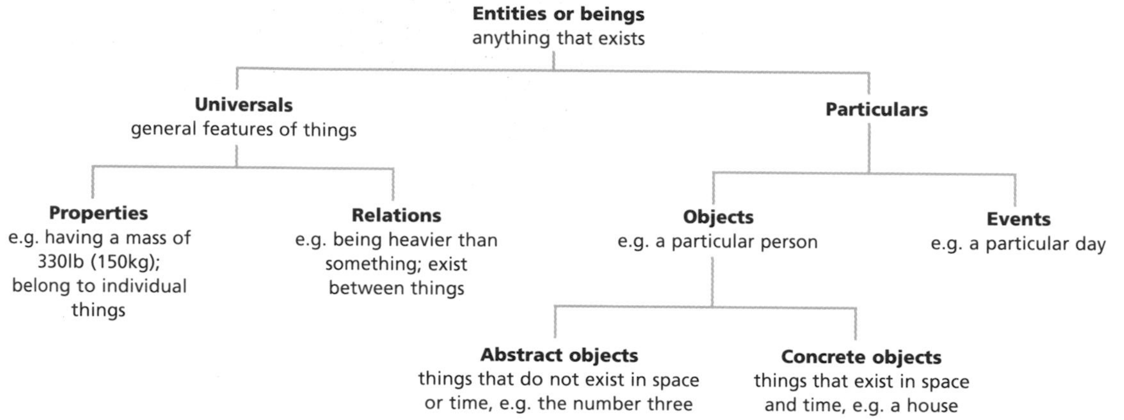

dualists, there are those who think that mental and material substances interact, and those who deny this. René Descartes (see pp.48–49) was the most famous "interactionist" dualist. Today, dualism is widely rejected by philosophers, and a form of materialist monism called physicalism is the norm (see pp.16–17).

Properties and objects

Dualism and monism are theories about substances, or the bearers of properties or attributes. But what about properties themselves? When we say that something has a property – for example, that it has a certain weight – what are we really saying? There are two kinds of answer to this question. The first (favoured by Locke, see pp.82–83) is to say that properties are not real entities in themselves, but are only the results of our classification of objects. By this view, there are no such things as weights: all that exist are objects that we classify as weighing x or y. This view is motivated partly by the unattractiveness of the view that things like weights might be entities – for what kind of entity could "weighing 1oz (28g)" really be? – and partly by the doctrine known as Ockham's razor. This doctrine (named after the medieval philosopher, William of Ockham) asserts that "entities should not be multiplied beyond necessity". In other words, our ontological theorizing should be parsimonious, and we should try to make do with as few kinds of fundamental entity as possible in our theory of the world.

The second kind of answer, which was favoured by Aristotle, says that properties are real entities in their own right. By this view, we will not have listed everything in the world if we only list the individual objects (the particular people, houses, trees and so on); we also need to list their properties. Thus – in contrast to the previous view – weights are real features of things: objects do not have weight because we classify them as having weight; rather, we classify them as having weight because they have weight. Properties such as weight are sometimes called universals, because they are general or universal features of things. Universals are contrasted with particulars, such as individual objects or people (see diagram, above).

Although this Aristotelian idea of a universal can seem somewhat mysterious, it is in a way more plausible than Locke's view because it better explains the fundamentally objective nature of reality and how it is independent of our systems of classification.

Aristotle

Aristotle was born in Stagira in northern Greece in 384BCE. He studied with Plato (see pp.76–79) in the latter's Academy in Athens for 20 years, until Plato's death. He returned to northern Greece in 335BCE to be tutor to Philip II of Macedon's son Alexander (later Alexander the Great). Aristotle returned to Athens in the same year to teach philosophy there, but when Alexander died in 323, Aristotle was charged with "impiety" by the Athenians, who were the enemies of Macedonia. Aristotle escaped but died a year later in 322, aged 62. Unlike many of the great philosophers, Aristotle was married (twice, in fact). By his second wife he had a son, Nicomachus, after whom is named his most famous ethical work, the *Nicomachean Ethics*.

Aristotle 384–322BCE

Probably the greatest philosopher who ever lived, Aristotle has had more influence on the development of Western civilization than any other. It is hard to exaggerate the importance and influence of Aristotle's work, which ranges from logic to science and ethics and even has relevance today.

Aristotle made lasting contributions to all areas of philosophy, including metaphysics, logic, ethics, aesthetics, political philosophy and the philosophy of mind. Some of his works take the form of finished treatises, while others are more like lecture notes or drafts for future work. Although the unfinished nature of Aristotle's texts can make it difficult to summarize his views on some subjects, in the core areas there remains a clear and strong vision of philosophy and the world that deserves the name "Aristotelian".

> *"If the eye were an animal, sight would be its soul, since this is the defining essence of an eye."*
>
> Aristotle, *De Anima*

The *Metaphysics*

In the most famous painting of philosophers, Raphael's *The School of Athens*, Aristotle and Plato are portrayed at the centre of a group of Greek philosophers. Plato's finger points upwards, while Aristotle's hand is held at waist height, stretched out towards the ground. This image symbolically encapsulates the difference between these two philosophers: while Plato took the genuinely real to be outside the world of experience, in the world of the Platonic "forms", Aristotle believed that real things, which he called "substances", are in the world around us. This is why so much of Aristotle's work covers topics that would now be the subject of empirical science – animal biology, the weather, planetary motion and so on. With his commitment to the reality of the ordinary things that we experience and his tireless need to classify, Aristotle was the first great systematic scientist of the Western world.

Aristotle's view that substances are the fundamental realities was put forward in his famous work, the *Metaphysics*. In the *Metaphysics*, Aristotle approaches the question of what it is for anything to be by describing the nature of the most fundamental beings, those he called "substances". The word "substance" has been used in many ways in philosophy, but in its most important use, a substance is an individual particular thing, such as an individual human being, for instance. This use of the term derives from Aristotle. For him, each individual substance is a combination of shapeless "matter" organized by what he called its "form". (Aristotle's view that the forms of things are in the things

Aristotle and medieval philosophy

Aristotle's works were lost in Europe after the end of the Roman Empire. They were rediscovered in the early Middle Ages through their preservation in the Islamic tradition, and the commentaries on them by Islamic philosophers – particularly Avicenna (Ibn Sina, 980–1037) and Averroes (Ibn Rushd, ca.1126–98)). As Aristotle's works gradually become known in the West, Christian philosophers struggled to understand them and reconcile them with Christian doctrine. Since many of these philosophers inhabited the medieval universities or "schools" of Oxford, Paris and Bologna, they have become known as "scholastics". The greatest scholastic philosopher was Thomas Aquinas (see p.112), whose work provided the Christian (and, later, the Roman Catholic) church with its official philosophy – a type of Aristotelianism – that persists even up until the present day.

One pressing problem for scholastic philosophers was how to reconcile Aristotle's theory of the soul with the Christian doctrine of life after death (see also pp.119–120). In Aristotle's view, form and matter are inseparable. Because the soul is the form of the body's matter (see below), there is a problem for the Christian view that, at death, the soul separates from and survives the body. The scholastics responded by emphasizing that souls are re-united with their bodies at the Day of Judgement. However, this does not explain how the souls of the dead can live without their bodies after death but before the Day of Judgement, and the ingenuity of the scholastics was greatly tested by this problem. The solution adopted by many — that the soul acquires a "spiritual body" which it inhabits before the Day of Judgement – would probably have been rejected by Aristotle.

themselves is therefore a major difference between his views and those of Plato. See also p.11.)

For Aristotle, the form of a substance is what makes the substance the thing it is; therefore it is also called the "essence" of the substance. For example, an axe is made up of matter organized in a certain way by its form so that it can be used for chopping; thus *to be used for chopping* is the essence of an axe. If it lost the ability to chop, then it would be an axe "only in name", as Aristotle puts it. The essence of a substance is expressed by its characteristic activity – in this case, by chopping. Further, a substance has this characteristic activity as its goal or purpose. For Aristotle, then, everything real had a purpose. Hence Aristotle's theory of substance, which effectively dominated metaphysics until Descartes' revolutionary ideas of the 17th century (see pp.48–49), is sometimes called a teleological theory: it describes a substance in terms of its characteristic goal, or *telos*.

The soul

Aristotle employed his distinction between form and matter to answer the question of the relation between the soul and the body. His general view was that the soul is the form of the body's matter. But Aristotle's conception of the soul was very different from that which later developed following Descartes' innovations.

For Aristotle, all living things have souls, but these souls are not all of the same kind: the nutritive (or vegetative) soul is responsible for growth and reproduction; the sensitive soul for perception and sensation; and the rational soul for thought and reasoning. Plants have only a nutritive soul, while animals have nutritive and sensitive souls, and humans have these plus the rational soul. These three kinds of soul (or, in humans, the three parts of the soul) can be thought of as the "forms" or governing principles of the characteristic activities of a living thing. It is hard to classify

Aristotle's view of mind and body in terms of the modern distinction between materialism and dualism. On the one hand, the soul has to have a material basis in the body: it is the form of the body's matter. But on the other hand, the soul (or mind) is not to be identified with the matter of the body: Aristotle explained the workings of the body in terms of the soul, and not vice versa.

Logic and the syllogism

Aristotle's systematizing approach extended to reasoning itself. Aristotle was the first philosopher to develop a system for studying the structure of logical reasoning, and for hundreds of years Aristotle's ideas constituted the heart of logic (in the 18th century, Kant remarked that there had been no progress in logic since Aristotle). These days, however, the logical theories of Bertrand Russell and Gottlob Frege (see p.58) are considered to have superseded Aristotle's logic.

One of the best known among Aristotle's many achievements in logic is his discussion of the syllogism, which he defined as "a discourse in which certain things having been stated, something else follows of necessity from their being so". What Aristotle was attempting to do in considering the different styles of syllogism was to classify examples of reasoning by their form alone – that is, without considering the specific content of the words. For example, a syllogism can have the general form:

All As are B
All Bs are C
Therefore: All As are C

Any argument with this general form is correct, because "All As are C" follows no matter what words we substitute for A, B and C. Aristotle thought that any argument where the conclusion follows from the premises can be represented as a syllogism.

However, this is now known to be false: a syllogism in Aristotle's sense can contain only general terms – that is, not specific names for individual things, such as "Aristotle", but only words that apply to many things, like "white". Ironically, perhaps the most famous example of a "syllogism" of all time – "All men are mortal; Socrates is a man; therefore Socrates is mortal" – is not a syllogism in Aristotle's sense at all, since it contains the name "Socrates".

> *"Human good turns out to be activity of soul in accordance with virtue, and if there is more than one virtue, in accordance with the best and most complete."*
>
> Aristotle, *Nicomachean Ethics*

Well-being

Aristotle's philosophy was not just concerned with abstract questions of logic and metaphysics. In his ethical writings, he was also deeply concerned with practical questions about how to live. His ethical theory aims to provide an account of *eudaimonia* – that is, well-being, or "the good life". Aristotle's view was that one should achieve well-being by living life in accordance with the virtues – traits of character such as courage, generosity or humility. Virtues are identified as a "golden mean" located midway between two vices. Thus, courage is located between the two vices of foolhardiness and cowardice; humility between false modesty and boastfulness; and generosity between meanness and profligacy. This attractive conception of the well-lived life does not depend on the particular traits Aristotle took to be virtues: an Aristotelian account of virtue developed in the present day would no doubt take different things to be virtues, but this does not undermine the general account.

Aristotle's political views developed along similar lines to his ethical views. A city-state has as a goal its own well-being. Democracy, Aristotle argued, would be a better way than oligarchy (government by a small elite) to achieve this goal.

Like many of Aristotle's views , these ethical and political ideas have had some echoes and adherents in modern times. However, we should not lose sight of the fact that Aristotle's views were rooted in his own time: it is unlikely that anyone would now endorse Aristotle's view that slavery is justifiable on practical grounds.

The physical world

We are all physical beings, inhabiting a physical world. But what does this world consist of? Is it solely made up of the things we can see and touch; or should everything described by science – and even supernatural entities – also be included?

What is the physical world? In one sense, it is the world of everyday physical objects around us. In a stricter, more scientific sense, it is the world as conceived of by the physical sciences. According to our everyday conception, physical objects or things are material objects: that is, made of matter. But in the stricter scientific conception, physical things need not be made of matter in any ordinary sense. An electric field is not made of matter, nor is a force like gravity; yet these are physical things.

Atoms and molecules form the building blocks of the physical world. But what else does reality contain?

These two understandings of the idea of the physical world correspond to two distinct philosophical doctrines – materialism and physicalism. Materialism, the doctrine that everything is material, goes back (in its broad outlines) to the ancient Greeks, and it became a prominent ontological doctrine in the 17th century. At this time materialist philosophers had a definite conception of what matter was: solid, impenetrable, conserved in interactions, interacting only on contact and deterministically. Gradually, however, physics began to chip away at this philosophical conception of matter. Newton's theory of gravitation destroyed the whole idea that matter must be in contact to interact, because gravity acts between bodies as widely separated as the earth and the sun. By the 20th century, physics had established a theory of matter according to which it is not solid (consisting at the atomic level of widely separated particles vibrating in empty space), not impenetrable (it can be penetrated by radiation, for example), not conserved (it can be converted into energy), and where its fundamental

We think of the physical world as made up of matter, but in fact modern physics recognizes things like forces and fields as equally part of the physical world. In deep space even more exotic material, such as invisible "dark matter", may also exist.

> *There is some unified body of scientific theories, of the sort we now accept, which together provide a true and exhaustive account of all physical phenomena… what scientists say nowadays to the contrary is defeatism or philosophy.*
>
> David K. Lewis, "An Argument for the Identity Theory" in *Journal of Philosophy* 63 (1966)

interactions (as described by quantum mechanics) are probabilistic rather than deterministic. And at the most fundamental level so far discovered, we find entities whose very nature is ambiguous: for example photons, the constituents of light, can be treated both as particles and as waves.

Physicalism

Given these discoveries about matter, a properly scientific materialism should therefore become a form of physicalism – the view that everything that exists is physical in the strict scientific sense, so that forces and fields exist on equal terms with matter itself. In fact, modern physics treats forces as among the most fundamental things there are. Current orthodox opinion is that there are four fundamental forces, not explainable in terms of others: gravity, electromagnetism, and the strong and weak nuclear forces (these less famous forces hold the inside of an atom together). The attempt to explain these four forces in terms of one ultimate force is sometimes called a "grand unified theory" (GUT) or (in an absurd exaggeration) a "theory of everything" (TOE).

But is the entire world physical? Some have argued that there are phenomena that exist outside the natural world altogether: ghosts, angels, spirits and so on. Most of these views, however, lack clear formulation and empirical support. A more serious alternative is the idea that mental phenomena (thoughts, feelings and so on) are not physical. Given the understanding of "physical" described above, then it is indeed unlikely that any mental phenomena are physical, since they do not figure in the categories of current well-established physics. However, physicalists have argued that there are ways of matching up states of mind described in mental vocabulary with states of the brain described in physical vocabulary. For example, one might identify the state of having a certain visual experience with a state of the visual cortex. Such a strategy aims to show that the mind does exist, but that it is really something physical. If this is correct, then the physical world may indeed be all there is.

The puzzles of quantum theory

Since its invention by Bohr, Schrödinger, Heisenberg and others, quantum theory – the physics of the very small – has always been philosophically controversial, because of its non-deterministic nature. But when we consider how quantum systems might interact with a "macroscopic" system (that is, objects at the ordinary level of experience), the theory becomes paradoxical.

For example, suppose we have a device that is set up to detect whether a certain atom undergoes radioactive decay; if the atom does decay, it triggers an atomic bomb to explode and destroy a whole city. So if the atom decays, then the city is destroyed, and if not, then not. But according to the laws of quantum mechanics, the atom can be in a "superposition" of states where it is both decayed and not decayed. But what has happened to the bomb and the city at that point? There is no such thing as being blown up and not being blown up – yet quantum theory allows that there are such states at the quantum level.

A famous and radical solution to the paradox of how to connect the quantum level with that of macroscopic objects is to say that it is our act of measuring the quantum state which makes it resolve into one or the other state. Another argument, put forward by Einstein among others, says that the solution must be in terms of our ignorance of some yet undiscovered factor or "hidden variable", and hence that, despite its empirical success, quantum theory is not yet complete.

The supernatural

Is there anything outside the natural world? Do ghosts, spirits and other "supernatural" phenomena really exist? Clarifying what such questions really mean is the first step towards answering them.

The supernatural is what is supposed to be above, beyond or outside the natural. But this idea is only as clear as the idea of the natural itself, and this idea too is somewhat vague. One plausible description of the natural is: the whole of reality. But this answer will not work in this context, because those who believe in the supernatural believe that reality contains both natural phenomena and supernatural phenomena. On this view, "nature" cannot mean the whole of reality, but rather something that is a part of this whole.

Believers in the supernatural often say that there is more to reality than is treated by science. So perhaps supernatural phenomena are simply those aspects of reality that lie beyond the reach of science? But this just changes the question into other ones: what is science, and what disciplines does it encompass? Defenders of the controversial discipline of parapsychology are often keen to emphasize its scientific status, pointing out that it uses scientific methods (experiments, statistics, theories) in its investigation of so-called "psi" phenomena, such as "extra-sensory perception" and "psychokinesis". So, if such things do exist, the parapsychologists surely would not object to their discipline being called a science – in which case it no longer counts as part of the supernatural. But if they do not exist, then parapsychology is studying nothing at all.

So there is little point in trying to define the supernatural in relation to science in general. But parapsychologists often say they investigate phenomena that are inaccessible to orthodox science. Even so, this does not give psi phenomena any special status as "supernatural"; rather, it is merely a criticism of some particular hypotheses of orthodox science and a proposal to replace them with other hypotheses. At most, parapsychology should be seen as saying that the rest of science has ignored something in nature that genuinely exists; consequently, it should have no need for the idea of the supernatural.

Belief in supernatural beings such as angels is still popular today – but, unlike in earlier times, we now have good reason to question such beliefs if they conflict with what we know from modern science.

Ghosts

Many people seem to believe that ghosts exist: numerous websites regularly report encounters with ghosts. So is there any truth in such stories? David Hume's famous argument about miracles (see also p.114) addresses this question.

Hume allowed that miracles are not logically or conceptually impossible. But nevertheless he doubted that we could ever have good reason to believe in the actual occurrence of a miracle. He ingeniously argued that, when we are presented with a report of a supernatural event such as a ghost encounter, we have always more reason to believe that some

confusion or fabrication has taken place, rather than that something so incompatible with our normal experience and the laws of physics really happened. "No testimony is sufficient to establish a miracle", Hume wrote, "unless the testimony be of such a kind, that its falsehood would be more miraculous than the fact, which it endeavours to establish." And there is always hugely more evidence to back up the claims of physics than can be gleaned from a typical report of a ghost sighting. In reminding us of where the burden of evidence lies, Hume's discussion still has much to tell us about the nature of our world.

The whole idea of the supernatural, then, is rather hard to make clear. We might do better to put the question of the definition of "supernatural" to one side, and consider some examples of things that believers in the supernatural generally take to exist, such as ghosts, spirits, angels and the like. Sceptics about the supernatural sometimes say that such phenomena are impossible. We should distinguish here between something's existence being logically impossible (such as a thing that is simultaneously square and not-square), and its being inconsistent with what we know. It is not logically impossible, for instance, that if you jump out of the window you will fly off into the clouds without any assistance, but it is inconsistent with what we know about gravity. Similarly, while the idea of (say) spirits may not be logically contradictory, if the supposed characteristics of such creatures are inconsistent with what we know from science, then we should not believe in their existence, even if they are in some sense logically possible.

Of course, the believer in the supernatural might say that this is exactly the point: supernatural phenomena show that the current laws of science are false. If we are even to consider this, then we need some serious evidence for the existence of the supernatural. But whatever evidence there is for supernatural phenomena, it is decidedly insubstantial compared to the overwhelming evidence for the dominant scientific theories – the atomic theory of matter, the DNA theory of the gene and so on. Moreover, modern technology has been built on these theories. In contrast, no technological consequence of supernatural phenomena has ever been demonstrated.

> *There are more things in heaven and earth than are dreamt of in your philosophy.*
>
> William Shakespeare, *Hamlet*

This last point could be pressed further. Many people claim to believe in ghosts and angels; but how many of them would be prepared to invest their money into a company that exploited the supernatural abilities of angels for some technological end? It is reasonable to speculate that an "angel-based" telecom company, for example, would not be a very promising business venture. If this is correct, then it suggests that belief in these things often has less to do with practicality than with a kind of wishful thinking.

Cause

Our world is one of causes and effects – things making other things happen. Causality, which Hume called the "cement of the universe", is what holds the world together. But, philosophically, the nature of this "cement" is deeply puzzling.

When something significant happens, we want to know what caused it. The idea of an uncaused event is not obviously contradictory, but it is nonetheless deeply mysterious to us. Normally, when we try to find out why something happened, what we are doing is looking for its cause. But what does it mean for one thing to cause another?

We might at first be tempted to think of causation in purely physical terms, as a force or energy passing between bodies. But it is clear that the transfer of energy is only an example of causation and cannot constitute its essence. In everyday life, we have no difficulty understanding claims such as "the country's strong currency caused investors to withdraw from its markets", which do not involve the physical transfer of energy. This is not because the world contains some mysterious "non-physical energy", but because causation is an idea that has a much wider application than just the transfer of energy or the work done by a physical force.

Cause and effect

Let us consider a concrete example of the search for causes. Imagine fire has destroyed a house and the investigators are looking for the source. What kind of thing would they be looking for, in the most general terms? Most obviously, it must be something that happened before the fire, because all causes must precede their effects. But the mere fact that an event, A, follows another event, B, is not enough to make A the cause of B. For example, someone might have been seen smoking a cigarette inside the house before the fire; the fact that this occurred before the fire is not enough to establish it as the cause. Assuming a causal relation here is a fallacy known as *post hoc ergo propter hoc* ("after this, therefore because of this").

As well as happening before the effect, then, a cause is something that brings about the effect. One traditional way of thinking of this is in terms of necessitation – that is, if the cause happened, then the effect must happen. So, if the intruder tossed a cigarette onto a pile of newspapers, then given the general facts about combustion and so on, they must burn. Here, the necessity is seen as a feature of the way the world is, rather than one of logic. But such "natural necessity" seems a very mysterious thing, and to explain causation in terms of it looks like explaining one obscure idea in terms of another. David Hume (see pp.24–25), with whom all modern discussions of causation begin, was sceptical about the existence of causal necessity. He argued that the appearance of necessity derives merely from expectations induced by our experiences. We think that there is some kind of necessary connection between fire and smoke, but in reality there is just fire followed by smoke, and our many past experiences lead us to expect fire to be followed by smoke. Fire and smoke are "constantly conjoined", and that is all causation amounts to.

Few philosophers have been happy with Hume's account of causation as constant conjunction, because sometimes a correlation is a mere correlation and not a direct sign of causation. For example, day is always followed by night, but day does not cause night; rather, both day and night are caused by the rotation of the earth. So constant conjunction cannot be all there is to causation.

So what alternative theory can we offer? One influential proposal developed in the 20th century starts with the very natural idea that a cause is "the thing that makes the difference". Throwing the cigarette onto the newspapers was the cause of the fire because it was the thing that made the

> *It appears that, in single instances of the operation of bodies, we never can, by our utmost scrutiny, discover any thing but one event following another; without being able to comprehend any force or power by which the cause operates. … One event follows another; but we never can observe any tie between them. They seem conjoined, but never connected.*

David Hume,
An Enquiry Concerning Human Understanding

Causation and determinism

Since the 17th century, it has been widely assumed by philosophers and scientists that causation is deterministic – that is, everything that happens is fixed by prior events and the laws of nature. On this view, if you knew all the laws of nature and the state of the whole universe at any one time, you would be able to deduce the entire subsequent history of the universe.

One consequence of this is that the same causes will always lead to the same effects. But is this in fact the case? We say that smoking causes cancer, for example; but not everyone who smokes gets cancer, so how can someone's smoking determine that they get cancer? Defenders of determinism reply that smoking will be a cause of cancer only in the presence of other factors – perhaps certain genes or lifestyle habits. In other words, when one of these (often unknown) further factors is missing; we are not really replicating the cause so we do not get the same effect.

This is plausible on the face of it; but how do we know whether there are always some hidden additional factors when events seem not to be caused deterministically? In particular, physicists have found that events at the subatomic level, such as radioactive decay, occur only with a certain probability. Here, no additional hidden factors have ever been found.

So what happens to causation when determinism does not seem to hold? Some say that events that are not determined are not caused; but this implies that nuclear explosions (which are produced by radioactive decay) are not caused, and this is surely implausible. The alternative theory is that there is indeterministic causation: causes do not determine their effects, but only make them more probable. By this theory, a nuclear explosion could said to be caused by radioactive decay, even though the decay process is based only on chance. And the same could be said for smoking and cancer: smoking makes it more probable that a person will get cancer than it would otherwise have been, and this is enough to make it a cause of that person getting cancer.

difference to whether there was a fire or not: if everything else had been the same and the cigarette had not been thrown, then there would have been no fire. This is called the "counterfactual" theory of causation, because it analyses causation in terms of what would have been the case if certain other things had been the case; that is, in terms of matters that are contrary to actual fact.

In the counterfactual theory, our fire investigators can cite the intruder's dropping the cigarette onto the newspaper as the cause because, if that had not happened, then the fire would not have occurred. But the theory will also count other things as causes of the fire: if the newspaper had not been dry, or the room had not been full of oxygen, then the fire would also not have happened. So all these factors are causes of the fire according to the counterfactual theory.

> *"The reason why physics has ceased to look for causes is that, in fact, there are no such things. The law of causality, I believe … is a relic of a bygone age, surviving, like the monarchy, only because it is erroneously supposed to do no harm."*
>
> Bertrand Russell, "On the notion of cause" in *Mysticism and Logic*

This is a problem only if an event must only have one cause – but there are no good reasons to think this. True, we do say things such as "the cause of the victim's death was…", but this is best regarded as loose talk. In fact, the victim died because his heart stopped, but he also died because he was shot; maybe he also died because he knew too much. It is a mistake to suppose only one of these is the "real" cause of death. Every event has many causes, so it is not an objection to the counterfactual theory that it would count factors other than the throwing of the cigarette as a genuine cause of the fire.

However, despite its evident appeal, the counterfactual theory is vulnerable to a decisive kind of counter-example. Consider a man who has two enemies, each of whom plans his murder. The man is crossing a desert on a trip. His first enemy fills his water bottle with poison. The second enemy, independently of the first, drills a very small hole in the water bottle. The poisoned water slowly drains away, and the man dies of thirst. Which enemy killed the man? Obviously, the second did. But the counterfactual theory has to deny this. For it is not true that if the second enemy had not drilled the hole, then the man would not have died; for he would have been poisoned instead. And this means, according to the counterfactual theory, that the drilling of the hole cannot be the cause of the man's death. But this is plainly wrong, so the counterfactual theory is unsatisfactory since it entails an obvious falsehood.

Fundamental concepts

The counterfactual theory has not been able to overcome this objection, and no adequate alternative theories of causation are forthcoming. So does this mean that we should try to eliminate the notion of causation from our account of reality? Those who think this sometimes claim support from Bertrand Russell's view that science no longer employs the notion of cause. Russell argued that the laws of physical science employ equations, but none of these mention the word "cause". However, we should not assume that because science does not mention something, it doesn't exist. In fact, physics describes the world using mathematical equations, but what these equations describe is the familiar world of causes and effects.

The notion of cause cannot be eliminated from our understanding of the world. If we cannot analyse it in terms of other notions, then maybe the correct conclusion is that is that causation is a fundamental notion for us. Many philosophers have argued that terms such as "truth" and "reality" cannot be defined, yet they are among the most important concepts we have. Similarly with "cause": perhaps there is no way to explain or define it in terms of more basic concepts.

A cause is what "makes the difference" – so without the cause there would be no effect. But what causes the waiter to drop the plates: the misplayed ball, the too-high stack, his being in the line of shot – or all of these?

Hume

David Hume was born in Edinburgh in 1711. After first studying law, Hume developed a strong interest in philosophy through reading Cicero. In 1734 he left Scotland to spend some time in France. There he wrote his *A Treatise of Human Nature*. Published in 1739–40, this work – which is now generally acknowledged as a masterpiece – met a famously poor reception: Hume himself wrote that "it fell dead-born from the press". Later on, having achieved more success with his *Essays Moral and Political* in 1741–2, Hume decided to reuse the material from *A Treatise of Human Nature* in his next two works: *An Enquiry Concerning Human Understanding* (1748) and *An Enquiry Concerning the Principles of Morals* (1751). These works achieved more success and are a more accessible introduction to his philosophy. Hume returned to Edinburgh in 1769, where he died in 1776. He was something of a worldly man with great personal charm, who enjoyed good living and had many friends.

David Hume 1711–1776

David Hume was one of the most brilliant and influential thinkers who have ever written in English. The leading thinker of the Scottish Enlightenment, his rigorous combination of empiricism and scepticism still carries much influence today.

Impressions and ideas

Hume was an empiricist – that is, he thought that all knowledge should be justified in terms of experience. He divided all the contents of the mind into impressions (essentially, the perceptions of the senses) and ideas (the "faint copies" of impressions created in thought, imagination and reflection). A fundamental principle of Hume's empiricist philosophy was that all ideas must derive from preceding impressions, so we could have no adequate idea of something for which there is no corresponding impression obtained from sense perception.

One of the main questions that any empiricist philosopher must face is how to account for knowledge – such as our knowledge of mathematics – that does not seem to be justified in terms of experience. We do not justify our belief that two plus two equals four by checking lots of examples of two things added to two other things and seeing whether they make four. Hume answered that this knowledge – called "*a priori* knowledge" – was not really knowledge of the world at all, but only of ideas and the relations between them and so did not need to be derived directly from experience. As well as providing an account of *a priori* knowledge, this view allowed him to exclude many traditional discussions in metaphysics and theology as bogus.

Many of Hume's ideas derive from his theory of impressions and ideas. A striking example is his analysis of causation – of one thing making another happen. Hume argued that we have no experience of a necessary connection (something that *must* happen) between cause and effect. Consider one billiard ball hitting another: all that we are given in experience is one billiard ball moving, and then the other one moving. We do not see the one ball *making* the other one move. "All events seem entirely loose and separate" Hume wrote, "One event follows another but we can never observe any tie between them." Hume concluded from this that our idea of causation is simply the idea of similar things following one another. This idea – the "constant conjunction" theory of causation – has been massively influential in the subsequent history of philosophy, despite many attempts to resist it.

> “*I was, I say, a man of mild dispositions, of command of temper, of an open social and cheerful humour, capable of attachment, but very little susceptible of enmity, and of great moderation in my passions.*”
>
> David Hume, *My Own Life*

Reason and nature

Hume's philosophy was dominated by his sceptical opinion of the power of reason to discern the real nature of things. Philosophers such as Descartes (see pp.48–49) and Spinoza (see pp.66–67) had tried to use reason alone to uncover the underlying nature of reality. Hume was doubtful about these attempts, and his theory of ideas and impressions was intended partly to show how empty they were. Hume extended his scepticism to religion, and wrote a notorious and influential critique of Christianity, *Dialogues Concerning Natural Religion* (*c.*1755), which contained a devastating critique of the traditional arguments for God's existence (see also p.110). Hume was well known as a religious sceptic, and the calmness with which he faced his own death was described by James Boswell with something approaching awe. But Hume was also a naturalist, in the sense of someone who thinks that the experimental methods of the natural sciences are the ways of acquiring true knowledge. It is this naturalism that makes Hume's philosophy so appealing to many philosophers today.

Hume's moral philosophy is without doubt one of his finest achievements. Our moral judgments, Hume thought, are derived from what he called a moral sense. “Morals and criticism” he wrote “are not so properly objects of the understanding as of taste and sentiment.” Moral judgments and practices are not derived from reason, he thought, because reason cannot by itself move someone to act. If you simply judge that someone is tormenting a child in the park, this will not move you to act against it unless you also have a desire, or “passion”, to prevent acts of that kind. This is the argument behind Hume's famous phrase, that reason is the “slave of the passions”.

Hume's moral philosophy is of a piece with his scepticism and his naturalism, because it recognizes the limits on what can be achieved by reason, and is based on what he takes to be the facts of human psychology. However, it is not a callow subjectivism or relativism – an “anything goes” theory of morality. Hume's life and personality make it clear that he was not the sort of person to endorse such a feeble and belittling account of moral life.

Hume's fork

Hume divided all knowledge into two kinds: knowledge of matters of fact, which is acquired through experience or experiment; and knowledge of relations of ideas, of which the prime example is mathematical knowledge. He thought that much traditional philosophy and theology claimed that there was other knowledge that did not fall into these two categories, and was neither experimental nor simply about ideas. At the end of his *An Enquiry Concerning Human Understanding*, Hume savagely attacked the idea that there was such knowledge:

“If we take in our hand any volume; of divinity or school metaphysics, for instance; let us ask, *Does it contain any abstract reasoning concerning quantity or number?* No. *Does it contain any experimental reasoning concerning matter of fact or existence?* No. Commit it then to the flames: for it can contain nothing but sophistry and illusion.”

This forced choice between the only two possible kinds of knowledge has become known as Hume's fork. It was Hume's attack on the pretensions of reason to achieve any substantial knowledge of the world that stimulated Immanuel Kant (see p.120) to defend the possibility of such knowledge in his masterpiece, *The Critique of Pure Reason*. As Kant himself put it, Hume awoke him from his “dogmatic slumbers”.

Idealism

In philosophy, idealism is the view that reality is fundamentally mental, rather than material. Despite its apparent strangeness, idealism can be seen as an intelligible response to some of the deepest problems of philosophy.

Philosophical idealism comes in many forms: from Berkeley's theory that "to be is to be perceived" (see pp.28–29), through Kant's view that the empirical world is a kind of appearance constructed by our minds (see box, below), to Hegel's theory that the world must be understood in terms of the unfolding manifestation of the *Geist* or world spirit throughout history (see p.30). But what is common to all forms of idealism is the denial of materialism – the view that matter constitutes the fundamental nature of the world. It might be objected that this view is incompatible with modern science. Hasn't science told us that the world is material? But this is to misunderstand the nature of idealism. Idealists do not deny any scientific theory. Rather, they claim that scientific theories, and the reality they describe, must ultimately be interpreted in mental terms.

So, why would anyone believe this? One argument derives from the distinction between appearance and reality. Some idealists (such as Berkeley) argue that we are immediately acquainted only with the appearances of things, not with how they really are; however, an object can presenting conflicting appearances from different points of view – so there can be no single real thing that has these conflicting properties. All that can be real are the appearances themselves, and these are purely mental entities (sometimes called ideas or perceptions).

But this argument is implausible. Why should we suppose that just because appearances can conflict, then what they are appearances of cannot be real? A plate can appear round from one angle, and elliptical from another: why should it follow that there is no such thing as the real, material plate? All that seems to follow is that things can look different from different angles – but this is an obvious truth that no one should deny, idealist or materialist.

Physical powers and the mental

Another, more contemporary, route to idealism starts with reflections about science itself, and the idea that physical science discovers only the

The transcendental idealism of Immanuel Kant

Immanuel Kant is the most famous and influential idealist in Western philosophy (see pp.141–143). Kant claimed to revolutionize our understanding of reality by putting the human mind at its centre, just as Copernicus had revolutionized our understanding of the universe by putting the sun, rather than the earth, at its centre.

Instead of asking how our knowledge can conform to a given world of objects, Kant argued, we should instead ask how objects can conform to our knowledge. Kant's answer was that all we can know are "appearances" or "phenomena", and that the nature of these phenomena is determined by the structure of our minds. For example, it is necessary that we perceive objects as being in space and time because space and time are the necessary forms of our perception. The nature of objects as spatio-temporal is therefore explained by something mental: the nature of our perception. However, Kant also argued that we have reason to believe that there must some kind of reality beyond the phenomena – this is the "thing-in-itself" or the "noumenal" world – but he denied that we could ever know this reality. Kant called his doctrine transcendental idealism; here, "transcendental" refers to the perspective from outside all possible experience.

For some idealists, reality is to be found not in an external world but in our perceptions and subjective experience.

powers or capacities of things. For example, the mass of an object is its power to affect the accelerations of itself and other bodies; and the same applies, in more or less complex ways, to all physical properties. But, intuitively, there must be more to reality than mere power: a universe of pure power would be a merely "potential" universe, with nothing really going on. Contemporary idealists argue that the only features of the world that cannot be understood as pure power are mental: a person's subjective experience consists of something more than power. They then argue that all the physical properties of the world must ultimately be understood in terms of how they affect subjective experience. Thus mass, for example, must ultimately be understood in terms of how it gives rise to subjective sensations of pressure; and so on.

This idealist argument, however, seems to conflate what there is in the world with how we know about it. While we come to know about the world through experiencing the powers that objects have, this does not imply that physical properties are mere powers. For example, the basis of sugar's solubility – its power to dissolve – can be found in its molecular structure, something that is not a power.

Idealism is a deeply strange concept of reality. Its chief strength as a philosophical system is in the challenge it presents to the common-sense view that the world consists of a realm of perceptible material objects such as trees, tigers and tables.

> “*What objects may be in themselves … remains completely unknown to us. We know nothing but our mode of perceiving them – a mode which is peculiar to us.*”
>
> Kant, *Critique of Pure Reason*

Berkeley

George Berkeley is one of the most controversial of all the great philosophers. Born in Ireland in 1685, he studied in Dublin and was ordained as an Anglican minister in 1709. He was made Dean of Derry in 1724, and spent some years in America trying to found a missionary college in Bermuda. The scheme eventually failed and he returned to Ireland in 1732, becoming Bishop of Cloyne. He remained there until 1752 when he moved to Oxford. He died in 1753.

> *For as to what is said of the absolute existence of unthinking things without any relation to their being perceived, that seems perfectly unintelligible. ....nor is it possible they should have any existence, out of the minds or thinking things which perceive them.*
>
> George Berkeley,
> *Principles of Human Knowledge*

Berkeley's major philosophical achievements were produced when he was a relatively young man: his first major work, *Essay Toward a New Theory of Vision*, was published in 1709, *Principles of Human Knowledge* in 1710 and *Three Dialogues between Hylas and Philonous* in 1717. The rest of his output is chiefly of historical interest – for example, *Siris*, his eccentric 1744 treatise on the medicinal benefits of "tar water" (water in which tar has been soaked) – although in *The Analyst* (1734) he produced an insightful critique of the contemporary use of infinitesimal quantities in mathematical calculus. Despite these other endeavours, Berkeley will be remembered chiefly for his idealism – the remarkable view that the only real things are mental things: ideas and the souls that perceive them.

To understand Berkeley's idealism, it is essential to see it as a reaction to the views of John Locke (see pp.82–83). Locke thought that material objects have two kinds of qualities: primary qualities, such as shape and size, that objects have independently of perception; and secondary qualities, such as colour or smell, that are dependent on being perceived. Locke thought there must also be something underlying the qualities, something that *has* these qualities. This thing was known as the "substratum"; but Locke encountered a problem in saying what the substratum was. For if we say anything at all about this substratum, then we are attributing qualities to it; but the substratum is by its nature something apart from its qualities. Locke concluded that the basis of mate-

Dr Johnson's misunderstanding of Berkeley

When first told of Berkeley's doctrine that everything is an idea, the 18th-century wit Dr Samuel Johnson famously kicked a stone, proclaiming "I refute him thus". Whether disingenuous or not, Dr Johnson's response expresses a common misunderstanding of Berkeley. For Berkeley did not deny the existence of stones, nor therefore the possibility of kicking one. Rather, he was proposing a theory about what stones and other physical objects most fundamentally are.

Of course, Dr Johnson's reaction is a very natural one, which many people have when faced with apparently outlandish philosophical theories. But to understand these theories, we must instead try to unpack the reasoning that has led to such strange conclusions. Whether right or wrong, Berkeley's idealism is one way of trying to answer some of the most difficult questions that there are, and should therefore be taken seriously. To refute him – as surely we must – requires finding out what is wrong with his arguments. Dr Johnson was too quick to announce his refutation.

George Berkeley 1685–1753

Berkeley is one of the greatest philosophers who ever wrote in English. Unlike his empiricist contemporaries David Hume and John Locke, however, he was an idealist: he thought that only mental things exist, and his controversial philosophy is captured by his famous slogan "to be is to be perceived". This apparently absurd doctrine was one that he defended with great brilliance.

rial objects is "something, I know not what".

Berkeley thought this was outrageous. To define an object as something unknown to us was, he thought, contrary to common sense and a source of unnecessary philosophical confusion. He also thought that Locke's theory gave rise to scepticism: for if we cannot know what the basis of material objects is, then how can we know they have any basis at all, or indeed that ordinary objects are any more than illusions?

The way to avoid these conclusions, Berkeley thought, was to reject the foundation of Locke's theory of matter: the distinction between primary and secondary qualities. Defenders of this distinction had often argued that in a world without secondary qualities (colours and so on), there would still be primary qualities, such as shape. But Berkeley challenged this: if we imagine a world without colour (including black and white), we will be imagining a world without shape too: for where would the boundaries of objects be perceived as lying? Having dispensed with the distinction between primary and secondary qualities, Berkeley argued that qualities must really be ideas. He had many arguments for this view, but a particularly striking one is based on the claim that only an idea can be like an idea. If this is correct, and if Locke was right that the ideas of secondary qualities resemble those qualities themselves, then it follows that these qualities themselves must be ideas. In his *Three Dialogues between Hylas and Philonous*, Berkeley sets out the following argument. Extreme heat is painful – but no one thinks that pain is in the object that causes it; so why should we think that extreme heat is in a material object? Berkeley concluded that "no object exists apart from the mind; mind is therefore the deepest reality". He thought this was closer to the common-sense view of the world than Locke's mysterious underlying "something".

But, we might naturally object, common sense does not think that objects depend for their existence on human minds perceiving them. Surely a tree in the courtyard continues to exist when no-one is perceiving it? Berkeley agreed that it did. Since for Berkeley a tree can be nothing but an idea, and all ideas are perceived, he drew the conclusion that the tree's continued existence is due to its being perceived by God. This argument was not frivolous or *ad hoc*: it was part of Berkeley's aim to put God back in the centre of philosophy. Locke's philosophy, he thought, gave too much succour to atheism.

Berkeley's system is, of course, very hard to believe, and few philosophers subscribe to anything like it today. However, there is one respect in which Berkeley is absolutely right about the merit of his view: it is the only kind of view that conclusively refutes the sceptical view that we have no knowledge of the world. For all sceptical arguments attack views that postulate a divide between the thinking mind and the world external to the mind. They then challenge us to defend our view that we have knowledge of this world. But if, like Berkeley, you deny that there is this gap between the thinking mind and the external world – since the world is simply constituted by the ideas of the thinking mind – then the challenge posed by scepticism vanishes. The price one pays for this victory over scepticism, however, is Berkeley's idealism. Many will think this too high a price.

Hegel

Georg Hegel 1770–1831

Georg Wilhelm Friedrich Hegel was one of the most systematic and ambitious thinkers of all time. His work attempts to tackle some of the deepest philosophical problems of all – the ultimate nature of reality, the foundation of morality and the nature of reason.

Hegel was born in 1770 into a middle-class German Protestant family in Stuttgart. He initially considered becoming a clergyman, and after giving up this ambition worked for a while as a tutor, schoolteacher and lecturer, and then as a journalist, before becoming a professor of philosophy in Berlin in 1818. He died in Berlin in 1831.

Hegel's most important works are *The Phenomenology of Spirit* (1807), *The Science of Logic* (1812-16) and *The Philosophy of Right* (1821). His aim in these huge and deeply learned works was nothing less than a rethinking of the whole of philosophy. Hegel argued that human thinking or reason is essentially determined by the forces of history. Indeed, he considered that the ultimate reality is what he called *Geist* (translated variously as "mind", "spirit" or sometimes "world-spirit"). *Geist* is one of the most complex ideas in Hegel's philosophy: it is both the force that operates through history, and something in which particular human minds participate. Hegel is an idealist because it is *Geist* that constitutes the most fundamental reality.

Hegel's conception of history was that its development was guided by an aim or purpose. The aim towards which history is progressing is the self-realization of *Geist*, its coming to know itself. The whole process has a certain kind of logical structure, which Hegel called "dialectical". Hegel's dialectic progresses by detecting internal conflicts or tensions within ideas, which must be resolved by moving to a higher – and to Hegel, more real – level of ideas. Conflicts are then found within these ideas, and resolved a still higher level; and so on, until we reach the ultimate reality that contains no conflicts, called the "Absolute".

The dialectic is sometimes described as the movement from an initial thesis, where an idea is asserted, through an antithesis, which opposes it, and resolved in a synthesis that in some way transcends the thesis and antithesis and combines elements of both. For example, when theorizing about morality, we might start with, as the thesis, the idea that the good is simply what maximizes pleasure. This idea, however, is riddled with tensions and contradictions, which we might try and escape by moving to, as the antithesis, Kant's morality of duty, which bases morality on pure reason. But this, too, is inadequate, providing only an empty, formal notion of morality, and we will only be satisfied when we move to, as the synthesis, the fully communal, historically situated morality that Hegel recommends.

Hegel's extraordinary vision of the world has had far-reaching influence – particularly through the work of Karl Marx (see pp.210–211). Marx's thought is called "dialectical materialism" because it combines Hegel's dialectical view of history with a recognition of the material basis of existence. For Marx, this was intimately linked to the importance of philosophy in addressing the problems of the world, notably the suffering of the working classes.

> "*Philosophy is its own time raised to the level of thought.*"
>
> Hegel, *The Philosophy of Right*

Phenomenology

The phenomenological movement, founded by Husserl, brought to philosophy the radical new idea of analysing the structure of experience itself. This movement was also the starting point for the intellectual tradition now known as continental philosophy.

The word "phenomenology" literally means "theory of appearance" (*phainomenon* is the Greek word for appearance). The word was invented by one of Kant's correspondents, the 18th-century German scientist J.H. Lambert, but it acquired a special meaning in the philosophy of Edmund Husserl (1859–1938) and his followers. For Husserl, phenomenology was a new and foundational method for the whole of philosophy. Although few philosophers went on to practice Husserl's phenomenological method as he had developed it, many of the most influential European philosophers of the 20th century – including Derrida, Heidegger and Sartre – began as followers or interpreters of Husserl and developed their ideas in reaction to his.

Phenomenology had its origins in the views of Husserl's teacher, Franz Brentano (1838–1917). In his most famous work, *Psychology from an Empirical Standpoint* (1874), Brentano argued that psychology should be based on a clear distinction between mental and physical phenomena, and that this distinction was to be found in what he called the "intentionality" of the mental. This term refers to the fact that any act of mind is directed to an object: that is, whenever someone wants, they must want something, whenever someone thinks, they must think something; and so on for all mental phenomena. Physical phenomena, Brentano argued, exhibit nothing like this intentionality.

Husserl developed Brentano's idea of intentionality, declaring it to be the distinguishing characteristic of consciousness and stating that "consciousness is always consciousness of something". But whereas Brentano was interested in the study of intentionality as an empirical phenomenon,

Continental philosophy

The tradition of thought running from Husserl, through Heidegger, to contemporary philosophers such as Derrida and Lyotard, is classified today as "continental philosophy". This is contrasted with "analytic philosophy", the mainstream style of philosophizing in the English-speaking world (typified by the work of Frege, Russell, Wittgenstein and, more recently, Quine, Kripke and Donald Davidson). These labels are inexact and in many ways inappropriate: the analytic philosophers Wittgenstein and Frege were Austrian and German respectively; and it is not clear that the word "analytic" denotes any very specific content. Nonetheless, there are broad differences of method, doctrine and style between the two traditions, however hard it may be to define these precisely. Some obvious differences are analytic philosophy's concern with theory-building, often governed by a desire to harmonize philosophy and science; its view of the importance of formal logic; and its general separation of philosophical questions from historical ones. These features contrast with continental philosophy's preoccupation with the question of whether philosophy is possible at all and a consequent scepticism about the possibility of philosophical theories; its tendency to conduct philosophical debates through "readings" of other philosophers; and its vision of philosophy as having a role in the wider intellectual culture. Continental philosophers also tend to be sceptical of the way in which analytic philosophy favours science as the most important source of knowledge. There are, however, exceptions to all these tendencies within both the analytic and continental camps.

A Maiden's Dream About a Lake by Max Ernst (1940). Surrealist painters shared with phenomenologists an interest in what was in the mind, irrespective of whether this was also present in reality.

Husserl eschewed the scientific investigation of consciousness and developed his "phenomenological method" as a philosophical analysis of the essence of consciousness. Husserl claimed that studying both states of consciousness (which he termed *noesis*, from the Greek for to perceive) and what is in consciousness (*noema*), the philosopher will gain knowledge of what enables consciousness to refer to objects outside itself.

Husserl argued that the study of consciousness, which he called the "phenomenological reduction", should involve reflection on the contents of conscious acts of the mind in their own right. That is, since the mind can think of objects even if those objects do not exist, the proper way to study the contents of the mind was by not assuming the real existence of anything outside the mind. This he called "bracketing": in investigating consciousness phenomenologically, the existence of things in the world should be "bracketed", or set to one side. The state of mind entered once the reality of the world was bracketed was what Husserl called the *epoché* ("withholding"). Husserl's phenomenological reduction is thus reminiscent of the position of the enquirer of Descartes' *Meditations*, who tried to establish the foundations of knowledge without assuming the existence of anything outside the mind (see pp.48–49).

> *Much closer to us than any sensations are the things in themselves. We hear the door slam in the house, and never hear acoustic sensations of mere sounds.*
>
> Martin Heidegger, *The Origin of the Work of Art*

Husserl acknowledged these Cartesian, almost solipsistic, origins of his phenomenology; but this standpoint was unacceptable to many of his followers. His most famous student, Martin Heidegger (1889–1976), rejected this viewpoint as the foundation for a theory of intentionality. In his *Being and Time* (1927), Heidegger argued that philosophy had lost touch with what he called "the question of Being", and Husserl's philosophy was no exception. For Heidegger, there could not be a phenomenological reduction because there is no perspective from which one can give an account of the data of consciousness, abstracted from the actual nature of our human way of being (which he called *Dasein*). We are thrown into a world of the everyday, and we cannot occupy the point of view of the disinterested, abstracted Cartesian spectator on the disembodied "objects of consciousness". When we give an account of our ordinary mode of being, our "everydayness", we come to realize that the fundamental nature of our intentionality is revealed by our immersion in the world, rather than by something that could be revealed in the Husserlian *epoché*. According to Heidegger, we do not experience mere sensations abstracted from the real objects of the world; rather, our experiences are of everyday objects in all their richness and complexity.

Existential phenomenology

So, although Heidegger was deeply influenced by Husserl and adopted many of his assumptions – for example, the idea that consciousness and Being should be investigated phenomenologically rather than scientifically – he ended up with a philosophical position very different from Husserl's. Another philosopher influenced by Husserl and Heidegger, who tried to reconcile some of their ideas, was Jean-Paul Sartre (see pp.156–157). Sartre agreed with Husserl that consciousness is always consciousness of something, but rejected Husserl's idea of *noema*. Maurice Merleau-Ponty (1907-61), who edited *Les Temps Modernes* with Sartre, rejected what he took to be the Cartesianism (separation of the mind from the embodied person) of Sartre's approach to intentionality, emphasizing instead the involvement of the body in all consciousness. In this, his approach was similar to Heidegger's insistence on the primacy of "being-in-the-world" – our active engagement with the world – as the basis of intentionality.

The philosophy of Heidegger, Sartre and Merleau-Ponty is known as "existential phenomenology" or "existentialism" (see also pp.154–155). These terms are perhaps somewhat too loosely defined to be of much help in clarifying their complex and conflicting doctrines, but what these thinkers do have in common is their rejection of the Husserlian notion of bracketing the existence of the world, and their insistence that real phenomenological discoveries will come only when we start with the actual phenomena of our existence, rather than with some preconceived notion of what the human subject is. This is one way to read the allusive existentialist slogan, "existence precedes essence".

Heidegger and Nazism

The nature and extent of Heidegger's relationship with Nazism has been a matter of some controversy. What is not in dispute are the following facts. In 1933, the year Hitler came to power, Heidegger became Rector of Freiburg University. In the same year he joined the Nazi Party and remained a member until 1945. Under Heidegger's rectorship, Husserl (who was a Jew) was forbidden to use the library of the university; Heidegger also issued a decree denying financial aid to Marxist, Jewish and other "non-Aryan" students. Heidegger resigned his rectorship in 1934, but he never offered a public recantation of his earlier Nazi beliefs, even after the war. Heidegger's evasiveness in post-war discussions of the matter did not help to remove the obscurity about his involvement with Nazism. His defenders say that his admiration for Nazism was short-lived and his use of its doctrines in the university merely expedient. Others see Heidegger's admiration for Nazism as of a piece with his apparent nationalism, his romanticization of the peasant life and his proclaimed distaste for technology and modern society.

Truth

Philosophers are interested in truth because – like other knowledge-seekers – they are engaged in discovering truths about the world. But more fundamentally, they are also interested in understanding the nature of truth itself.

How are we to understand the nature of truth? One common contention is that the widespread disagreement about what is true shows that truth is relative to a community or even to an individual. On this view, nothing is true absolutely: only "true-for-me" or "true-for-us". In fact, this view is based on a confusion. Consider two people who disagree about how many people have swum the English Channel. This disagreement does not entail that there is no absolute fact of the matter. Perhaps 3,000 people have swum the channel – in which case, if someone says that only 2,999 people have done it, they are (absolutely) wrong. Disagreement does not imply relativity: the truth may be hard to discover, but this does not mean that it is relative to anything other than the facts, or how things are.

The question of the nature of truth is quite distinct from the question of how we know what is true. Consider, for example, one traditional theory of truth: that truth consists in the coherence of a set of beliefs. Given this definition, deciding which beliefs are "true" means identifying those that cohere. In practice this may prove difficult, but that is no argument against the underlying idea that truth is nothing but coherence. In fact, this theory is no longer widely accepted, but not because it makes particular truths hard to know.

An alternative analysis of truth is in terms of a correspondence between a statement and a fact ("what is"). However, the trouble with this "correspondence theory" of truth is that it seems to be empty of content. If the notion of a "fact" is to provide an informative analysis of truth, then it must have some content that is independent of the notion of truth; but it is hard to define "fact" as anything other than "what a true statement states". The correspondence theory of truth thus seems to be just another way of saying that true statements are true because of how things are in the world. This is undeniable, but it hardly deserves to be called an analysis or theory of truth.

The liar paradox

According to St Paul, Epimenides the Cretan stated that all Cretans are liars. If Epimenides was speaking the truth, then – since he was a Cretan himself – he must have been lying. This paradox can be expressed neatly as follows: if someone says "I am now saying something false", what they say is true only if they are saying something false - which is a contradiction.

Apart from being intrinsically puzzling, the liar paradox poses a problem for any systematic attempt to construct a semantic theory – a theory of the relationship between a language and reality. Because it is concerned with reality, any such theory must employ the concept of truth, and must find therefore a way of dealing with the liar paradox.

Polish logician Alfred Tarski (1902–83) dealt with the paradox by showing that, if a language does not contain words that talk about its own sentences (such as "I am now saying…"), then the liar paradox does not arise in that language. Tarski's proposal does not apply to "natural" languages, such as English or French, because they obviously do contain such words, but it has provided a powerful solution for the formal languages of mathematics and logic. A solution to the paradox that applies to all languages has yet to be found.

According to pragmatism, the fact that a bridge functions establishes the truth of the principles behind its construction.

Minimalism and pragmatism

Some philosophers have argued that it is futile to hope that truth can be analysed at all. The influential minimalist theory of truth states that truth is not a substantial property or feature of beliefs and statements (unlike, for example, the property of being interesting or morally important), so there is no "hidden nature" that a theory of truth would need to uncover. Minimalists argue that asserting that a particular statement is true is just another way of asserting that statement: the statement "it is true that fish swim" does not really say anything different from the statement "fish swim"; someone could express their belief that fish swim by making either statement.

One problem with the minimalist theory of truth is that if truth is not a substantial feature of our beliefs, then why should anyone try to seek the truth? And it seems that people do seek the truth: truth is the aim of many of our activities. So how can the minimalist explain this? One answer, called pragmatism, locates the value of truth in the role that true beliefs have in making our actions succeed: "truth is what works", as William James put it.

> *True and false are attributes of speech, not of things. And where speech is not, there is neither truth nor falsehood.*
>
> Thomas Hobbes, *Leviathan*

These two approaches, minimalism and pragmatism, can be combined in the following way: a belief is true when actions based on this belief succeed, as this implies that things are as the belief says they are. This combined approach agrees with the pragmatist view that the value we place on the search for truth is explained by the role of true beliefs in helping our actions to succeed; and with the minimalist view that there is no need to postulate some "hidden nature" to truth. So the ultimate explanation of the nature of truth may be based on nothing more mysterious than linguistic economy and the practical realities of human action.

Mathematics

Counting things is such an everyday part of our lives that it is easy to overlook how deeply puzzling numbers are. Mathematicians and philosophers have struggled to define the concept of number in a way that makes intuitive sense and is mathematically sound.

What is mathematics about? The natural answer is: numbers. But what are numbers? What, for example, is the number three? We can count three apples on the table – but these are just three things, not the number three itself. We do not change the number three by eating these apples, or by changing any other three-membered collection of objects. So the number three must be something distinct from all the collections of three objects; but what kind of thing is this?

One traditional philosophical view says that numbers must be real, non-physical things, located outside space and time. This view is called Platonism, in honour of Plato's view that ultimate reality lies outside ordinary experience (see pp.76–79). The problem with Platonism is that if numbers exist in their own Platonic realm, how does anyone ever come to know about them? You cannot know that the number three is prime by seeing it, since on the Platonist view it is nowhere to be seen, being outside space and time. In fact, since we cannot causally interact with things that are not in space and time, we cannot have any kind of causal interaction with numbers at all.

There is nothing puzzling about a collection of any three objects – but what exactly is the number three itself?

Some philosophers and mathematicians have reacted to this problem by asserting that mathematics is a matter of the conventions governing the use of certain symbols. This view is called formalism, since it treats mathematical statements as concerning only certain symbols or forms. The problem for this view is how to explain why mathematical truths (such as that two plus two equals four) appear to be necessarily true. If mathematics is just about conventions about how to use symbols, why could there not be different conventions, with the result that different mathematical truths are true? Moreover, it is not clear that formalism can explain why mathematics applies to the world – that is, why, for example, bridges built using mathematical calculations do stand up.

These questions are answered by the one serious philosophy of mathematics that remains. This is logicism, the view associated originally with Bertrand Russell and Gottlob Frege (see p.58). Logicism attempts to explain all mathematics in terms of self-evident truths of logic. This explains the necessity of mathematics in terms of the necessity of logic; and mathematics applies to the world, logicists say, because the world itself has a logical structure. Unfortunately, however, Russell showed that this approach led to a contradiction, and therefore logicism cannot be correct.

Given the failure of logicism and formalism, there is no alternative, it seems, but to return to the Platonist view that numbers are real. Indeed, this is what many mathematicians assume in their dealings with proofs and numbers. The mathematician Paul Erdos used to talk about the best mathematical proofs as coming from a book written by God.

The infinite

Is the infinite real, or just a fabrication in our minds? Infinity has been an object of suspicion among philosophers and mathematicians for centuries – yet it is an essential concept in mathematics and in thinking about space and time.

The idea of infinity has often been treated with scepticism by philosophers and mathematicians. The German mathematician Karl Gauss said that "the infinite is but a figure of speech". Aristotle distinguished between the actually infinite – something that goes on forever – and the potentially infinite (such as a series of numbers that could go on forever), and denied that there are any actual infinities. This way of thinking had lasting influence, although in the 17th and 18th centuries philosophers tended to understand infinity as something emanating from God's mind. Isaac Newton, however, was bold enough to claim that space was infinite, and his invention of the differential calculus used the idea of an infinitesimal quantity: one larger than zero but smaller than any finite number. In the 19th century, this relatively mysterious concept was replaced by the well-defined concept of a limit. Later in that century, some of the mysteries of the infinite in mathematics were resolved by the German mathematician Georg Cantor (1845–1918), who really invented the mathematics of the infinite, along with set theory. Nonetheless, the mathematics of the infinite remains deeply puzzling – for example, it seems there can be infinities of differing sizes.

The arrangement of stars and planets as we view them is represented by this celestial globe. But, like the globe, is space itself finite in extent?

We also encounter the infinite when thinking of space and time in the universe. If the age of the universe is finite – having a beginning and end in time – then we must ask: what happened before it and what will happen after it? Kant was surely right when he argued that these questions provoke one of the deepest paradoxes in our reasoning about the world.

Interestingly, infinity in space is not the same as having no boundaries or limits. Consider the surface of a sphere of finite size: wherever you are on that surface, you can always go further – yet the surface is finite. (And, of course, if you kept on walking on the surface in the same direction, you would eventually encounter the same place – not so with a true infinity, such as the number series 1, 2, 3, 4... and so on, where you would never encounter the same number.) So, by analogy, the fact that wherever you are in space you can always go further does not show that the universe is infinite: space might be, as it were, the three-dimensional surface of a four-dimensional universe; it would be finite but unbounded. This is, in fact, how many cosmologists think the universe is.

> *"Something is infinite if, taking it quantity by quantity, we can always take something outside."*
>
> Aristotle, *Physics* book III

Leibniz

As well as being a brilliant philosopher and mathematician, Leibniz was an inventor, diplomat and courtier. There is a striking contrast between the rarefied abstractions of Leibniz's philosophical thought and the practical politics that occupied him for much of his life. He never held a position in a university, but worked for most of his life for the dukes of Mainz and Brunswick, travelling frequently on diplomatic missions. He was also very interested in technology and experimented with engineering inventions, including a scheme to drain mines using wind power.

In his prime, Leibniz was clearly a man of considerable charm and sophistication: referring to him, the Duchess d'Orléans observed that "it is so rare for intellectuals to be smartly dressed, and not to smell, and to understand jokes". His philosophy, by contrast, was resolutely abstract. Leibniz never wrote a large, substantial treatise, but set out his philosophical ideas in letters, short articles and commentaries on the work of others. But from these hundreds of scattered pieces – many still to be published – emerges a metaphysical system of great originality and strange beauty.

Gottfried Wilhelm Leibniz 1646–1716

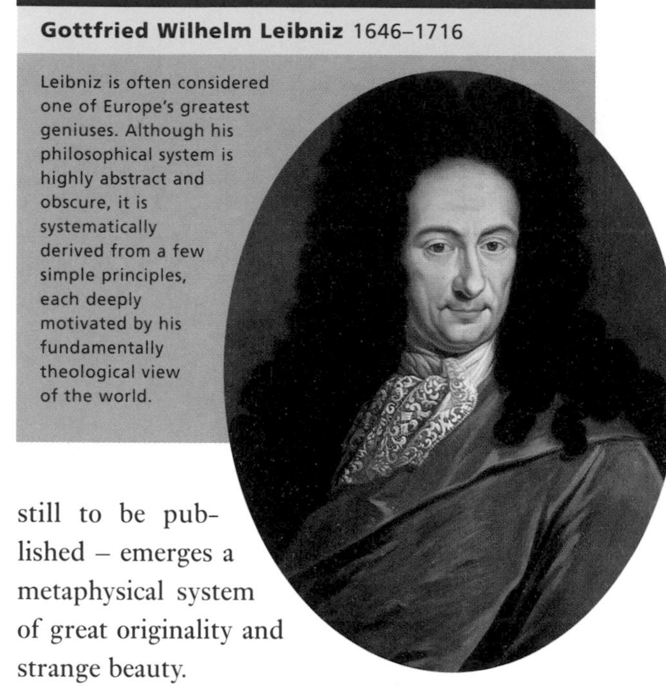

Leibniz is often considered one of Europe's greatest geniuses. Although his philosophical system is highly abstract and obscure, it is systematically derived from a few simple principles, each deeply motivated by his fundamentally theological view of the world.

The discovery of calculus

Leibniz made many mathematical discoveries, but the most important is without doubt the method known as calculus. This is still widely used to calculate the rates of change of any varying quantity, or find its total sum over time. Leibniz discovered calculus a few years after Isaac Newton (1642–1727), although he published his results before Newton. Newton's notation was cumbersome, and it is Leibniz's which is used today. Although their discoveries were independent, Newton and his followers publicly accused Leibniz of plagiarism, an accusation Leibniz angrily denied. The Royal Society in London formed a committee to assess the allegations and found in favour of Newton, as did an anonymous review published in the society's journal. It later emerged that both the committee's report and the review had been written by Newton himself, using his position as president of the society.

Possible worlds

As with many philosophers of his era, the notion of God was central to Leibniz's philosophy. He believed that God chose to create our world out of an infinity of other "possible worlds" – that is, possible ways the world could have been. For example, God chose to create the world in which Caesar crossed the Rubicon, as opposed to the world in which he did not. In addition, Leibniz claims that God must have had a reason to create this world rather than any other. This is a consequence of his "principle of sufficient reason", which asserts that when something is true, there is always a reason why it is true rather than not. Now since God is perfectly good, his reason for creating this world must have been a moral reason. And it would be incompatible with God's goodness not to bring the best possible world into existence, hence Leibniz's well-known view that this is the best of all possible worlds. (Although this does not make it a perfect world: Leibniz believed that only God could be perfect, so anything that is distinct from God must be imperfect in certain ways.)

The view that God could not have created a better world leads to a distinct problem for Leibniz: how can his philosophy make sense of the idea that things might have been different from the way they are? For example, what would have happened in World War II if Count von Stauffenberg had succeeded in assassinating Hitler in 1944? Such speculations make perfectly good sense to us, but they presuppose that much of history is contingent: that is, it might have been otherwise than the way it actually is. Truths that are not contingent are necessary: they could not be otherwise. (Mathematical truths, such as 7 plus 5 equals 12, are examples of necessary truths: it makes no sense to speculate about how these truths could be otherwise.)

The problem for Leibniz's philosophy is that it seems to make all truths necessary. For given God's goodness and the principle of sufficient reason, God could create no other world than our own. Furthermore, it was Leibniz's view that every genuine individual person or object (both referred to as "substances" by Leibniz) had what he called a "complete notion": everything that is, was and will be true of the individual. The complete notion is what makes each individual what he or she is. So it follows that von Stauffenberg could not have succeeded in killing Hitler; if he had, he would not have been the same individual. This theory seems to imply that nothing could have been different from the way it actually is: contingency is impossible. A further consequence of this is that human freedom is impossible: the complete notion of an individual appears to make it impossible for anyone to have done otherwise than they actually did.

Leibniz was, of course, fully aware of these difficulties. He saw that his commitment to certain fundamental principles – such as the principle of sufficient reason – required that he explain how there can be contingent truth. His explanation appealed to the nature of God. Leibniz held that, because God's mind is infinite in scope, he can logically deduce any truth from any other, even if this would take an infinite number of steps. However, our minds are finite and there are therefore some truths that cannot be deduced by our reason alone. These truths, which we have to know in other ways (for example, by our senses), are the contingent truths. So the reason that it is contingent that von Stauffenberg did not kill Hitler is that we cannot deduce it in a finite number of steps. This solution to the problem of contingency demonstrates the interconnectedness and unity of Leibniz's thought.

“ *There is a world of creatures … in the smallest part of matter. Every portion of matter can be thought of as a garden full of plants, or as a pond full of fish. But every branch of the plant, every part of the animal, and every drop of its vital fluids, is another such garden, or another such pond.* ”

Leibniz, *Monadology*

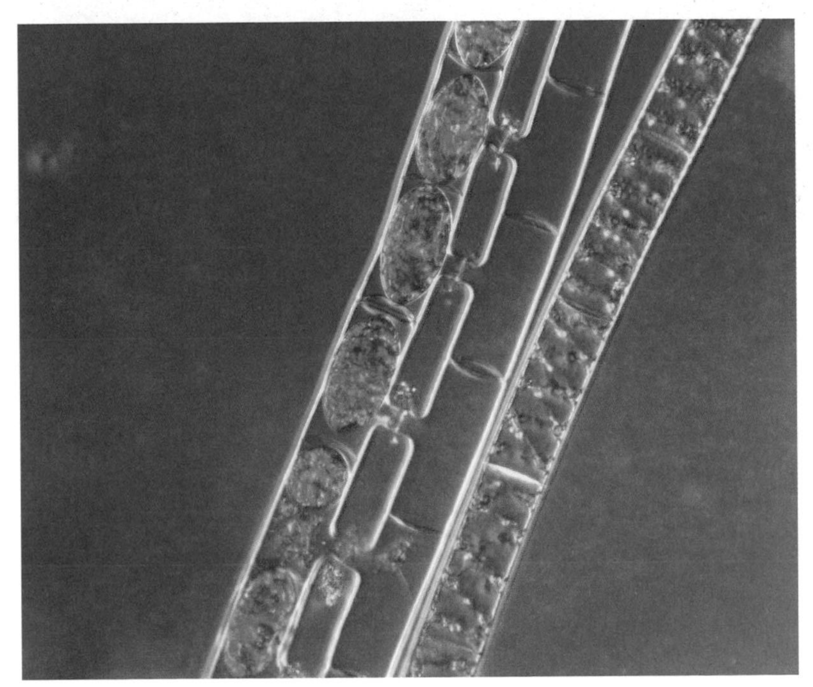

Time and space

Thinkers from the ancient Greeks onwards have argued about the nature of space and time. Today, physics treats time as the fourth dimension of "spacetime", but puzzling questions remain: why, for example, do we experience time as "moving" in one direction only?

Could the universe have begun five minutes earlier? Could it be moved one mile to the right? And do these mind-boggling questions make any sense? Leibniz (see pp.38–39), who first raised such questions, thought not, and argued that space and time are constructions from the spatial and temporal relations between objects and events, not entities in themselves. Without events, there would be no time; and without objects, there would be no space; so it makes no sense to suppose that the universe might have begun five minutes earlier.

We often represent time using a spatial dimension, as in this image sequence showing the phases of the moon day by day.

Leibniz was attacking the views of Isaac Newton, who thought of space and time as real things – the "containers", so to speak, in which objects exist and events occur. Kant (see pp.141–143) gave an important argument in defence of Newton's conception of space: if the only thing in the universe were a single glove, there would be the question of whether the glove was right-handed or left-handed. Yet the spatial relations between the parts are the same for the right-handed glove and for the left-handed glove; therefore spatial facts (such as whether a glove is right- or left-handed) cannot be reduced to spatial relations between the parts, as Leibniz supposed.

Of course, Newton's conception of space and time has now been superseded by Einstein's theory of relativity, which treats time as the fourth dimension of a single entity, "spacetime". To say that time is the fourth dimension of spacetime is just to say that it is one way in which things can fail to coincide, just as they can fail to coincide by being in different locations in one of the three spatial dimensions. However, time seems to differ from the spatial dimensions by having a direction: events seem to "move" in time from the past into the present and future. But what does it really mean to say that events "move in time"? An event cannot move in time in the sense in which a person can move in space, so perhaps we should say that time itself "flows". But this idea is also strange: if time flows, at what rate does it flow? The obvious, facetious answer – "at the rate of one second per

Zeno's paradoxes

Zeno of Elea (ca.470BCE) was one of the earliest Western philosophers whose ideas have survived. He is known chiefly for his famous "paradoxes of motion" (a paradox is an unacceptable conclusion drawn from apparently true assumptions by apparently sound reasoning). These arguments aim to prove that motion is impossible and to ridicule the idea that space and time are infinitely divisible.

The most famous of these concerns Achilles and a tortoise. Achilles is racing the tortoise, and gives it a head start. To overtake the tortoise, Achilles has to run the distance between himself and the tortoise, by which time the tortoise has moved on a little, so Achilles has now to cover the new distance to the tortoise; and so on. It follows that Achilles can never catch up with the tortoise, never mind overtake him. This paradox still has no agreed solution, testifying to the underlying strangeness of the idea that space and time are infinitely divisible.

second" – highlights the emptiness of the question: "flowing" is a process that takes time; time cannot itself take time.

Time travel

Although it is difficult to understand and make clear, something askin to the idea that time flows or has a direction is deeply embedded in our thinking. For example, we know that it is perfectly possible to travel in any direction in any of the three spatial dimensions around us. But try as we might, we can travel only in one direction in time: into the future, but not into the past. Does this impossibility indicate a deep metaphysical fact about time, or only the current inadequacy of our powers of travel? Talk of travelling into the past or future, as in science fiction, assumes that the distinction between past, present and future has a basis in reality, but some influential philosophers have argued that this is an illusion. In the early 20th century, J.M.E. McTaggart argued that every event has the property of being past, present and future at some time or other. Since these properties are incompatible, and since nothing can have incompatible properties, past, present and future do not exist.

The four-dimensional picture given by modern physics also denies the reality of past, present and future. In this picture, events can be said to be earlier than or later than each other, but no event ever has the privilege of being in "the present" or "the past". This is because being in the present

is the same as happening now. In the four-dimensionalist picture, happening now is analogous to happening here, and objective reality no more contains a "here-ness" than it contains a "now-ness": whether an event is "here" or "now" are matters of a person's perspective on reality, and not part of reality itself.

So the four-dimensional way of thinking of space and time reveals why there is no such thing as the flow of time. But if it is to be ultimately satisfactory, this picture must also reveal why we are under the illusion that time, in some sense, flows.

Chapter 2

MIND AND BODY

What is the mind?

There are many different things in the world – such as tigers, tornadoes and football matches. There are also things that are mental: sensations, thoughts, ideas and so on. These mental things exist in packages we call minds. But what place do minds have in the physical world?

It is well known that minds bear an intimate relation to brains. We often read about scientists discovering brain regions that underlie our mental capacities. But how do electrochemical events in brain cells relate to our pleasures and frustrations, our insights and anxieties? This is one way of stating what philosophers call the "mind–body problem".

The mind–body problem is challenging because minds possess properties that do not seem to be found elsewhere in the natural world. For one thing, many of our mental episodes are conscious: it feels like something to hear a favourite song, or to mull over the possible options for dinner this evening. In contrast, it surely does not feel like anything to be a pebble or a teacup. Mental states also have the property of representing things – that is, of being about objects or events. While we can have a perception of a sunset or be angry about an insult, pebbles and teacups do not harbour inner states that are about anything. So how do consciousness and representation arise in a physical world?

Many philosophers of the past were dualists: they held that mind and body are fundamentally distinct. René Descartes (see pp.48–49) is the author of the most famous argument for dualism. Descartes begins with the observation that we can doubt the existence of our bodies, or indeed the existence of every physical object in the world—but we cannot doubt the existence of our own minds, because the doubt itself would be a mental state and would therefore confirm the mind's existence. This is the core idea expressed by Descartes' "*Cogito ergo sum*" ("I think, therefore I am"). Since bodies are dubitable and minds are not, Descartes

Other minds

As Descartes pointed out, none of us can doubt the existence of our own mind, because we experience it directly. But we cannot experience the thoughts of others directly, so how can we know that they too have minds? The position called solipsism – in which each person can regard him or herself as having the only mind in the universe – is widely regarded by philosophers as preposterous, but also hard to refute. In other words, it is a central problem for philosophy.

John Stuart Mill (see pp.139–140) and Bertrand Russell (1872–1970) thought that we could prove that other minds exist by arguing from analogy. For example, I know that I have a mind, and that I wince when I am in pain, and I can therefore infer by analogy that you are in pain when you wince. The problem with this argument is that I can observe the correlation between my mental states and behaviour, but not between anyone else's mental states and behaviour. Left to a single case, the argument from analogy is very weak.

Instead of regarding others' behaviour as evidence for the fact that they have minds, Gilbert Ryle (1900–1976) argued that behaviour has a necessary connection to the mental. On this "behaviourist" approach, wincing is not just evidence of pain: it partly constitutes it. In a similar spirit, Wittgenstein argued that we learn words for mental states only by pointing to the behaviour of others – so wincing is part of the meaning of "pain". If these authors are right, we can literally observe mental states of others, and the problem of other minds dissolves.

But even if mental states are intimately linked to behaviour, the fact remains that each of us also has a special, direct way of accessing our mind: we do not need to see ourselves wince to know we are in pain. And as long as we can doubt whether others have this special way of knowing, the problem of other minds remains.

> *The mind by which I am what I am, is wholly distinct from the body, and is even more easily known than the latter.*
>
> René Descartes, *Discourse on the Method*

reasons, they must be distinct. In this argument, Descartes attempts to move straight from conceivable difference to actual difference, but this move is invalid. The fact that you can doubt the existence of your body but not your mind does not prove that your mind could exist without your body. After all, someone knowing little chemistry might doubt that there is H_2O in the Amazon river but not doubt there is water there – but of course it is not possible to have water without H_2O. So the fact that we can conceive of two things existing apart from each other does not prove that they are truly distinct.

Mind, brain and body

Many philosophers today think that there are other reasons to reject dualism. Intuitively, we know that mental states can have causal effects on the physical world – as when my decision to raise my arm causes my arm to lift. But it is unclear how mental states could have physical effects if they existed in an entirely separate realm. Moreover, every change in my body has an identifiable physical cause, due to the links between the body and the nervous system. When my hand rises to lift a cup of tea to my lips, there is a prior state of the neurons in my brain and nervous system that can explain this action, so my mental intention to raise the cup appears irrelevant. Dualism seems to imply that mental states, as they are not identical to physical states of the brain, are causally inert and therefore superfluous.

Some of Descartes contemporaries embraced this reasoning. Leibniz (see pp.38–39) suggested that mind and body are causally independent, and that God creates a pre-established harmony between them so that they appear to interact. Other philosophers have tackled the problem of mind–body interaction by rejecting dualism, preferring a "monist" view whereby only one kind of substance exists. Berkeley (see pp.28–29) argued for idealism, according to which the only substance that exists is mental. On this view, "physical" bodies are nothing but ideas in the mind, so it is no wonder that they can be influenced by our thoughts and intentions.

These views may seem bizarre to modern readers, and today another form of monism is more popular: materialism, according to which only matter or physical stuff exists. But once again, how can material things have consciousness – how do we get

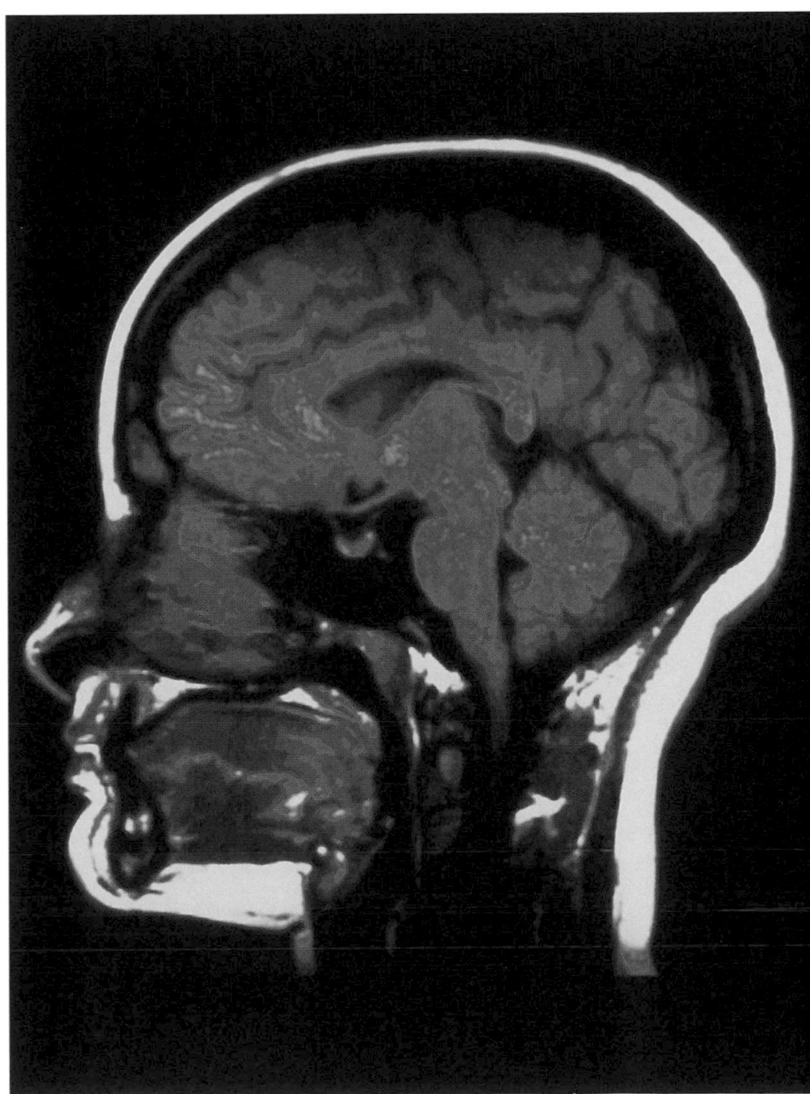

Modern brain imaging techniques allow us to see the brain at work – but where, and what, is the mind?

Artificial intelligence and the "Chinese room"

Computers can make predictions, diagnose diseases and defeat chess masters. In short, they can perform in ways that seem highly intelligent. But should we conclude that they are intelligent and can really think?

Philosopher John Searle is sceptical. He asks us to imagine being an English-only speaker inside a room filled with a huge number of rule books that together can supply a response in Chinese to any question written in Chinese. If someone outside the room were to slide such a question under the door, you would be able to look it up in one of the rule books, find a reply and send it back out – but you would have no idea what either the question or the reply said. Merely manipulating symbols in this way, which is all that computers do, does not confer understanding. Searle concludes that computers cannot be intelligent, and that real intelligence requires biological brains.

Searle's argument can be challenged. An English-only speaker trapped inside a Chinese speaker's brain would not understand Chinese, but it does not follow that the Chinese speaker would not understand Chinese. Also, there is a strong argument in favour of thinking computers. Suppose we replaced each neuron in your brain, one by one, with a silicon chip. You would end up with a computer for a brain – but, intuitively, there would be no point in the process at which you stopped thinking, demonstrating that intelligence does not depend on biological materials. This undermines Searle's main conclusion, and opens up the possibility that we might be able to create artificial intelligence.

mind from matter? Current debate on the mind–body problem largely concerns this question.

We now know that a great correspondence exists between mental phenomena and brain processes. It appears that every mental episode can be correlated with activity in some region of the brain. For example, the experience of "illusory contours" in certain optical illusions is correlated with activity in an area called V2 at the back of the brain, while holding a phone number in your head before dialling is associated with activity in the frontal cortex. Such remarkable correlations suggest that mental states could be identical with states of the brain. Materialists who think that we can identify mental states with brain states are called identity theorists.

> “... *it may be the true nature of our inner experiences, as revealed by science, to be brain processes, just as to be a motion of electric charges is the true nature of lightning, what lightning really is.*”
>
> J.J.C. Smart, *Philosophy and Scientific Realism*

One difficulty with identity theory is that no two human beings have identical brains. The belief that snow is white is correlated with different patterns of neuronal activation in different people, even if they are identical twins. Therefore, that belief (and all other beliefs) cannot be identical to some particular brain state. Another difficulty is that mental states can exist in creatures whose brains are entirely different from ours. Suppose we discover a species of intelligent aliens whose brains are made of vibrating crystals, and that we encounter one such alien who is very gloomy and complains that life is just not worth living. Surely we should describe the alien as depressed – but identity theorists could not do this, because the alien's brain does not contain the same biochemical components as a depressed human's brain.

Function and experience

Such concerns have led materialists to adopt a theory of the mind–body relation called functionalism. According to this idea, what makes something count as a particular inner experience or mental state is not its biochemical composition but the role it plays in our mental life and consequent behaviour. In contrast to identity theorists, who identify mental states with specific types of brain states, functionalists identify mental states with whatever physical states happen to be playing the appropriate role. Vibrating crystals in aliens qualify as states of depression when they play the role associated with depression; patterns of neuronal activation in humans qualify as the belief that snow is white if they play the role associated with that belief. Consider: what makes something count as water is its chemical constitution, H_2O. But what makes something count as a heart is the role it plays in the circulatory system – whether it is made of muscle, plastic or anything else. Identity theorists think mental states are like water, and functionalists think mental states are like hearts.

Functionalism overcomes problems with identity theory, but it faces an objection of its own. Suppose we take two twins at birth and implant special lenses that invert the colour spectrum into the eyes of one of them. So, when one twin has a red experience, the other has what we would call a green experience. But because the twins are unaware of the surgery, these distinct experiences come to play the same functional role: both twins walk when there is a green light and stop at a red light. But their inner experiences are not the same at all – so different experiences can play the same role. If functionalism were correct, this should be impossible: the role should determine the experience.

Functionalism and identity theory are the two leading forms of materialism, and both are problematic. But a combination of these theories may be better than either alone. Some mental states can be identified by the way they feel and others by the roles they play. Many mental states have both attributes: pain, for example, involves both a feeling and a disposition to seek remedies. We can use identity theory to explain feelings and functionalism to explain roles. On this approach, functionalism and identity theory are not equally flawed competitors, but compatible partners providing explanations of different aspects of our mental life.

This depiction of the Grand Canal in Venice by the 19th-century painter J.M.W. Turner is deeply subjective and clearly expresses his inner experience of the scene. Exactly how such inner experience is linked to states of the brain continues to be a controversial issue.

Descartes

René Descartes was born in 1596 in La Haye (now called "Descartes") in the French province of Touraine. Having obtained a degree in law in 1616, he travelled to Holland two years later. There he met Isaac Beeckman, a Dutchman engaged in a project to explain physical phenomena mechanistically in terms of matter in motion.

Excited by his discovery of Beeckman's "remarkable science", Descartes resolved to develop a unified system of knowledge on new foundations. In 1629, having settled in Holland, he began work on a manuscript entitled *The World* in which he planned to explain all natural phenomena in terms of matter moving according to fixed laws established by God. By November 1633 the work had grown to include an explanation of human physiology, and was nearing completion. But that same month Descartes received the shocking news that Galileo had been condemned in Rome for maintaining that the Earth was in motion. This changed his plans completely: in *The World*, Descartes envisaged the solar system as a giant fluid in which the Earth and other planets are carried around the Sun in a spinning vortex. The movement of the Earth was so central to this description that he chose to suppress the work rather than publish it in a mutilated form. Instead, Descartes embarked on a long-term campaign to win acceptance for his new scientific and philosophical system.

René Descartes 1596–1650

Often regarded as the father of modern philosophy, Descartes set out to establish a system of knowledge that broke the link with medieval thought. Although today he is best known for his ideas about the mind and his "method of doubt" that attempted to put philosophy on a secure footing, his aim was to revolutionize the physics of his time.

Building the new foundations

In 1637, *Discourse on the Method* was published anonymously. Intended to "prepare the way and test the waters", this semi-autobiographical work expresses Descartes' dissatisfaction with the constant disputes in existing philosophy and presents the results of his search for more stable philosophical foundations for science. These investigations are described more fully in *Meditations on First Philosophy*, published in 1641.

In *Meditations*, Descartes guides the reader towards discovering the ideas of mind, matter and God that is innate in the understanding. The overt aim of *Meditations* was to offer proofs of the existence of God and the soul, consonant with religious orthodoxy. The covert aim was to lay the metaphysical foundations of his mechanical physics, and to replace the prevailing medieval philosophy – a fusion of Christian theology with Aristotelian thought – with his own system. In the work, Descartes constructs an ingenious argument that provides divine validation of human intellectual powers, in particular of the "clear and distinct" ideas innate in our minds. This conclusion provided Descartes with secure foundations from which he could depart from the theological philosophy of his day.

In his next major work, *The Principles of Philosophy*, Descartes uses God to validate his conception of matter as "pure extension", and to ground the basic laws governing its motion. Since God is unchanging, Descartes argues, he keeps the same amount of motion within the matter of the universe. This vision of a physical universe governed by simple mathematical laws was influential in the development of Newtonian physics.

Even more profound was Descartes' impact on the development of philosophy. The sceptical doubts introduced in *Meditations* to clear the ground took on a life of their own, providing the foundations for a new, rational theory of knowledge. But his ideas also raised new problems: in particular, it was not clear what link there could be between the two quite separate realms of matter and the mind. Descartes' last work, *The Passions of the Soul*, published in 1649, was an attempt to address this question and explain how an immaterial mind could act on a material body.

> *… this proposition I am, I exist is necessarily true whenever it is expressed by me or conceived in my mind.*
>
> René Descartes, *Meditations on First Philosophy: Meditation II (3)*

Descartes died of pneumonia in 1650, while staying in Sweden at the invitation of Queen Christina. Although his physics was superseded, the problem of accommodating the conscious mind in a material universe proved a lasting legacy.

The *Meditations*

Descartes' masterpiece, *Meditations*, is designed to guide the reader toward discovering the ideas of mind, matter and God innate in the understanding.

In the first meditation, designed to clear away preconceptions, Descartes presents reasons to doubt what seems most evident to us. He argues that there are no sure signs to distinguish waking experience from dreams, and that all our experience may therefore be an illusion. To reinforce this doubt, Descartes imagines that he is deceived by an evil demon of great cunning.

In the second meditation, Descartes makes the discovery that doubt itself yields certainty of his own existence: even to be deceived he must think, and to think he must exist (hence "I think, therefore I am"). Since he can be certain of his own existence while doubting the existence of anything material, Descartes concludes that he is a thing whose whole nature consists in thinking. This result is used in the final meditation to argue that mind and matter are distinct substances that can exist apart, thus allowing Descartes to conclude that the soul is immortal.

In the third meditation, Descartes argues that he is the creation of a benevolent, non-deceiving God. Finding in himself an idea of a perfect being, God, he claims that only such a being is able to cause this idea: the idea of God innate in our minds is the trademark that God has left on his work. The argument is unconvincing to us because it rests on a dubious assumption about the causation of ideas, but its conclusion – that, as long as we rely on ideas that are clear and distinct we cannot go wrong, since God is no deceiver – is of profound importance for Descartes.

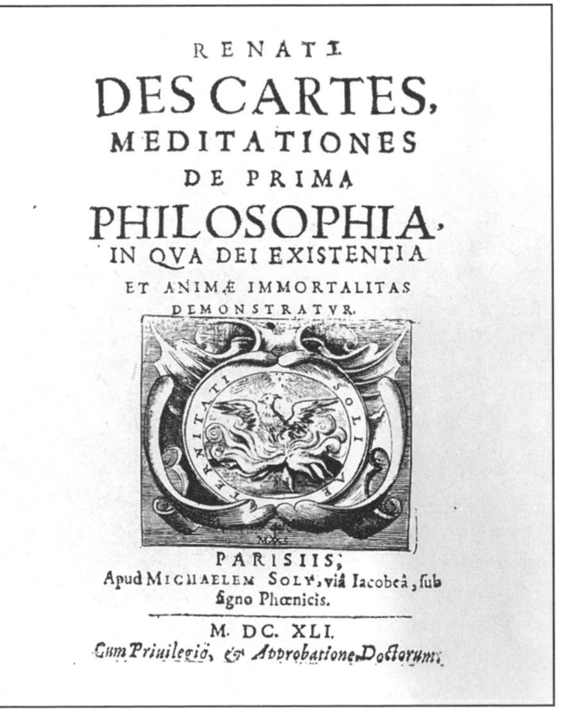

RENATI
DES CARTES,
MEDITATIONES
DE PRIMA
PHILOSOPHIA.
IN QVA DEI EXISTENTIA
ET ANIMÆ IMMORTALITAS
DEMONSTRATVR.

PARISIIS,
Apud MICHAELEM SOLY, via Iacobæa, sub signo Phœnicis.
M. DC. XLI.
Cum Priuilegio, & Approbatione Doctorum.

Thinking

Thoughts swim through our minds constantly, but their nature is somewhat elusive. Are thoughts images in the mind's eye or verbal narrations in the mind's ear? And is language essential to thought – or just a dispensable convenience?

Most living things get through life without thinking. Plants certainly do not think, and it is highly questionable whether insects do. These life forms are able to obtain nourishment and reproduce without the benefit of thought. But this does not mean it is useless to think. Animals that think can adapt to novel situations in a flexible way, and humans regard thinking as valuable in its own right. Most of us enjoy reflecting on things and trying to make sense of the world we inhabit. Philosophy is perhaps the ultimate example of doing this. But what exactly is thinking?

One traditional answer, defended by David Hume (see pp.24–25) and other philosophers of the British empiricist school, is that thoughts are mental images – pictures in the mind's eye. On this view, thoughts are copies of sensory experiences. That does not mean we cannot think about things that we have never perceived. New thoughts are created by combining familiar images in new ways: we can think about golden mountains by combining an image of gold with an image of a mountain.

Not everyone has been convinced by the image theory of thought. Some of our thoughts seem too abstract to have a perceptual foundation. What picture corresponds to the thought that honesty is a virtue, or democracy is a stable form of government? Even some concrete thoughts seem to outstrip images. As philosopher Jerry Fodor (see p.52) puts it, a picture needs a caption to tell us what it means. The point can be dramatized by a mental image of a cat on a mat. Is this the thought that the cat is on the mat, or that the mat is under the cat, or that cats are able to sit on mats? We can also ask whether such an image counts as the belief that the cat is on the mat, the desire that the cat should sit

Can animals think?

We are often tempted to attribute complex, human-like beliefs to animals. This is not unreasonable: after all, non-human mammals have brains that are organized in much the same way as ours, and even bee brains metabolize similar neurochemicals. Even so, there are obvious mental differences between humans and animals. We do not find philosophers, physicists, and poets among the beasts. So what is the mental dividing line between animals and humans?

One intriguing possibility is that human thought is qualitatively different from animal thinking because of its tendency to go beyond superficial appearances. When we see a tool, we automatically think about its causal powers: how will the tool perform in use? And when we see other people, we automatically attribute inner mental states to them: if we notice a person looking in a particular direction, we wonder what she or he is seeing. This ability to go beyond appearances may be missing in other species – even chimpanzees. Primatologist Daniel Povinelli has shown that chimpanzees often fail to understand simple properties of physical objects (such as that a rigid hook makes a better tool than a flimsy one), and do not recognize the simple fact that eyes are used for seeing: a chimp will make begging gestures in front of a blindfolded person.

In contrast, humans effortlessly and habitually seek to explain everything around us. If animals do not think in this way, their thoughts are very unlike ours. Perhaps there are no animal philosophers and physicists because these activities are manifestations of a thinking style that is distinctively human: our thoughts penetrate beneath the surface of things.

How many stripes? It is possible to see the details – and count the stripes – on a real picture of a tiger, but can we do this with a mental image? Daniel Dennett argues that we cannot, because mental images lack the necessary detail. His conclusion, that thoughts therefore are not "inner pictures", is contrary to what many previous thinkers have supposed.

on the mat, or a passing fantasy that the cat is on the mat, and so on.

Other thinkers have doubted whether the concept of mental images really makes sense. Could there literally be images in the head, when there is no mind's eye for seeing? The American philosopher Daniel Dennett has argued that, when we think we are picturing something, we are merely describing it to ourselves in great detail. To support his thesis, he argues that there are fundamental differences between real pictures and alleged mental pictures – you can count the stripes in a picture of a tiger, but you cannot count the stripes in a tiger that you merely imagine. Like verbal descriptions, imagination leaves many details out.

Language and thought

If thoughts are not merely images, what might they be? Dennett's critique points to one suggestion: perhaps thoughts are linguistic? Unlike images, thoughts and sentences can both express facts very precisely, and they both lend themselves to logical inferences. These parallels have led some philosophers to conclude that we think in language.

If this is so, then language may have a profound effect on the way we understand the world. Schopenhauer (see p.173) claimed that language imposes a distorted idea of reality, with spurious boundaries and a false sense of order. The idea that language determines thoughts is also found in the linguistic relativity hypothesis. of linguists Edward Sapir and Benjamin Lee Whorf, who argued that different languages result in different ways of experiencing the world. For example, Whorf claimed that Inuits experience snow differently from monolingual English speakers because they have many words for snow. It turns out, however, that differences in the size of snow vocabulary have been greatly exaggerated, and that no cognitive differences between English and Inuit speakers have been found. If such differences were to be found, they could be explained by appeal to culture or environmental differences. Overall, while linguistic differences can have subtle effects on what we notice or remember, there is little evidence that language shapes thought. This suggests we may not think in the languages we speak. To say that thought has a linguistic form does not require that we think in English, or French, or Swahili. We may think in a universal language of the mind.

> “*The feeling entertained by so many that they can think, even reason, without language is an illusion.*”
>
> Edward Sapir, *Language*

Fodor

Jerry Fodor was one of the first philosophers to emphasize the analogy between minds and computers. Fodor thought that human minds may qualify as computers, in the sense that our minds contain inner symbols and an inner mental logic. This idea is called the computational theory of mind.

The suggestion that the mind contains symbols may sound odd: if we look inside the brain, we do not see any marks or inscriptions. But the same is true for computers, which contain nothing but electrical circuits. In a computer, a pattern of electrical pulses corresponds to a symbol, which forms an instruction in a programming language. Likewise in the mind, where symbols are electrochemical events in the brain. The mind can therefore be understood as a program run by the brain.

According to Fodor, the main goal of psychology should be to describe the program that constitutes the mind, not the physical materials that happen to be running that program. Just as computers can be made out of vacuum tubes or silicon chips, the mind could have been made out of something other than neurons and neurotransmitters. To describe the mind, we need only describe the program, and we can leave details about the hardware out of the story. Thus, Fodor believes, psychology will never be replaced by neuroscience.

If we think in symbols, it would be natural to infer that we think using the very languages we speak; these, after all, are made up of symbols, known as words. Fodor resists this conclusion. To learn a language, he believes, we must be able to translate words into a symbol system that we already understand, so we must have an innate language. Fodor calls this the language of thought.

> *My view is that you can't learn a language unless you already know one – the language of thought is known … but not learned. That is, it is innate.*
>
> Jerry Fodor, *The Language of Thought*

Jerry Fodor 1935–

According to the American philosopher Jerry Fodor, the mind is essentially a computer. Like a computer, it uses sequences of symbols in a rule-governed way. These are not the symbols and rules of a computer programming launguage, but of the "language of thought" – an innate, inner language that we all share.

Fodor has also defended an influential theory of how the mind is organized. He asks us to consider an optical illusion in which one line appears longer than another, even though they are equal in length. The striking thing about the illusion is that it persists even after we learn that the lines are equal: our knowledge cannot correct our experience.

Fodor uses evidence of this kind to argue that perceptual systems are modular – that is, they are isolated from the knowledge contained in our "central systems" where judgment and reasoning take place. Modules, according to Fodor, are fast, innate and dedicated to particular kinds of inputs.

Some philosophers and psychologists now argue that the entire mind is modular; even reasoning systems subdivide into isolated processing systems that carry out specific tasks, such as social reasoning, thinking about numbers or avoiding dangers. Brain injuries can lead to selective impairments in particular cognitive abilities, such as social reasoning or mathematics, suggesting that these abilities may indeed be modular. But Fodor is sceptical: he believes that only perception and motor control systems are modular, and argues that we need a general-purpose central system to decide what module to use for a given task.

Consciousness

How do electrical and chemical events in grey matter come to be experienced as red roses and euphonious symphonies? Even a complete neurological account of consciousness would not solve this fundamental problem.

Consciousness comes in various forms. For example, we can be conscious of our perceptions, as when we notice a red traffic light; or we can be conscious of ourselves, as when we reflect on our thoughts. In recent years, philosophers and scientists have been searching for a theory of consciousness, but so far have had limited success.

One major problem is that even if neuroscientists were able to come up with a good theory of how and when consciousness occurs, there would still be a big mystery about conscious experience. Suppose we know that consciousness occurs only when neurons fire 40 times per second. This still does not explain why our brains produce inner subjective experiences at all.

The American philosopher Thomas Nagel dramatizes the challenge of explaining consciousness by posing the question, what is it like to be a bat? Suppose we have read every scientific study of bat sonar and have complete understanding of the neuronal processes involved. Do we thereby know what it is like to experience the world from a bat's point of view? It seems not. There is an explanatory gap between understanding the physical world and understanding conscious experiences.

One can respond to the mystery in several ways. One can abandon the idea that consciousness has a physical basis that can be identified with particular brain processes. Or one can press on with trying to explain the mystery. Brain science is still in its infancy, and perhaps neural theories of consciousness will be more explanatorily satisfying as we learn more about the brain. Third, one can embrace the mystery. British philosopher Colin McGinn suggests that our inability to understand how consciousness could arise from physical processes may just reflect a limitation on human understanding. Just as dogs will never understand calculus, we may lack the mental machinery to make sense of how consciousness emerges in a physical world.

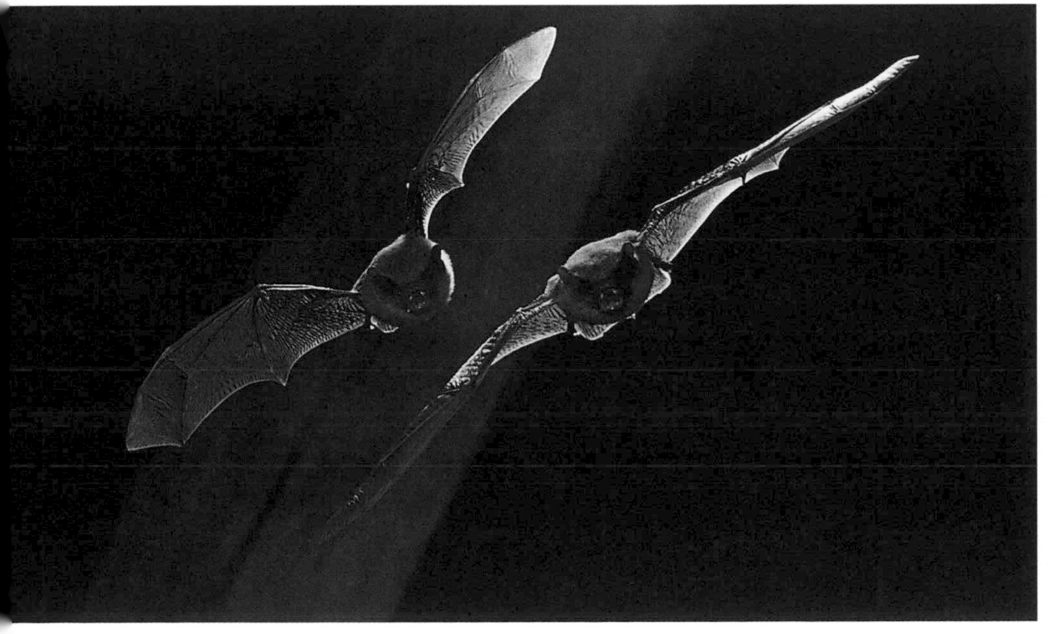

What is it like to be a bat? As philosopher Thomas Nagel points out, even if we knew everything about bat brains, and knew that certain brain processes were occurring when a bat uses sonar, we still cannot infer what it feels like for the bat. This makes subjective experience – consciousness – deeply mysterious.

Feelings and emotions

Feelings come in at least two basic varieties. We have sensations, felt through our senses; and we have emotions. But how do these two types of feelings relate to each other? And how do feelings relate to thoughts?

You can feel hungry, aroused or lightheaded. You can feel a sense of déjà vu, a thrill of elation or the sun on your back. At first sight, feelings appear to be a rather strange assortment, with little in common. So is it just an accident of language that we use one word to talk about all of them?

On closer analysis, some similarities emerge. The feeling of the sun is a sensation: it depends on the sense of touch. Feeling lightheaded, hungry or aroused may also be sensations, but from a sense that is directed towards our inner condition, rather than the external environment. Arousal and hunger also reflect our internal states and prod us to act: they are motivations. They seem similar to elation, which is an emotion or a mood. Déjà vu may be an emotion too – a slightly unnerving, feeling of familiarity. But a puzzle remains. Although there seems to be a continuum from sensations to emotions, bridged by various appetites, there is still no underlying feature that all of these feelings have in common. So why should a pinprick and a panic attack be put in the same category?

> *"Emotions are judgments. If I do not believe that I have been wronged, I cannot be angry."*
>
> Robert Solomon, "Emotions and Choice"

In the late 19th century, William James (1842–1910) tried to bridge the sensation-emotion divide. He observed that emotions often involve various changes in the body. When we are angry, our muscles tighten, our heart rate increases and our brows lower; we may even bare our teeth. Common sense has is that all of these bodily changes are effects of our emotions. James suggested that exactly the reverse is really the case: emotions are feelings caused by changes in the body, not the other way round. Anger is the feeling of our fists clenching, our hearts racing, and our brows lowering. It is the sensation of our bodies getting ready for a fight.

James's justification for this proposal is simple. Imagine being in an emotional state, he says, and then in your mind subtract all your bodily sensations. Imagine, for example, terror without the

Our facial expressions communicate our emotions to others – unless we take steps to hide them.

Can there be unconscious emotions?

We usually think of emotions, like perceptions, as conscious states. However, psychological studies have shown that we often perceive things unconsciously, as when we take in information while our attention is elsewhere. So are there unconscious emotions too?

Sigmund Freud (1856–1939) claimed that unconscious emotions are impossible. One might feel anxious and not know why; but for Freud this is because emotions are typically caused by thoughts, and these can be unconscious: we are conscious of the feeling, but unconscious of the thought behind it.

Since Freud, many experimental studies have shown that we often act on preferences of which we are unaware. For example, one famous experiment showed that people judge faces to be more attractive if the pupils of the eyes are dilated, although they will not consciously notice this difference. But whether this is really unconscious emotion, or simply conscious emotion with an unconscious cause, remains unclear.

More convincing evidence for unconscious emotions comes from a recent study on drug addiction. In the study, cocaine addicts were allowed to take intravenous "hits" from two solutions, only one of which contained minute amounts of the drug. After repeatedly sampling both solutions, the drug addicts concluded that both were drug-free, but, without realizing it, they had actually taken more hits from the solution containing cocaine. This behaviour suggests that they unconsciously found one solution more pleasant, implying that we can indeed experience pleasure unconsciously.

strained breathing, the wide eyes, the racing heart and so on. Without the bodily changes, says James, there will be nothing left that you can call an emotion. If James's argument is correct, emotions are just a special class of bodily sensations. This theory, which has recently been revived by neurologist Antonio Damasio, has the virtue of unifying emotions with other kinds of feelings. To support his case, Damasio cites evidence that the emotional circuits in the brain include structures associated with the perception and regulation of bodily states.

The cognitive theory of emotions

Despite its advantages, the Jamesian theory has been challenged on the ground that it does not do full justice to the nature of emotions. Notice some differences between an emotion such as anger and a sensation such as lightheadedness. Anger can be justified or unjustified, as when one gets angry at an alleged injustice, while lightheadedness can be neither. Anger is generally about something, as when you are angry when someone didn't return your call; lightheadedness is not about anything. Anger can occur without obvious bodily perturbation, as when we say we are angry about the new government tax policies; lightheadedness is constituted by a bodily perturbation. These contrasts suggest that emotions may have an essential cognitive (thought-based) dimension. Aristotle suggested that anger arises only when we believe that we have been insulted. Similarly, fear may involve a judgment of danger, while delight occurs when we recognize that a goal has been achieved. In this view, the traditional contrast between having an emotion and thinking breaks down: emotions are thoughts.

The cognitive theory has some advantages over James's bodily theory, but it leaves two things unexplained. First, if emotions are thoughts, why do we classify them as feelings, along with sensations? And, second, why are emotions often associated with bodily changes? Some psychologists and philosophers offer a simple answer: emotions are complex psychological states containing thoughts bound to sensations of the body. The conscious experience of anger is a cognitive component (the thought that you have been insulted) combined with a bodily sensation (a racing heart). At times, these two components come apart. In states of mild agitation, we can have some of the bodily sensations of anger without the thoughts; and, when we hear that government has ignored something we care about, we may have "angry thoughts" without actually feeling angry (diplomats are masters at this). By this approach, emotions do not undermine the dichotomy between sensation and thinking; they show only that the two often travel in pairs.

Language

Philosophers have had a long-standing interest in language. In the 20th century, many philosophical problems were reinterpreted as problems about the meanings of words. With this transition, language itself became a topic of extensive philosophical investigation.

Philosophical questions are difficult to answer using the methods of science. If you want to know what goodness is, or what actions count as free, there is no obvious experiment to perform. Philosophers typically investigate such questions by analysing concepts – for example, by asking what people mean when they use the word "good". In the 20th century, linguistic analysis began to dominate philosophical methodology – a trend fuelled by advances in logic. Philosophers also began to regard language as a phenomenon of interest in its own right. In addition to asking what particular words mean, philosophers have become very interested in the nature of meaning itself.

How do words, which are just marks on a page, sounds or gestures, come to mean what they do? The word "cat" represents a cat when uttered by most English speakers, but the almost identical sound means "adequate" in French (*quate*). It is natural to assume that words acquire their meaning from the intentions of their speakers. Philosopher Paul Grice developed an influential version of this idea in the 1950s. A word, he said, means whatever the speaker intends listeners to understand by his or her production of that word.

Grice's theory is intuitively very appealing, but it turns out to be vulnerable to counter-examples. For example, if you use incorrectly words of a foreign language you barely know, but with a particular intention, the words would retain their actual meaning in the language despite what you intended them to mean. One response to this problem favoured by many philosophers is to say that meaning is determined, not by a speaker's current

Language deconstruction: Jacques Derrida

English-speaking philosophers often assume that language allows us to readily convey thoughts and refer to the objective world around us. In the late 1960s, French philosopher Jacques Derrida launched an attack on this assumption. For him, language is not a window onto an objective world; rather, it imposes structure on the world by creating divisions that would not exist without language. We are never able to think without language, so we have no direct access to an objective world. In this sense, the world is itself a text—a set of objects, properties and events that acquire their meaning through language.

Derrida also thinks that there is no absolute truth about what our words mean. Meanings change from context to context, and in any particular context the meaning of a word may be irresolvably ambiguous. Derrida also criticizes the assumption that the speaker of a word (or the author of a text) has a privileged role in determining what those words mean. Meanings are determined, in part, by listeners and by social practices that a speaker cannot control.

Derrida's philosophical methodology is innovative. Rather than attempting to defend his views using clear analytic arguments, he tries to "deconstruct" language. He uses words in novel ways, makes puns, breaks up words in unusual places, exploits ambiguities and traces inventive etymologies that reveal connections between words that were not obvious before. This method is known as deconstruction because it is designed to undermine presuppositions about meaning and disrupt attempts to achieve clarity through language. Some readers find his deliberate obscurity and language play frustrating. His style is closer, at times, to avant-garde poetry than to traditional philosophy. But Derrida's work poses a challenge to widespread assumptions that is hard to ignore.

Great speakers, such as statesman John F. Kennedy, skilfully exploit the meanings of words. But what exactly is meaning?

intentions, but by the intentions and linguistic practices of a whole community of language users. On this view, a word gets its meaning from the fact that it is *ordinarily* used with certain intentions.

Reference and sense

So what, then, are meanings? In developing a theory of meaning, it is natural to begin with the supposition that a word means nothing more than what it refers to. You can specify what a word means, on this view, by just pointing to its referent – the object that the word designates. Many philosophers, however, believe that this theory of meaning is inadequate. The logician Gottlob Frege devised an influential argument for this conclusion. Consider the sentence "Lewis Carroll is Lewis Carroll." This is obviously true. But now consider "Lewis Carroll is Charles Dodgson." This is true, since Lewis Carroll was the pen-name of Charles Dodgson. But if reference were all there was to meaning, then the latter sentence should also be self-evidently true. But it is not universally known that the two names refer to the same person. So there must be more to meaning. What, then, is the missing ingredient?

> *A painter, a horseman, and a zoologist will probably associate different images with the name 'Bucephalus'. Thus, the image is fundamentally different from the sense of the sign, which can be the joint property of many people.*
>
> Gottlob Frege, "On Sense and Reference"

A natural suggestion is that the meaning of a word is the idea it expresses, where ideas are regarded as images in the mind. The problem with this proposal is that images can vary from person to person, but when two people use the same word they seem to be capable of conveying the same meaning. Meanings are shared; mental images are not. This problem led Frege to postulate something called senses. Senses are not objects in the world, like referents, or ideas in the mind, like images. Although it is not always clear what senses are supposed to be in Frege's work, it can be helpful to think of them as sets of properties in virtue of which a particular word denotes its referent. "Lewis Carroll", for example, picks out the person who has the property of being the author of *Alice's Adventures in Wonderland*, while "Charles Dodgson" picks the person who teaches logic at Oxford. These two sets of properties are possessed by the same individual, so the names co-refer, but they differ in sense.

Frege's theory has come under attack in recent decades. One concern is that, just as images vary from person to person, different people may associate the meaning of a word with different collections of properties. If meanings comprise senses, and senses vary from person to person, then it is not clear how meaning can be shared by users of the same language. Another worry is that senses are very hard to constrain. People often associate many properties with the words that they use. For example, we know a tremendous amount about cats – their diets, behaviour and so on. But which aspects of this encyclopaedic knowledge constitute the sense of the word "cat"? There seems no principled way to separate knowledge that is part of the meaning of the word from facts that we just happen to know about cats. The sense of a word begins to look a bit unwieldy. If senses encompass everything we know about a class of objects, how do we bring senses before our mind when processing the meaning of the words we hear?

A third problem for Frege's theory concerns the relationship between sense and reference. Frege argued that sense determines reference, so that any two words with the same sense must refer to the same thing. The American philosopher Hilary Putnam developed a thought experiment to refute Frege's assumption. Here is a version of his argument. Imagine that there is an isolated island where a species of cat-like animals live. "Myowies", as the islanders call this species, are not cats: although they are outwardly indistinguishable from cats, they have a different genome and a different evolutionary history. They are a different species, so our word "cat" does not refer to them, and the islanders' word "myowie" does not refer to cats. Nevertheless, English speakers and islanders conceptualise these creatures in exactly the same way, so "myowie" and "cat" have the same sense – but different referents. It follows from this that sense cannot determine reference.

If the sense of a word does not determine its reference, then we need another account of how words refer. Many philosophers now think reference is determined by historical relations. On this view, "cat" refers to cats and not to myowies because the word "cat" was originally introduced while pointing to cats. When someone utters the word "cat" today, their use of that word can be traced back to that original introduction of the word.

This theory takes up the idea that words mean what members of a language community generally intend, and the literal meaning of a word is usually what the people who coined it intended it to convey. So meaning is normally determined not by the current contents of our minds, but by history. Those who are mistaken about what their words were used to represent in the past may be mistaken about what they are saying now.

Language and logic: Frege's influence

Gottlob Frege (1848-1925) was a German mathematician and philosopher who made a major impact on the course of 20th-century philosophy. His work provided the foundations for the philosophical study of language and set the stage for the emergence of analytic philosophy, which uses the tools of logic to characterize the meanings of words.

Frege cared about logic because he was convinced that it provided a foundation for some branches of mathematics. Many of Frege's contemporaries believed that mathematics and logic had psychological foundations, and that if we had different kinds of minds, logic might be different. Frege opposed this view, believing that the rules of logic were absolute and universal. He sought to translate the basic rules of arithmetic into the language of logic and thereby derive all arithmetical truths. This was a breathtakingly ambitious effort, which captivated philosophers at the turn of the 20th century. Although the project was ultimately unsuccessful, along the way Frege showed that logic could be used in constructing proofs of mathematical theorems. This obviated the need for writing proofs in everyday language, which were notoriously difficult to verify.

While Frege's innovations on logic were revolutionary, his influence in other areas of philosophy has been equally significant. Frege demonstrated that one could gain insight into the meaning of a word by breaking it down into its logical components. Where philosophers had once asked questions such as "what is existence?" or "what is knowledge?", they began to ask questions such as "what does 'exist' mean?" and "what does 'knowledge' mean?" This may look like a retreat from the world into language, but it proved a very valuable approach. Logical analysis allows philosophers to formulate precise and illuminating answers to questions that originally seemed vague and impenetrable.

Wittgenstein

Wittgenstein inspired two different schools of thought. His early contributions inspired logical positivism (see p.92), while his later contributions inaugurated the movement called ordinary-language philosophy and anticipated themes in contintental philosophy such as deconstructionism. Wittgenstein had a distinctive approach to writing philosophy, emphasizing provocative conclusions rather than arguments. His works are immensely challenging, and he raises fundamental questions about the nature of philosophy itself.

Ludwig Wittgenstein 1889–1951

Ludwig Wittgenstein is perhaps the most remarkable figure in 20th century Western philosophy. Wittgenstein's first book had a major impact on the philosophical world. Later, he became very critical of his earlier views. His new ideas culminated in a posthumously published book that would change philosophy for a second time.

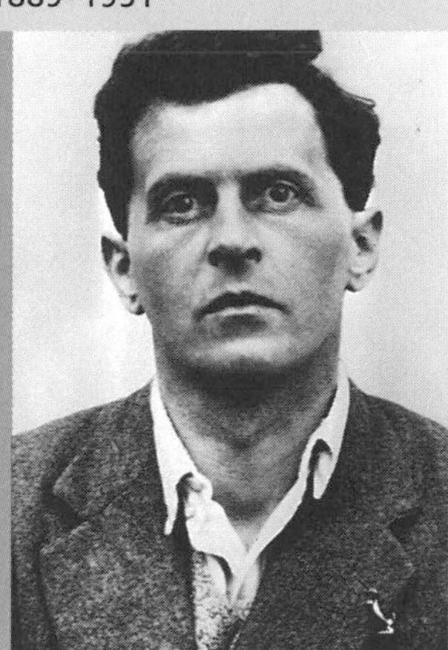

Wittgenstein was born into a prominent Viennese family of Jewish and Catholic descent. He was the youngest of eight siblings, several of whom were artistically talented. On the darker side, three of his four brothers committed suicide.

Wittgenstein initially took a degree in engineering, but by 1911 he was studying philosophy under Bertrand Russell at Cambridge. When World War I broke out, Wittgenstein joined the Austrian army. In 1918, while on leave, he completed his first book, the revolutionary *Tractatus Logico-Philosophicus*, which was published in 1921.

In the *Tractatus,* Wittgenstein claimed that the world is made up of facts, not objects as we normally assume. If it were made up of objects, the relationship between sentences and the world would be obscure. But sentences express facts, so if the world is made up of facts, we can say that sentences and the world have a similar form.

By this view, to understand a sentence is to know what fact would have to be the case for that sentence to be true. Wittgenstein infers from this that sentences can represent only contingent facts, facts that could be false. This does not mean there are no necessary truths – but only that such truths cannot be conveyed using language. For Wittgenstein, the rules of logic are like this: they are not facts but overarching principles that dictate the structure of facts. Wittgenstein suggests that ethical truths may also fall into this category of necessary truths hovering above the changing world of facts.

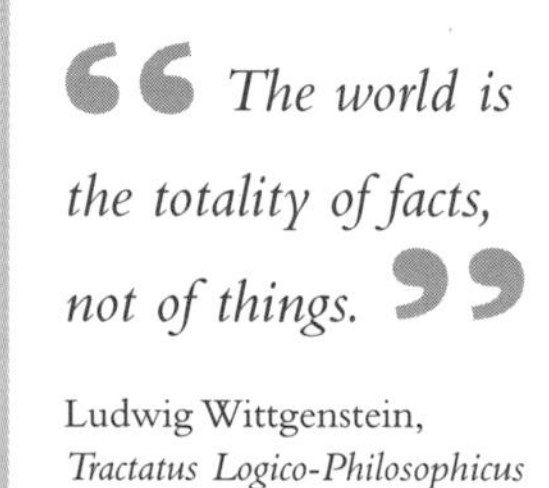

"The world is the totality of facts, not of things."

Ludwig Wittgenstein, *Tractatus Logico-Philosophicus*

The *Tractatus* is a challenging read that vexes students and scholars alike. Even Bertrand Russell, who wrote the original introduction, may not have fully understood it. Wittgenstein himself said cryptically of the *Tractatus* that its real import lies in what it does not and cannot say.

The *Philosophical Investigations*

At the time of its publication, Wittgenstein believed that the *Tractatus* had solved the fundamental problems of philosophy. Convinced that his work was done, he spent the following years working outside the academic world. He returned to a post at Cambridge in 1929, by which time his views were beginning to change. The numerous lectures Wittgenstein gave at Cambridge on his new ideas ultimately evolved into the *Philosophical Investigations*, published posthumously in 1953.

The *Philosophical Investigations* is written as a series of numbered, interrelated aphorisms. Wittgenstein rarely presents an argument and insists, emphatically, that he is not constructing a theory, but rather challenging the reader to give up assumptions that are pervasive in philosophy. There is considerable debate about what Wittgenstein was trying to convey in many passages, but little debate about the importance of the work, which engendered an entirely new approach to philosophy that dominated the English-speaking philosophical world for years after its publication.

> *What is your aim in philosophy? To show the fly the way out of the fly-bottle.*
>
> Ludwig Wittgenstein, *Philosophical Investigations*

Philosophical Investigations is, in part, a challenge to the views in the *Tractatus*. There, and throughout philosophy, it had been assumed that language is primarily in the business of representing things: sentences state facts. In *Philosophical Investigations*, Wittgenstein says this is a distorted conception of language. The meaning of a word is determined not by the object it represents, but by the way it is used in language games – the various conversational contexts in which a word may appear. The same word can be used in many different language games, and this variability means that many words cannot be given precise definitions, because their meaning will vary with context. However, the collective set of meanings of a word will resemble each other, much like members of a family. The word "game" itself is a case in point. In trying to define "game", one might propose that games have two sides; this is refuted by the example of solitaire. One might say that all games can be won or lost, but that leaves out the game of throwing a ball back and forth. For any alleged defining feature, one can find counterexample, and there is no feature that all games have in common. This does not make the word "game" incoherent. Rather, it is a feature of language that words are associated with loose clusters of features, instead of specific defining features.

Wittgenstein's new conception of language led him to conclude that many philosophical problems were based on confusions. Philosophers, he suggested, become mired in language by assuming that every word must be referring to something, and they spend generations trying to figure out what

Can there be a private language?

Of all Wittgenstein's philosophical contributions, none has been more widely discussed than his so-called private language argument. There are many interpretations of this argument, but a standard reading can be summarized as follows.

Imagine a person who decides to invent a language that only he can understand. One day he experiences a particular sensation and he gives it a name. Then, on a later occasion, he experiences a sensation that he takes to be just like the first, and he calls it by the name that he coined on that earlier occasion. Can we say that he was correct in re-applying the term? Wittgenstein thinks that we cannot; nor can we say he was incorrect. Words, he argues, can only be correctly or incorrectly applied if there are public criteria for using them correctly. Suppose, for example, that the man had misremembered his earlier sensation. We might be tempted to say he is wrong to use his private word now. But perhaps his private word refers to a larger class of sensations and applies correctly to both? No one other than him has any authority on this, but he too cannot be sure when he is getting it right. Real languages are public, and communities of language users collectively determine when words can be used. Wittgenstein concludes that a truly private language, usable by only one person, would not count as a language at all.

While many philosophers were persuaded by Wittgenstein's argument when it first appeared, today many find the argument flawed. Imagine a person who has an abnormal olfactory system that causes her to hallucinate a distinctive smell from time to time. It seems perfectly plausible that she could introduce a word for this smell and refer to it whenever the smell occurred. Even if she inadvertently uses the word to refer to other sensations, that does not show the word is meaningless – only that she can be mistaken. And if we are good at identifying our own sensations, as seems plausible, the chances of such an error are slim.

For Wittgenstein, chess is a game because of features it shares with other games – but no features are shared by all games.

those things are. Wittgenstein says that language is not in fact a tool for referring, but rather a collection of practices used to coordinate our actions with those of others. Philosophy, he said, should be transformed into a form of therapy whose primary function is to cure philosophers of the confusions caused by their misunderstanding of language.

This directive is put into practice throughout Wittgenstein's mature philosophy. In the last months of his life, he wrote a collection of remarks that were later published under the title *On Certainty*. Wittgenstein argues here that the debate between sceptics and defenders of commonsense is confused. Sceptics say that we cannot know that there is an external world, and that we must even doubt the existence of our own bodies. Their opponents try to show that scepticism is wrong by constructing proofs for the existence of the external world. But, says Wittgenstein, both sides are mistaken. In ordinary language we use words such as "doubt" and "know" to describe things about which we can be uncertain, so it is an abuse of ordinary language to say "I doubt that I have two hands" or even "I know that I have two hands". Similarly, the word "uncertain" is not ordinarily applied to fundamental commonsense beliefs, such as the belief in an external world. If we want to know what is certain and what is uncertain, we need only look at how these terms are ordinarily used. Wittgenstein argues that both sceptics and their opponents use such words in deviant ways in their debates, thereby changing their meaning and shifting the topic of discussion. Followers of Wittgenstein today continue to adopt this model of philosophizing, and they try to dissolve age-old philosophical debates by showing that both sides misuse the key terms.

> *By liberty, then, we can only mean a power of acting or not acting, according to the determinations of the will; that is, if we choose to remain at rest, we may; if we choose to move, we also may. Now this hypothetical liberty is universally allowed to belong to everyone who is not a prisoner and in chains. Here, then, is no subject of dispute.*
>
> David Hume, *An Enquiry Concerning Human Understanding*

Free will

Intuitively, we feel that we have free will: we can choose what we say or do. But religion and science both call into question the very notion of free will, implying that our choices are predetermined by factors beyond our control. So is our sense of free will an illusion?

Historically, the problem of free will was first recognized by the founding fathers of the Christian Church. They saw that free will is in tension both with God's omniscience and with his omnipotence. If God is omniscient, he must have foreknowledge of our choices, and if he is omnipotent, our actions must have been determined along with the rest of his creation. In the face of these threats to free will, Augustine (see pp.116–117) maintained that humans are at least free to accept divine grace and redemption.

Later Christian theologians aimed to defend a more thoroughgoing freedom. In the 13th century, Thomas Aquinas (see p.112) and his followers argued that God exists outside time, and so his powers do not imply any kind of predetermination. While he knows all things, the world he has created includes exercises of free will unconstrained by prior circumstances. In this respect, God's knowledge might be compared to his viewing a film: although he sees everything that happens, he has no influence on the action.

While God's existence outside time may successfully accommodate his omniscience, the threat to free will posed by his omnipotence is not so easily removed. In the 16th century, both Martin Luther and John Calvin argued that God has indeed preordained all our choices, and that therefore it is predestined who is saved and who is damned. Catholic orthodoxy continued to uphold the notion of free will, and the great ecclesiastical Council of Trent, begun in 1545, emphatically repudiated the doctrine of predestination.

After the scientific revolution of the 17th century, science replaced religion as the major threat to free will. The mechanical philosophy of the new science implied that movements of matter are always determined by prior material circumstances. To the extent that human beings depend on their material bodies, it would seem to follow that all our choices are determined by circumstances beyond our control. In response to this scientific threat, some philosophers accepted that our choices are indeed determined and that therefore we have no free will. For example, the 17th-century Dutch philosopher Spinoza (see pp.66–67) concluded that free will is an illusion.

Most modern philosophers, however, have sought to defend free will against scientific determinism. There are two quite different ways of doing this. Libertarians agree with Spinoza that determinism would leave no room for free will, and deny that human beings are in fact determined. By contrast, compatibilists are prepared to accept that human choices are determined, but they deny that this rules out human free will.

Mental autonomy?

At first sight, it might seem as if the libertarian view is supported by the 20th-century discovery that the physical world is fundamentally chancy at the sub-microscopic "quantum" level. (We know that, even with complete information, the behaviour of sub-atomic particles can be described only by laws of probability, so their precise behaviour cannot be predicted.) Some thinkers such as Roger Penrose have argued that this deterministic "gap" could in fact be the basis for the freedom we all seem to experience in our own mental lives. However, such quantum haphazardness seems a poor basis for free will. Suppose you choose one job rather than another because by chance an electron in your brain moves one way rather than another. This does not seem an exercise of your

In Christian theology, God – depicted as the divine draughtsman of creation in this 13th-century French illumination – is both omnipotent and omniscient, raising the question of whether there is room for human free will. Today, the same problem is posed by scientific materialism.

free will, but more like an outcome decided by the toss of a coin. Genuine free will would seem to demand an autonomous self that actively resolves to go one way rather than another, not some purely random means of deciding the issue.

To uphold free will, libertarians need to view the human mind as somehow separate from the material realm of modern science. Once humans are regarded as purely material beings, there is no room for the kind of autonomous control libertarians require – whether matter is governed by deterministic laws or otherwise. In line with this, Descartes (see pp.48–49) argued for the dual nature of mind and body. By this view, mind and body are separate substances, but they can interact. In particular, the mind can autonomously resolve to move the body as it wills. Although similar "dualist" views have been defended by some modern thinkers including Karl Popper (1902–94) and John Eccles, this is now very much a minority stance. Physiological research has simply given no reason to suppose there is a separate mental realm: changes in the physical brain are clearly linked to changes in the mind.

Free will as preference

Instead, most modern-day defenders of free will are to be found in the compatibilist camp. The compatibilist response to the problem of free will goes back to Thomas Hobbes (see pp.184–185) and David Hume (see pp.24–25); more recent defenders include A.J. Ayer (1910–89) and the contemporary American philosopher Daniel Dennett. Unlike libertarians, compatabilists do not resist determinism but seek a place for free will within it. To see how this could be, contrast choices that are intuitively within your control, such as which of two job offers to accept, with things that are intuitively beyond your power, such as running a three-minute mile or bringing about world peace. The obvious difference is that which job you decide to accept depends on your preferences, while whether you run a mile in three minutes does not.

> "*…from the fact that my action is causally determined it does not necessarily follow that I am constrained to do it: and this is equivalent to saying that it does not necessarily follow that I am not free.*"
>
> A.J. Ayer, "Freedom and Necessity" in *Philosophical Essays*

Note that this contrast does not require that your wants themselves be undetermined. Perhaps your genes and personal history make it inevitable that you would prefer one job to the other. Still, it remains the case that you chose that job because you preferred it. Your action may have been determined, but at least the determination went through your wants and was not independent of them. Provided your action flows from your preferences, argue the compatibilists, then you are free, even if your preferences are determined by your past.

> *The will is by its nature free so that it can never be constrained.*
>
> René Descartes, *The Passions of the Soul*

Not everybody is convinced by this compatibilist version of free will. Intuitively, when we say that people act freely, we hold them responsible for their actions and blame, praise, reward or punish them accordingly. However, if their actions are determined by their previous history, even if this process is mediated via their wants, then attributing blame and praise seems inappropriate – somewhat akin to praising someone for a sound upbringing. To this extent, the compatibilist version of free will appears to omit an essential feature of true free will.

The problem of free will thus resists any easy solution. On the one hand, libertarians seek the kind of free will that makes an autonomous difference to the course of nature, even though it is unclear that modern science leaves any place for such free will. On the other hand, the kind of compatibilist freedom that remains strikes many as a pale shadow of the real thing.

Free will and justice

If the preferences on which we act are themselves predetermined, can we in fact hold people responsible for their actions? American trial lawyer Clarence Darrow (1857–1938) used this as a standard line of argument in defending his clients. He urged juries to remember "that we are all the products of heredity and environment; that we have little or no control, as individuals, over ourselves; and that criminals are like the rest of us in that regard". None of Darrow's clients in murder cases ever received the death penalty.

Some compatibilists, by contrast, uphold traditional responses to wrongdoing. The American philosopher C.L. Stevenson (1908–79) pointed out that the actions the compatibilist counts as "free" – those that issue from agents' preferences – are precisely those where there is some *point* to ascribing praise and blame, since they are just the cases in which we can influence agents by altering their preferences.

But are Stevenson's "praise" and "blame" themselves the real thing? To "blame" people purely as a way of manipulating their behaviour is not the same as actually resenting their deeds. Oxford philosopher Peter Strawson has argued that Stevenson's "detached" versions of blame and praise fall far short of such genuinely "reactive" attitudes as resentment, anger and gratitude. Strawson observed further that these reactive attitudes are basic to human relationships, and that it would be quite inhuman always to take a detached attitude toward those close to you, treating them as objects whose behaviour is to be manipulated. He concluded that abstract philosophical arguments involving determinism cannot possibly show that it would be right always to suppress our natural reactive responses in favour of detached manipulation.

Still, even though such reactive attitudes come naturally to human beings, this does not mean that they are always morally justified. Insofar as the misdeeds of criminals are a predictable upshot of heredity and environment, it may indeed be unfair for the legal system to hold criminals to account for their crimes. Strawson is undoubtedly correct to point out that it would be inhuman to adopt a detached perspective in all our personal relationships. But this does not mean that the detached suppression of reactions such as resentment and anger may not be an appropriate attitude for those designing systems of law and punishment.

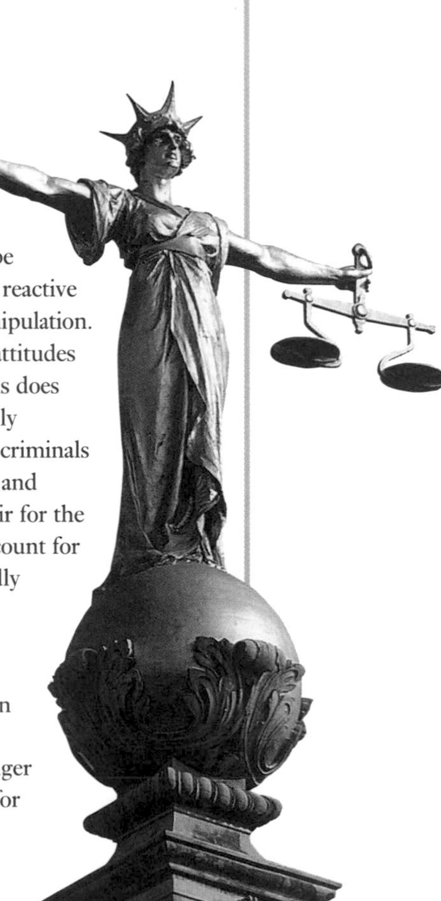

Spinoza

Spinoza was born in Amsterdam to a Jewish family who had fled Portugal because of persecution by the Spanish Inquisition. He received an education within the Jewish community, studying the Talmud and Jewish philosophers such as Maimonides. He also developed a keen interest in Descartes' work. As a young man, he publicly defended a number of views that were at odds with prevailing Jewish orthodoxy, rejecting the immortality of the soul and regarding biblical stories as parables. In 1656, he was excommunicated from the synagogue for his views. He adopted the Latin name Benedict in place of his given name Baruch, and took up work as a lens grinder to support himself while continuing to study philosophy. Spinoza died of lung disease at the age of 44. His major work, *Ethics*, was published posthumously.

Benedict (Baruch) Spinoza 1632–1677

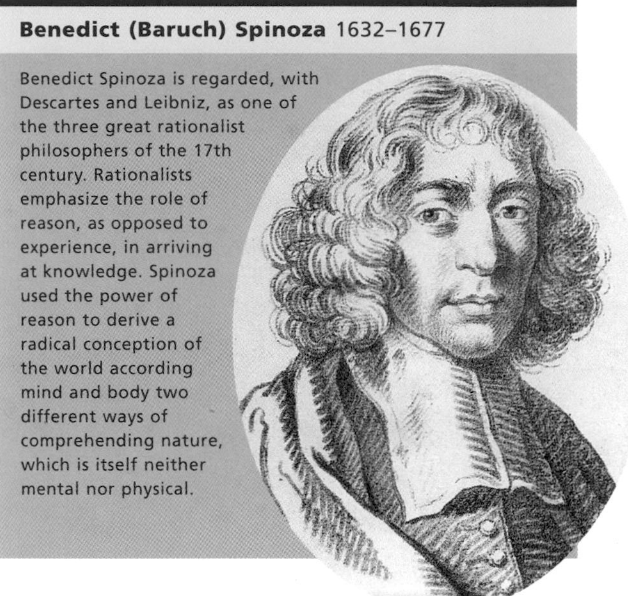

Benedict Spinoza is regarded, with Descartes and Leibniz, as one of the three great rationalist philosophers of the 17th century. Rationalists emphasize the role of reason, as opposed to experience, in arriving at knowledge. Spinoza used the power of reason to derive a radical conception of the world according mind and body two different ways of comprehending nature, which is itself neither mental nor physical.

Ethics is a daunting read, because its style is that of a mathematician. Spinoza begins with a small set of basic principles and definitions, then derives further conclusions from these using complex proofs. The book blends lessons from Descartes with ideas inspired by Jewish philosophy and Greek stoicism. The result is utterly original, and a major contribution to the history of Western philosophy.

Central to *Ethics* is the notion of a substance. Descartes (see pp.48–49) defined substances as things whose existence does not depend on anything else. According to Descartes, mind and body

Spinoza's passionate psychology

In *Ethics*, Spinoza advanced a novel theory of human psychology. He claimed that our behaviour is driven by a striving for self-preservation, or *conatus*. This can be understood as an effort to achieve greater control or power. Desires are experiences of this striving. For Spinoza, there is no distinction between belief and desire, no way of passively entertaining a thought. Every idea is marked by dispositions to act. Some of our actions lead to an increase in power; these cause joy. Other actions and events decrease power, which is experienced as sadness. Spinoza regarded joy and sadness as fundamental emotions from which others can be derived. For example, he defined pity as sadness caused when another person is injured, while love is joy coupled with an awareness of the thing that causes the joy.

For Spinoza, emotions reflect the downside of the human predicament: they are responses to events that are outside our control. But feeling despair in our losses and jubilation in our successes is unwarranted, given the ultimate necessity of all things. To react emotionally is to harbor the illusion of freedom; and the only true freedom we can achieve is knowledge of this necessity. When this knowledge comes, it can also bring a kind of calmness. We recognize that all our hopes and fears are in vain, since we have no power to change the course of nature. Given our inability to change the world, we should strive to restrain our emotional responses as much as we can. This flight from passion echoes the views of the Stoics (see p.138) and some traditions in the East. Spinoza joins a long line of thinkers who regard emotions as essentially confused.

are fundamentally different substances – that is, they have no attributes in common. Spinoza disagreed, arguing that there could be only one substance, and that substance is God. God, after all, is perfect, and perfect things must have all attributes. If substances are distinguished by their attributes, then there can be no substance other than God, because there can be nothing with attributes that God lacks. Mind and body, then, are not distinct substances at all; rather, they are two different ways of conceiving the one true substance, God. Since God is everywhere and everything in this view, Spinoza equated God with nature as the only existing substance.

Spinoza's view is called neutral monism, meaning that only one substance exists and it is neither mental nor physical. It contrasts with dualism (the view that mind and body are separate substances); materialism (the view that there is one substance and it is physical); and idealism (the view that there is one substance and it is mental). Spinoza's account of the mind–body relationship is intended to circumvent Descartes' difficulties with mind–body causation. If mind and body are distinct substances and substances are, by definition, independent, then one should not be able to affect the other. By embracing monism, Spinoza lifted this barrier, but the resulting position may seem equally odd. On Spinoza's view, mind and body do not exactly interact, rather, they are parallel but distinct perspectives on the same thing.

> *Men are deceived if they think themselves free, an opinion which consists only in this, that they are conscious of their actions and ignorant of the causes by which they are determined.*
>
> Benedict Spinoza, *Ethics: Part II* (35)

Freedom in a determined world

Spinoza's theory of reality has important implications for free will. Because everything that exists is part of God, humans have no independent reality: we are all just "modes" in the one true substance, like wrinkles in a great cloth. Human actions are completely determined by God or nature, and freedom is, strictly speaking, an illusion arising out of ignorance. We think we are free because we fail to discern the causes of our actions.

Spinoza did not regard our lack of free will as a cause for despair. There is, he claimed, a kind of liberation that we can obtain through knowledge. When we fail to recognize the causes of our actions, we are passive or unwitting victims of those causes. But when we recognize that everything we do is determined by things outside us, we can claim to be active participants in the causal ebb and flow, rather than passive victims. We can choose to act as we are determined to act. Paradoxically, we can achieve a form of freedom through the knowledge that we are not free.

Spinoza regarded joy and all other emotions as inherently misleading, because all things happen through necessity.

The self

Each of us assumes that we are the same person, or self, today as we were last week. But are we really entitled to that assumption? Finding a source of continuity connecting us to our past and future selves turns out to be very difficult.

Over time, as we accrue new experiences and forget old ones, we change psychologically. Suppose that, as a result of these gradual changes, our identities change. If this is right, then a different person inhabited my body a few years ago, and another will occupy my body a few years from now. Should I care about either of these "other" people, if they are not the same person as I am today?

John Locke (see pp.82–83) wrote a seminal discussion of personal identity in which he suggested that memory is the key to survival of the self. You are the same person today as you were in the past, because you remember your past. But the 18th-century philosopher Thomas Reid pointed out that memory, unlike identity, is not transitive. Suppose now you recall your teenage years, and as a teenager you recalled your early childhood. It does not follow from this that you remember your early childhood. If you do not, then Locke must say that you are your teenage self, your teenage self is your childhood self, but you are not your childhood self. This cannot be right, because two things that are identical to a third thing must be identical to each other.

One might try to account for Locke's reasoning by saying that we are identical to our past selves because there is a continuous string of memories linking us together. This is better, but still faces difficulties. The Oxford philosopher Derek Parfit argues that there is no sense in which a person at one time can be the same person at a later time if the latter has no recollection of the former. Consequently, he says, we must accept the conclusion that our bodies contain not a single continuous self, but rather a collection of successive selves. It may be irrational, he adds, to care more about the person who inhabits your older "self" than for another person, as neither one of them is you.

The 1957 film *The Three Faces of Eve* was based on a real-life case in which one woman lived as three different "selves". This psychological condition is called dissociative identity disorder.

In contrast, the British philosopher Bernard Williams has argued that memory is inessential to identity. Imagine, he says, being told that an evil scientist is about to erase all of your memories, and just afterwards he will inflict excruciating pain. If you identify with your memories, the threat of the excruciating pain should not cause you any more anxiety than learning that a complete stranger is to be tortured. This is surely disturbing, but your own comfort would not be at stake. But in the imagined scenario, it seems that the pain inflicted would be your pain: you would be the one to suffer. Williams invites us to consider the idea that we identify with our bodies, not with our memories.

Sanity and insanity

According to our normal notions, sane people are in control of what they are doing, while insane people need treatment and may not be responsible for their own actions. But this description leaves the central concepts unclear. So what exactly is it to be sane or insane?

The term "sane" is inherently contrastive: it cannot be defined without referring to its opposite. Today, we rarely use the word "insane". Instead, we talk of psychiatric disorders and see such conditions as illnesses. Most of us regard this medicalization of insanity as progress. It removes blame from those we diagnose as mentally ill and may offer new options for treatment. But medicalization has its critics: some have argued that in fact the division between normal and pathological in the mental realm is constructed by cultures, not discovered by science as the medical model suggests.

Defenders of the medical model often try to show that mental disorders qualify as diseases by identifing a physical basis underlying the psychological symptoms. For example, researchers have found distinctive abnormal patterns of brain activity in schizophrenics and people with manic depressive disorder. But there are psychiatric conditions for which no distinctive physical marker has been found; and even if there were a distinctive biological sympton for every psychiatric condition, we could not infer that those conditions are illnesses, because physical difference by itself does not entail pathology. If liberals and conservatives have different brains, it does not follow that one of these groups is sick.

An alternative account of mental disorder is the social constructionist view, which takes note of the cultural variablility of such concepts. For example, in Western culture there has been a huge increase in the diagnosis of dissociative identity disorder, and a radical decline in hysteria diagnoses. According to social constructionists, the division between sanity and insanity reflects a cultural group's decision to value certain psychological traits above others. One of the most vocal defenders of the social constructionist view is psychiatrist Thomas Szasz. He argues that mental disorders cannot literally be forms of illness, because illness is defined in terms of the body. Since most mental disorders are not physical pathologies, medicalization is no more than metaphor. Szasz thinks that the illness metaphor is dangerous because it is used to defend policies that take rights away from people deemed insane and to absolve them of responsibility when they violate social rules. French philosopher Michel Foucault (see p.88) has also defended a social constructionist view of insanity, and urges that people we regard as insane have legitimate persectives on the world that deserve to be heard.

The American philosopher Susan Wolf has argued that the criminal definition of insanity may point to a definition that has advantages over both the medical and constructionist accounts. To be criminally insane is, in effect, to be incapable of understanding things that others understand – in particular, what one is doing and the moral significance of one's actions. So perhaps mental disorders in a broader sense are like this. Their victims have a less accurate understanding of the world than others do: schizophrenics hear unreal voices, depressives see their endeavours as hopeless, and so on. If insanity involves systematic error, sanity may just be a matter of being able to understand the world more or less as it really is.

> " *Strictly speaking, disease or illness can affect only the body; hence, there can be no mental illness.* "
>
> Thomas Szasz, *The Myth of Mental Illness*

Life and death

What is life? What is death? These questions may seem to have easy answers, or at least answers that can be readily determined by science. In actuality, both have proven difficult, and definitions of life and death remain surprisingly elusive.

Philosophers are known for pondering the meaning of life. They also have something to say about the meaning of "life". That is, in addition to asking what makes life worthwhile, they ask a more basic question about what it is to be a living thing.

In a sense, life presents an analogue of the mind–body problem. Just as many cannot understand how mental states could be electrochemical processes of the brain, people have wrestled with the idea that life could be explained by mechanical or chemical processes of the body. In many cultures and times it has been presumed that life requires a special, non-physical life force. This idea, known as vitalism, was popular in 19th-century Europe. Vitalists at that time claimed that compounds such as urea and acetic acid could be produced only by a living thing. When scientists began to synthesize these compounds in the laboratory, many concluded that vitalism must be mistaken. Further, as scientists began using the resources of biology and chemistry to explain the processes found in living organisms, it became evident that all aspects of living things can be explained without postulating a hidden "life force". Vitalism has therefore fallen into disfavour in the Western scientific community.

Viruses seem to be on the borderline between life and non-life: they can reproduce only by hijacking the host cell's mechanism.

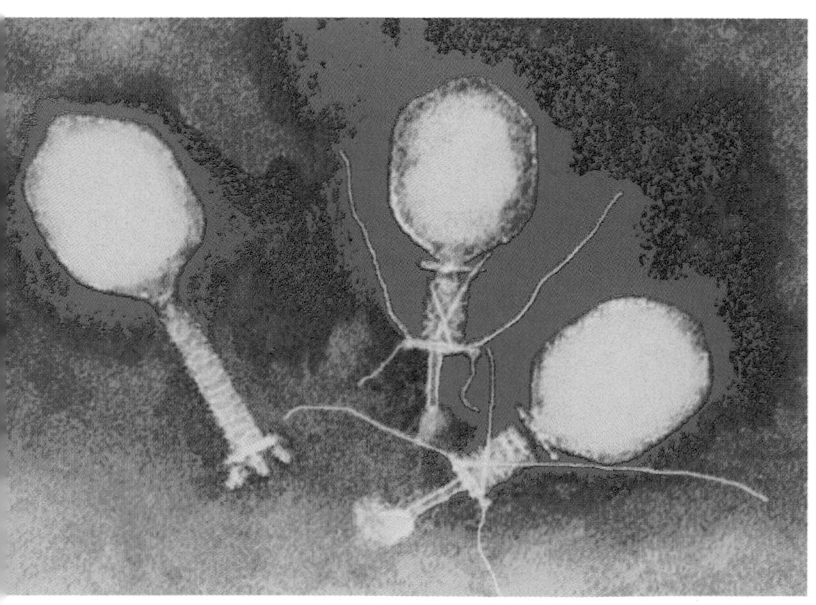

If there is no such thing as the life force, then we need a different definition of life. One strategy is to define life in terms of certain physical processes. Living things grow, move, metabolize and reproduce, so perhaps a living thing is just something that exhibits these processes? One problem with this definition is that some living things may fail to qualify. Consider an old, paralysed mule: it cannot move or reproduce and it may have stopped growing, but it is certainly alive. A second problem is that some non-living things also exhibit these processes: cars metabolize in so far as they use up energy and expel waste; and computer viruses can reproduce, move from computer to computer and grow over time. Similarly, wars between nations can spread, change locations, trigger other wars and even consume energy and produce waste. But we should not accept any definition of life that forces us to say that wars are alive.

One further definition of life is available. Intuitively, living things strive towards ends. They do so even if they lack mental states – even plants strive to maximize sunlight – while rocks and chairs do not. Called teleology, this feature of striving towards an end can be explained in purely physical terms by appeal to Darwin's notion of natural selection. A trait that increases an organism's prospects for survival or reproduction is likely to be passed on to the next generation, so such a trait has an evolved purpose in that it helped past

Fear of death

Assuming that there is no afterlife and that death is final, is it rational to fear death? To some people, the answer is obviously "yes". Death is the loss of life, and life is what we value most. Still, many philosophers have argued that we should not fear death.

Epicureans held that, if death is a state of nothingness for the dead, it is nothing to fear. Fear of death, they surmised, was fear of painful dying. Death itself is not bad for the dead, because they are dead, and not bad for the living, because no living person can be dead. In response one might point out that, while the living are not dead, they do die, and dying is a terrible thing. It brings all of our hopes, ambitions and pleasures to an end. But that still does not mean that it is rational to fear death. Stoics said that death should not be feared because we cannot do anything about it. It is irrational to fear the inevitable, because fear gives us the false impression that there is an escape route. Nietzsche said we should embrace death joyfully, by choosing when to die. Other existentialists said that death should be a source of dread because it reveals the ultimate absurdity of existence. More optimistically, they viewed death as a motivation to live life more fully.

Fear of death can also be addressed from a Darwinian perspective. We are programmed by our genes to procreate and to try to stay alive. Fear of death may be instinctive to help achieve this end. It may be as natural as the desire for sex, and, in this Darwinian sense, it may be perfectly rational. In response, one might argue that natural selection generates only the fear of danger, not the fear of death. Voltaire argued that we are the only creatures that can contemplate our own death. But we are not the only creatures that work hard to stay alive, so working hard to live evidently does not require the fear of death. It seems more plausible, then, that fear of death is not an evolutionary adaptation, but an inevitable byproduct of our evolved ability to think and reflect.

generations survive. So perhaps we can say that to be alive is to have traits with teleological ends in this Darwinian sense. However, this definition is vulnerable to a serious objection. Suppose that an organism is created in a laboratory. That organism will not be the product of natural selection, so its traits will have no evolved purposes. If having such traits is essential to being alive, this organism cannot qualify as living. This is problematic, as the definition of life should not rule out the possibility that scientists could create living things, so having traits with evolved purposes cannot be a necessary condition for being alive.

Perhaps one of these definitions of life is reparable, or perhaps another definition can be developed. Until that happens the meaning of "life" will remain an unsolved problem.

Defining death

But what is it for a living thing to cease being alive – that is, to die? For bacteria, death may involve the cessation of motion and metabolism. For human beings, however, these criteria do not seem appropriate, as loss of motion is not sufficient for death, and loss of metabolism may not be necessary.

The definition of death that has become accepted by the health professions is that of brain death – the irreversible cessation of the functions of the entire brain. If circulation, respiration and metabolism can be maintained, but brain function cannot, a person qualifies as dead. This definition is, of course, hard to reconcile with the intuition that life centrally involves biological processes such as metabolism and growth, which can persist without a brain. It also means that our criteria for remaining alive are inconsistent: in humans, preservation of brain function is crucial, but in other species different criteria are used. This suggests that, in our own case, the concepts of life and death are closely tied to the concept of having a mind.

> “*What has this Bugbear Death to Frighten Man,*
> *If Souls can die, as well as Bodies can?…*
> *From sense of grief and pain we shall be free;*
> *We shall not feel, because we shall not Be.*”
>
> Lucretius, *De Rerum Natura* (John Dryden translation)

Chapter 3

KNOWLEDGE

What is knowledge?

We believe many things about the world, for a great variety of different reasons. But to call a belief "knowledge" means that it must have certain features in the way it relates to the facts. So what is it exactly that makes a belief count as knowledge?

If you want to know who to ask for advice on a topic, you look for someone who knows about it. We often say things like "Ask Marina, she knows all about Thai cooking" or "that's what Marcus says, but it's just his opinion; he doesn't really know." So one fundamental reason why we classify our beliefs and opinions into knowledge and less-than-knowledge is that we are interested in classifying one another as reliable and unreliable sources of information on specific topics.

We can clarify what counts as knowledge by thinking about what is not knowledge. False beliefs are obviously not knowledge; more subtly, a true belief that is obtained by guesswork is also not knowledge. A person who guesses that a tossed coin will come down heads does not know this, even if it does in fact land heads. Some connection between the fact and the true belief is needed for knowledge. One such connection is provided by evidence: if a person sees a Thai restaurant with a glowing newspaper review posted in the window, then that person can link a true belief about where the best Thai restaurant is located with evidence tracing back to the facts.

Throughout the world much knowledge is held within a community, rather than by individual experts. Such "traditional" knowledge is often the basis for methods of agriculture and food-preparation, such as the grain-sifting carried out by these Egyptian farmers.

Defining "know": two scandals?

Knowledge is a central philosophical concept, and philosophers always insist on the need to define one's terms. So it is striking, perhaps shocking, that until the late 20th century nearly all philosophers used the words "know" and "knowledge" without even trying to define them. Most philosophers thought that there was a simple and obvious definition: a belief is known when it is true, and reasonable. Then, in the 1960s, prompted by a single short paper by Edmund Gettier, philosophers suddenly woke up to the fact that this answer is neither obvious nor true. There are many cases of true, reasonable beliefs that we would not call knowledge. Suppose, for example, a very trustworthy friend tells you some juicy gossip, which you believe. In fact, the friend was lying, for the only time in her life, but the gossip just coincidentally is true. Your belief is true, and reasonable (because your friend is generally trustworthy), but it is not knowledge.

Philosophers then set to work and produced many possible definitions of knowledge, all of which proved vulnerable to increasingly complicated and subtle counter-examples. But instead of giving up, or trying a different tack, numerous philosophers are still working away, refining their definitions and generating more counter-examples. Is this perhaps as great a scandal as not even trying to achieve a definition?

Evidentialism and traditionalism

There is thus an ideal, "evidentialism", according to which a person's belief counts as knowledge if there is enough evidence that it would be unreasonable not to believe it. According to evidentialism, a belief without this kind of evidence is mere opinion, not knowledge. But this is a rather extreme position: it would mean that beliefs that we acquire from the testimony of others are excluded from knowledge, unless we have independent evidence that what these others say is true. In fact, according to evidentialism, very little of what any person believes will count as knowledge.

> "*Man by nature desires to know.*"
>
> Aristotle, *Metaphysics*

We can contrast evidentialism with traditionalism, which advances an ideal in which people are members of communities that pass on reliable information to one another and that jointly possess more evidence than any one person can summon. Traditionalism makes it easier to understand why many people believe themselves to know, for example, the basic principles of science, although very few could cite the experimental data on which they are based. But traditionalism often seems to make knowledge too easy: any prejudice that is prevalent in a community could be defended along traditionalist lines. So most philosophers take knowledge to be described by criteria that lie somewhere between the stringency of evidentialism and the permissiveness of traditionalism.

One major focus of the theory of knowledge has been the idea of a rational reason for a belief. The assumption here is that a belief cannot count as knowledge unless it is rational and based on reasoning. This assumption, however, can be challenged (and is implicitly challenged by traditionalism, because communities themselves do not reason). An individual person believes many things about the world without producing anything as intellectual as a chain of reasoning to defend them. The simplest example of this is perception: we just see and hear how things are, and the processes of perception are generally reliable ways of learning about the world – at least as reliable as our capacities to carry out complex reasoning. We also have social reactions that tell us when to believe, trust or fear, one another, and these too are roughly accurate, although obviously not infallible. In fact, at least as many of our beliefs based on information from our senses and social intuitions are likely to be true as those reasoned laboriously from a small amount of very carefully obtained data. And it makes sense to honour those "intuitive" beliefs that are true with the label of knowledge, despite the lack of reasoning involved.

Plato

Plato is the central figure in ancient Greek philosophy and the original writer on many strands of the European philosophical tradition. He came from an aristocratic Athenian family and distrusted the democracy of his native city. His political writings describe a variety of alternatives to democracy, and Plato made one disastrous attempt to serve as a philosophical advisor to a political leader, the tyrant Dionysius of Syracuse. The greatest influence on his life was his revered teacher Socrates, whom he immortalized by making him the central figure of many of his dialogues. His own teaching took place in the Academy, a distant ancestor of modern universities.

Plato's thinking revolves, on one topic after another, around questions of the limits of human knowledge. And though the details vary with the topics, and from one work to another, Plato suggests that genuine knowledge is at once surprisingly attainable and startlingly unreachable. He articulates an ideal of perfect infallible knowledge and suggests that on some subjects – notably mathematics, ethics and metaphysics – that we have a chance of attaining such knowledge, while at the same time insisting that most of the world around us is simply not capable of being known.

Plato's starting point was the teachings of Socrates, whose theme was not knowledge but rather intellectual humility. Instead of arguing for any positive philosophical doctrines, Socrates debunked the pretensions of other intellectuals of his time who claimed to be able to understand morals, politics and the universe and to be able to transmit their understanding to others. He developed a technique of probing questioning that revealed that its victims did not have grounds for the assumptions on which their assertions rested, and usually did not understand their own central concepts. They did not know as much as they thought they did. Socrates, on the other hand, claimed to "know only that I know nothing". Socrates' assertion does not contradict itself: he has no knowledge of what people often claim to know, but does have knowledge of a different kind concerning the relation between the mind and reality. For Socrates, this second, attainable, kind of knowledge is very limited and serves mainly to limit our ambitions in the sphere of knowledge. In Plato's hands, though, the distinction between what people think they know and what philosophers can hope for becomes much more dramatic.

Plato *ca.*429–377BCE

Plato contrasted the changing world of appearances with unchanging ideas or "forms", such as goodness and the truths of mathematics. The forms are known by reason, which allows us to grasp mathematics and begin to see what is good in individual and political life. But for Plato the changeable nature of the world around us gives the mind no hold by which to know it.

The knowable and unknowable

The complex of ideas that is usually taken as "Plato's philosophy" is worked out in a series of dialogues – fictional discussions usually led by the figure of Socrates – that were written in the middle of Plato's career. The essential points are: the "forms" (of which more later); the soul's affinity to them; and the unknowable world of appearance. To introduce the forms, consider Socrates' demonstration of his opponents' ignorance: they do not even understand the ideas, such as "virtue", "justice" or "courage" about which they are pronouncing. To understand these ideas, according to Plato, would be to possess adequate definitions of them and to be able to arrive at absolutely certain conclusions about some of their properties. To show that this is possible, Plato shifts the focus to mathematics, where we can prove that some claims are true in a way that gives us a firm grasp on them.

We can know, for example, the Pythagorean theorem in a way that is much less tentative and speculative than our knowledge of anything in the physical world. And so, in a crucial yet tendentious move, Plato stipulates that real knowledge is typified by that which mathematical proofs give us. Thinking that results in anything less is incomplete and unsatisfactory. So, he argues, when we do know anything it is something that, once grasped by the mind, cannot be taken away. The subjects of this knowledge are things that cannot change (knowledge cannot be un-known): these are the forms. They can be thought of as abstract qualities such as triangularity, virtue or courage; or as ideal models of things as varied as humans, societies, and everyday objects.

> “*Bodily exercise, when compulsory, does no harm to the body; but knowledge which is acquired under compulsion obtains no hold on the mind.*”
>
> Plato, *Republic*

Plato shifted, from one work to another, in his description of the forms, and it is very hard not to read into his texts ideas that appear in later philosophical thought. But for Plato, the essential characterization of the forms is: what can be known. That is, he insists that we can have knowledge, but this must be about rather different things from those things we think about in everyday life.

The knowable forms thus contrast with the unknowable world around us. We think we are surrounded by physical objects whose properties we know through our senses. But in fact, according to Plato, this domain is unsuited to being known, for two reasons. First, it changes. Objects have properties at one time and then have the opposites later: they go from young to old, small to big to small; they change in location and arrangement. As a result, anything we conclude about them may have to be retracted later. Second, it is a domain of appearances. Things look different from near or far, in one light or another, or to one person or another. As a result, all evidence about physical objects will have to be tentative, taken as a report of just one of perhaps infinitely many perspectives. Plato did not clearly separate these two obstacles to knowing the world. He characterized the world as a place of seeming and becoming, unfriendly to the mind.

Love and knowledge

The most literary of Plato's dialogues is the *Symposium*, which describes a long drinking party in which the participants give their deepest thoughts about love – all types of love: carnal, homosexual, heterosexual, asexual. Socrates' speech at the party is meant to bring out the links between love of a particular other person and love of something abstract, such as truth, beauty or justice. (It is significant that Socrates says, in the somewhat misogynistic atmosphere around his male companions, that what he knows about love he was taught by a wise woman, Diotima.) There are two ways of interpreting what Socrates is saying. The one which has greater superficial coherence with the rest of Plato's philosophy is that, when we think we are loving another human being, we are really loving something much more abstract, such as the form of beauty. But another, not inconsistent, reading is that when we are moved by love for something abstract, such as truth, it is real physical love of the same kind as moves us towards another person, with the same psychological origins. So, for Plato, the human capacity to know and the human capacity to love are interdependent: we could not have one without the other.

In fact, he sometimes suggests that the familiar world may itself be an illusion that hides unchanging reality. He can suggest this because he takes the fact that objects look different under different circumstances to be an intrinsic property of them, closely linked to the fact that they change, rather than as a relation between objects and people, mediated by sensory impressions, as modern philosophers would. In addition, it is hard to avoid the impression that he thinks that the slow and messy business of sorting through varying and contradictory data about the sensible world, to draw a few tentative conclusions that have not yet been refuted by some observation from some point of view, is beneath the dignity of a noble mind.

Sources of knowledge

So if we do not gain knowledge through our experience of the world, how then do we get it? The simple answer for Plato is: through thinking. But to think we have to think about something: and how do we manage to get an "about" relation to the forms? It seems evident to Plato that if the mind or soul were simply a thing in the world of change, it would never be able to have knowledge. So in order for the soul to think about the forms, it must be distinct from the body. While the body is part of the changing physical world, the soul is more like the forms and thus can interact with them. The soul is in fact as complex as reality: there is an aspect to it that is like the unchanging forms and as a result can know them, and there is an aspect that is like the changing illusory world and the body, and as a result can take part in the play of images and illusions from the sensible world.

Plato was very interested in images and illusions, and often uses metaphors of image-making to describe the relation between the forms and perceptible things. Most famously, in the *Republic* dialogue, Plato uses a metaphor of projected shadows to explain how we can make the transition from focusing on the physical world to focusing on the forms. Imagine, he says, people chained in a cave so that they can see only a wall, which is illuminated by the light of a fire, close to which objects are carried so that their shadows fall on the wall. They would take these shadows to be real things. However, if their chains were broken, they would turn and recognize the objects themselves as the originals of the shadows: a real sword is more sword-like than the shadow of a sword. But until they had done this, they would not know what real things, as opposed to shadows, were. Similarly we, condemned to live in the movie theatre of everyday life, can know that there are forms but find it hard to know what they are. All we can say is that they are more authentic examples of things and qualities – such as triangularity, virtue or justice – than anything we meet in perceptual experience. Similarly, a carpenter making a bed is trying to make as bed-like an object as possible. Plato describes this as the carpenter trying to imitate the form of "bed". When the carpenter succeeds, a bed is produced. This, however, is in the world of change and will thus never be an absolutely perfect bed, so for Plato it as an imperfect copy of the form of bed.

Immortality and mathematics

Plato holds that we can know mathematical facts by reasoning and not by perception. In his dialogue *Meno* he illustrates this by having Socrates elicit from a slave who has had no experience of mathematics a theorem about how to make a square of twice the area of a given square. But how can an intellectually untrained person even understand the concepts needed for this? Plato's answer is that, before we are born, our souls are in contact with the forms. Though someone may be a slave in this life, before this life his soul was mingling with the ideas of length, area and shape. But in the process of being born into a human body we forget what we have learned of the forms, so that in order to know about mathematics we have to laboriously remember, by subjecting ourselves to proofs and demonstrations. This doctrine of metaphysical amnesia and remembering (*anamnesis*) can be seen in two ways. You can see it as Plato extracting himself from a philosophical tight spot by appeal to a mystical doctrine, or as Plato arguing for the existence of an immortal soul from the fact that we are capable of understanding mathematics.

For Plato, our knowledge of the real world is very limited: it is as if we see only shadows of things, not the things themselves.

The forms of virtue and justice remind us that Plato is as much concerned with moral and political issues as he is with mathematics. Indeed he wants the two to be intimately connected. In *Republic*, he describes a city-state ruled by philosophers whose education is largely in mathematics and abstract issues of political philosophy. As a result, he argues, these benevolent dictators will be able to make the best decisions and produce the best lives for everyone in the state. The whole state, in fact, and the mind of each person in it, will be a rough image of the abstract form of justice. To us today this seems as politically naïve as it is metaphysically extravagant, but there is an important point from which this reaction should not distract us, which is that moral thought has many similarities with mathematics. In both cases we are not trying to find out how things actually are in the world around us but how they must or should be; and in both cases we proceed by applying abstract principles. For example, in deciding if a social institution is just, we compare it to criteria of justice, such as impartiality, and consider imaginary variations on it that might affect its acceptability.

In expounding this metaphysics of knowledge that is at the heart of his philosophy, what Plato says about knowledge is rarely separated from what he says about reality or goodness. In one later dialogue, *Theaetetus*, Plato discusses knowledge for its own sake. But what he says there does not make a dramatic contrast between the knowable forms and the unknowable world. He does not mention the forms at all. He argues that perception is not a good source of knowledge, but does not deny that there might be knowledge of ordinary things by some other means. (An example, not Plato's, might be knowing that it is 5 miles from A to C because B is 4 miles due east of A and C is 3 miles due north of B.) Given that believing something on the basis of perception is not knowledge, even if the belief is true, Plato tries to find a better definition of knowledge. Plato suggests tentatively that to know is to believe with a reason for believing. Not any reason will do; it has to be the kind of reason that supports knowledge. Plato leaves the discussion at this point, having shifted some of the force of the question from "what can we know?" to "what is a good reason for believing something?"

> “*Thus the soul … has seen all things both here and in the other world. …All nature is akin, and the soul has learned everything, so that when a man has recalled a single bit of knowledge – learned it, as we ordinarily say – there is no reason why he should not find out all the rest.*”
>
> Plato, *Meno*

Perception and experience

How do we obtain information about the world around us? Perception – using our senses – is obviously a very important source of such information. But is all knowledge derived from perception alone?

Perception is where the world meets the mind: light and sound from objects travel through the air and impinge on our eyes and ears, which set off a chain of events in the nervous system, which results in our seeing and hearing. These processes have evolved over millions of years to be robust and reliable; usually the beliefs they give us about the immediate environment are accurate. Moreover, information obtained from the senses often seems to be quite resistant to other influences. If you think that maple leaves turn blue in the autumn and then see a red maple leaf, it will look red to you and you will have a strong tendency to believe that at least some maples have red leaves sometimes. You can try to resist that tendency, either by thinking that what you saw was not a maple leaf or by dismissing the whole experience as an illusion, but the perceptual information is likely to remain persuasive. The stubbornness of perception is naturally taken as a sign of honesty: it reports what it reports, however surprising or unpopular the news.

However, it is doubtful that perception on its own can account for our whole knowledge of the world. In fact, very few beliefs can be based entirely on perception: for example, we need reasons for thinking that the tree from which the red leaf comes is a maple. It is possible that these reasons can themselves be derived from perception, but it will be via long twisting routes where many things can go wrong. In addition, the very stubbornness of perception can as well be taken as dogmatism rather than honesty – like someone always telling the same story, whatever the evidence. If there is some basic feature of the world that perception systematically misleads us about, the very stubbornness of perception would then be a disadvantage, blocking our realization of how things really are. Some philosophers have argued that this is indeed our situation. Descartes (see pp.48–49), Locke (see pp.82–83) and many contemporary philosophers argue that colours and tastes are not real features of things – yet perception presents objects as if they were simply red, green, sweet or sour.

Is seeing always believing? Here, our knowledge overrides our perceptions: we do not think the buildings curve in reality.

Sight and seeing

The 17th-century philosopher John Locke suggested an interesting experiment. As he puts it: "Suppose a man born blind, and now adult, and taught by his touch to distinguish between a cube and a sphere ... Suppose then the cube and sphere placed on a table, and the blind man be made to see: quaere, whether by his sight, before he touched them, he could now distinguish and tell which is the globe, which the cube?" Locke continues with his assessment of the likely results: "[I] am of opinion that the blind man, at first sight, would not be able with certainty to say which was the globe, which the cube, whilst he only saw them; though he could unerringly name them by his touch..."

In the 1960s it became possible to carry out this experiment when people suffering from life-long cataracts were operated on. The results are only partially favourable to Locke. On gaining the use of their eyes, people can usually tell the difference between simple shapes through sight alone with very little training. On the other hand, they never manage to make full use of their eyes. Seeing requires a coordination with other senses, and this may be impossible to acquire as an adult.

The account of knowledge first put together by John Locke in the late 17th century and developed in the next generation by Berkeley (see pp.28–29) and Hume (see pp.24–25) was a response to these problems. These philosophers tried to describe how beliefs can be based on perception in the most direct way, so that their influence is not diluted by influences from other sources and the issue of the fundamental accuracy of perception can be faced squarely. According to this approach, known as empiricism, the first step in perception is the reception by the mind of simple perceptual ideas. These ideas are completely immune to influence by beliefs and expectations and represent nothing but the way a person's subjective experience seems to him or her.

The most important feature of this level of perception is its infallibility. For example, if you are seeing a red leaf, you cannot be mistaken about the redness and shape you are seeing, even if you can make a mistake about whether it is in fact a leaf you are looking at or even whether it is a physical object. You still know with complete certainty that your experience of the moment is characterized by this colour and this shape. According to empiricism, these infallible perceptual data can used as a basis for inferring other, more substantial beliefs, such as that what we are seeing is a real leaf from a real maple tree.

Most philosophers today reject the empiricist approach of grounding all knowledge on perceptual foundations, and see traditional empiricism as misconstruing the nature of perception, which does not start with infallible data about perceptual appearances. Rather, it consists of innate processes that give us beliefs about the locations, colours and movements of things in the world around us, processes which are extremely reliable (although not perfectly so). Sometimes our knowledge of the world gives us reason to believe that some perception is not reliable, and sometimes a scientific investigation allows us to understand better exactly how and when the use of the senses will give us true beliefs. So, on this alternative picture, inference passes both ways between beliefs and perceptions, and in the process we manage to find evidence for most of what we know.

> *"Let us suppose the mind to be, as we say, white paper, void of all characters, without any ideas. How comes it to be furnished? ... To this I answer in one word, from experience."*
>
> John Locke,
> *An Essay Concerning Human Understanding*

Locke

John Locke was the first philosopher to articulate the central ideas of modern empiricism, according to which very few issues can be settled without careful and unbiased consideration of evidence obtained from the senses. Born in 1632, he wrote at a time when Newton's physics was replacing the science of Galileo and Descartes, whose ideas owed more to reason than empirical evidence. In supplying the ideology to accompany Newtonian science, Locke made the empiricist attitude part of educated common sense. The same anti-dogmatic attitude shaped Locke's influential ideas about religious tolerance: when it is so hard to know what the truth is, Locke argued, people should as far as possible be left to believe what they choose.

John Locke 1632–1704

Locke 's theory of empiricism is a complete account of the mind and its relation to its environment. According to Locke, the mind obtains all its ideas through perception and reflection. Even with these capabilities there are definite limits to what we can know, and beyond these limits, he believed, we must tolerate one another's opinions.

Locke's central claim about knowledge is that there are no innate ideas. He meant two things: first, along with many other philosophers, Locke held that we have to learn our beliefs in various ways through our experience of the world; second, and more fundamentally, he insisted none of the concepts which we use in our beliefs are present at birth. Many had assumed that basic concepts, such as identity, were just part of the mind's thinking equipment. Locke argued that even these concepts need to be acquired: at birth, the mind is a *tabula rasa*, a blank slate.

In his *An Essay Concerning Human Understanding* (1690), Locke gave a number of reasons for denying the existence of innate ideas. He points out that children do not acknowledge abstract principles involving basic concepts until they have been taught. Two-year-olds do not say "everything is identical to itself" or "four right angles make a complete revolution." Newborns, he further points out, do not seem to think in terms of any concepts at all – for they do not seem to think. As for the ideas of properties of objects, such as shape, weight and solidity, he argues that what we sophisticated adults have in mind here are in fact complex combinations of ideas. The idea of a triangular shape, for example, is based partly on what various triangular objects look like when seen from various angles, partly on what they feel like, and partly on what it is to walk around triangular routes. It is only when a person can combine all of these images that they have the idea of a triangle.

In Locke's view, children at birth lack the basic concepts of colour and shape and must acquire these through experience.

Sources of knowledge

So, if there are no ideas at birth, where do they come from? Locke's answer is that the mind has innate capacities to acquire ideas from perception of the external world and from reflection on itself and its contents. So after a very little time in the world, a child will have what Locke calls "impressions", which are the the simplest ideas produced by sensation and reflection. Sensation gives impressions such as particular colour shades, and reflection gives an impression of the self. By combining these impressions we formulate complex ideas, such as those of physical things and of their properties. So a child can combine the simple ideas of grey and large with the ideas of shape and solidity to get the more complex idea of an elephant and of a trunk, and to form the belief (which Locke would also call an idea) that elephants have trunks. In this way, the whole rich content of our thinking is built up from simple elements received passively via perception and reflection.

> *"There is a great variety of opinions, concerning moral rules, which are to be found among men … Which could not be, if practical principles were innate, and imprinted in our minds immediately by the hand of God."*
>
> John Locke,
> *An Essay Concerning Human Understanding*

This position satisfies the empiricist slogan "everything comes from experience". But Locke's empiricism was in one way less extreme than that of many other empiricists, as he did not think that our reasons for holding all our beliefs come only from perception. Instead he held that, once one has the idea of a triangle and the number three (for which perception is essential), one can then know just by reflecting on these ideas that all triangles have three sides.

Locke regarded knowledge gained from reflection as not limited to the physical world. By reflecting on ideas of right and wrong, we can discover some important facts, such as that cruelty is wrong. However, there are some questions, Locke thinks, to which we will never know the answers; and such questions are at the heart of many religious disputes: we cannot prove that the soul is immortal or that one or other form of religion is right. This idea leads Locke to a political consequence of empiricism. Locke believed that some uniformity of belief was necessary for social harmony, and thought that belief in the existence of God and enough Christian doctrine to underwrite morality should be required of citizens. But, he proposed, most other religious matters should be left to the conscience of the individual. Three hundred years later this may be uncontroversial, but in Locke's day it was a truly daring claim.

Primary and secondary qualities

On Locke's account of perception, to perceive is to have ideas, which are aspects of the mind. Locke held that some ideas match the properties of actual objects: his list was solidity, extension (length), figure (shape), motion or rest, and number; these are the "primary qualities". Others – colours, sounds, tastes, and so on – do not: these are the "secondary qualities". We think of secondary qualities as being real features of things, but this to Locke is an illusion. "The leaf is red" just means "the leaf looks red to humans". So Locke thinks that leaves are not really green or red, and food is not really sweet or sour.

This distinction between primary and secondary qualities is still accepted by many philosophers today – but is it correct? On the one hand, if you look at a red maple leaf under an electron microscope, its redness disappears. On the other hand, the same is true of its shape. If you shine coloured light on the leaf it looks a different colour – but then, if you take it to the moon it will have a different weight. It seems the world as depicted by science is utterly different from the world as it appears to our senses – so different that it is hard to find a sharp divide between properties that really do match their appearances and others that do not.

Scepticism

There are surprisingly strong arguments for scepticism – the idea that human beings know very little at all, not even that we inhabit a physical body in a physical world. So how much of what we take as knowledge should we trust?

We are very sure of some things. Only insane people would doubt that they have heads on their shoulders, or that water is wet. Indeed, we would have concerns about the sanity of anyone who doubted many less obvious things, such as that babies form within the bodies of their mothers, or that the moon orbits the earth. Yet since ancient times, sceptical philosophers have expressed doubts about our grounds for such beliefs.

There are some standard "thought experiments" that philosophers use to make vivid our possible lack of knowledge. Consider a brain kept alive in a vat of nutrient fluid on Alpha Centauri, being fed stimulation to its optic and other sensory nerves from a powerful computer. The brain could have sensations just as if it were living on earth, perhaps reading a book called *Philosophy*. But, in fact, its belief that there is a book in its hands would be false, for there would be no book and it would have no hands.

The important point here is not that such a brain would have very little knowledge, although indeed it would not. The vital point is that an ordinary person in an ordinary body, such as you or me, cannot rule out the possibility that we are brains in vats. So, even if our beliefs are in fact true, they will not count as knowledge – because our evidence for them is the same as the evidence that the brain in the vat has for its false beliefs, and this does not seem enough to prove to anyone that he or she is not a brain in a vat.

> *"How do I know that [God] has not brought it about that there is no earth, no sky, ... while ensuring that these things appear to exist just as they do now? ... may I not similarly go wrong every time I add two and three, or count the sides of a square?"*
>
> René Descartes, *Meditations on First Philosophy*

Resisting scepticism

There are three main responses to the sceptical predicament. The first is to find some way of proving that we are not brains in vats or victims of any similar deceptive situation. Descartes (see pp.48–49) tried to do this, arguing that we can prove by the power of pure reason alone that God exists and that God would not permit any such trick to be played on us. But this response fails, because it turns out to be circular: in order to show that God exists and wants us to have true beliefs, Descartes has to make assumptions that would be false if we were brains in vats.

The second response is to argue, based on a reinterpretation of the brain's thoughts, that a brain in a vat does, after all, have as much knowledge as you or me. For example, when the brain thinks "there is a book in my hands", perhaps we should interpret this thought as about the presence of a book in the subjective image which is being produced by the computer. And of course there is a book in this subjective image, and moreover the brain in the vat is perfectly placed to know this. So if that is what the thought "there is a book in my hands" is, it is something the brain in a vat does know. The upshot is that the brain in a vat has just as much knowledge as a person on earth, but knowledge of a different reality. This line of thought can be found in the writings of Kant (see pp.141–143) and more recently in the work of the contemporary American

The Matrix is a film set in a future in which machines have taken over the earth and keep human beings hooked up to life-support machines, feeding them illusory experiences from a supercomputer. When the viewers of the film see the "action" that occurs within this virtual reality, they need to remember that they are merely being presented with the illusions experienced by the captive humans.

philosopher Hilary Putnam. However, there is something disappointing about this response to scepticism. It is not much consolation to be told that you know a lot of things, if your knowledge is solely about the way the world appears to you subjectively rather than how it is in reality.

The third response is to argue that we do have good, if not conclusive, evidence that we are not the victims of any conspiracyinvolving vats. We do not need certainty in order to know, and the "hypothesis" that one is living in a human body on earth is part of a body of beliefs that explain the details of one's experience better than the hypothesis that one is a brain in a vat. The main advantage of this response is that it does reveal the hidden and dubious sceptical assumption that what is known must be certain. There is a worry, however: does this response do anything more than show us that we are justified in believing that we are not being deceived, as opposed to showing us that we reliably know this?

All but the first of these responses gives some material for resisting scepticism, but none of them seems a knock-down refutation of it. Suppose that it cannot be refuted: would that be an intellectual disaster? We would then have to accept the possibility that we have almost no knowledge, if we take the word "knowledge" in a strict and demanding way. But it would still be the case that we have more evidence for some beliefs than others, that some beliefs are well founded and others insane, and that there is no serious reason to believe that we are being systematically deceived. As the contemporary American philosopher Peter Unger puts it, the concept of knowledge would then be like that of flatness. Nothing is completely flat, since the smoothest surface in the world has tiny imperfections and at the atomic level an array of atoms can never form a precise plane. But that does not prevent us saying that deserts are flatter than mountains, or that the standards of flatness for the mirrors of reflecting telescopes are very high.

Relativism

Relativism is the idea that when people have very different opinions, each is right relative to their own point of view. Some versions of relativism are very subtle and profound, while others are simply crude mistakes.

Not so very long ago, the most intelligent and well-informed people believed that the earth was at the centre of the universe. They were wrong, we say now, but they had reasons for this belief. Similarly, in many cultures past and present, the belief that there are many gods who rule over the affairs of humanity is prevalent among respected thinkers, who also have reasons for thinking this. Are these people simply wrong? Some people – firm monotheists and atheists – will be sure that they are, as in their view it is false that there are many gods. Others will balk at saying this: the belief in question is part of a whole system of beliefs that is very different from our world view, so to dismiss it as false rather than simply different seems to ignore the possibility of understanding the world in any way except the one we happen to hold to at present.

We may disagree about the exact height of Mount Everest or who first climbed it, but for an anti-relativist there must be a fact of the matter – whether we know it or not.

Relativism and anti-relativism

Relativist theories of truth view the truth of statements or beliefs as relative to the circumstances of those making the statements or holding the beliefs. Of course, the truth of some statements can depend in a very straightforward way on the circumstances of the person making them: the statement "the red buoy is on the left" is true when you are leaving the harbour, but false when you are entering it. Most relativist theories, however, go much further than this in allowing that beliefs can be true for one person and false for another, and often involve a relativist claim about the nature of truth itself. One very basic relativism about truth says that, because we can almost never

Alien viewpoints

Perhaps the most profound versions of relativism focus on the limitations of the human perspective. Even many anti-relativists with respect to other human cultures think that our beliefs must be evaluated relative to a human point of view, and not invalidated by the possibility of non-human ways of thinking. As human beings, we are equipped with particular sensory organs and our brains are wired up in a manner that makes it possible to think in some ways and impossible to think in others. We can imagine that there might be intelligent creatures that perceive different things and think in different ways; but we find it almost impossible to imagine the thoughts of these creatures. Suppose, for example, that, for understanding the universe, the best belief humans can have (in terms of fitting the facts we know) is that the universe consists of zillions of fundamental particles. And suppose the best belief for the aliens is that the universe consists of one thing, related to itself in ways we cannot conceive. Well: can there be just one thing and zillions of things? A non-relativist response is to say that one of these views is true, though humans may not be capable of knowing which. A relativist response is to say that each is true, relative to its own point of view.

be certain what is true, we might as well just mean by true "true for B" where B is a person who has the belief. Most philosophers see this as a confusion: the fact that we cannot tell whether a claim is true has no bearing on whether it is in fact true. A slightly more subtle relativism argues that the truth is different for different people because different people mean different things by their words. So if by "gods" you mean "important factors affecting human life" then "there are many gods" is true.

In contrast, an anti-relativist about truth is someone who thinks that whether a belief is true can in principle be answered in absolute terms, irrespective of who holds the belief. Importantly, an anti-relativist need not hold that our current opinions about what is true are correct. Future science may refute most of our beliefs, and may employ methods that we have not thought of. What an anti-relativist must hold is that, ultimately, there is always a fact of the matter: if future science differs from present-day science on some point, then either it is true or present science is true: no fence-sitting of the "each is true in its own way" sort is allowed.

> *"Relativistic theses often come in two forms: a bold and arresting version, which is proclaimed, and a weaker, less vulnerable version, which is defended – with the first having a tendency to morph into the second when under attack."*
>
> Chris Swoyer, "Relativism" in *The Stanford Encyclopedia of Philosophy*

Reason and evidence

One can also be a relativist about reasons, as well as about truth. In medieval times in Europe, almost everybody took the Bible and the declarations of the church as sufficient proof for their belief, while today empirical scientists support their theories by appeal to experimental evidence. One might say that medieval people were wrong to take these as proofs for their belief because we now know that scientific reasons are the only good ones. But why should we say this? Science has produced a large and coherent body of beliefs with many practical applications, but a stubborn medievalist could always say "there's no reason to believe any of it". One possible answer is the fact that radically different attitudes can converge over time. Many philosophers believe, or perhaps simply hope, that if people who base their beliefs on very different evidence from ours were to encounter more facts and the pressure of difficult problems, then eventually their attitudes will approach ours. If these optimists are right, then instead of saying "that was evidence for them but not for us" we can say "that was what they mistakenly took to be evidence."

Foucault

> *Truth is a thing of this world: it is produced only by virtue of multiple forms of constraint.*
>
> Michel Foucault, *Truth and Power*

People in different times think different thoughts, and find the thoughts of other times very hard to understand. We think of Harvey's discovery of the circulation of the blood in the early 17th century as step towards a modern understanding of the world – until we learn that he thought that blood circulates because the heart is like the sun and the blood is like the planets circling it.

Harvey's ideas form part of what French philosopher Michel Foucault called an "episteme", a complex of beliefs and methods of inquiry characteristic of a culture and defining what counts as rational for that culture. Foucault's greatest influence is as a philosopher of sexuality, in particular as a debunking historian of ideas about homosexuality. Especially in his later career, until his death from AIDS, he was a heroic figure to those wanting scholarship to engage with the attitudes of the non-scholarly world.

Foucault's early work focuses on the institutions that dealt with madness and illness in earlier European culture. Foucault argues that there has been no single constant conception of what madness or illness is throughout history. In particular, Foucault points out that, until the 18th century, madness was seen as a rejection of the norms of rational or orderly behavior. Society's response to such rejection is to exclude the affected person; but when madness comes to be seen as disease, the social response becomes that of confinement. A conceptual change is thus linked to the invention of the asylum. All Foucault's themes are here: a social institution, usually involving the restriction of individual liberty, depends on and also supports a system of ideas.

Foucault puts these themes together in different ways in different works, such as *Madness and Civilization* (1961), *The Order of Things* (1966), and *The Archeology of Knowledge* (1969), but there is a consistent picture that emerges from the totality of his writings. We have to distinguish between two kinds of knowledge, *connaisance* and *savoir,* that together generate intellectual life with a common episteme. *Connaisance* is the largely unexpressed assumptions that shape everyday activities and create limits within which the more explicit and formal kind of knowledge, *savoir*, can be formulated. So *savoir* produces the explicit beliefs that justify social institutions, and *connaisance* enables actions that make these institutions function. So restrictions on what we are allowed to do produce restrictions on what we can think.

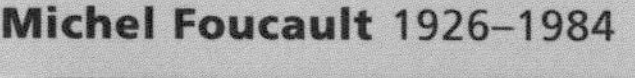

Michel Foucault 1926–1984

Foucault's philosophy ties the limitations of thought to limitations of freedom. In a culture of a time and a place, there are things you are unable to think and acts you are prevented from carrying out. Each reinforces the other so that, ultimately, power shapes truth.

These ideas express a radical relativism about the authority of reason. Foucault often gives the impression that he thinks that truth is also relative to an episteme, so that when people reason in accordance with the practices of their time then their conclusions are true, for them. But it is not at all clear to interpreters of Foucault whether he has in fact any grounds for taking truth to be relative. The simplest way to read him is to take him as agnostic on the question of whether there are any facts that are independent of how we describe them. The word "truth", as he uses it, is then best understood as "what people think is true".

Quine

W.V.O. Quine was the dominant American philosopher of the late 20th century. From the 1940s to the 1980s he produced a stream of influential books and articles, notably *From a Logical Point of View* (1953), and *Word and Object* (1960). His earliest works were in logic and the philosophy of mathematics but his later ideas about language, knowledge and science were equally influential.

For centuries, philosophers have argued that we know some facts – such as that cats are animals – simply from the meaning of words. These facts are traditionally labelled "analytic", and all others "synthetic". Quine's central contribution to philosophy is to have broken this distinction. According to Quine, even the assertion that cats are animals counts as substantive knowledge about the way the world is, as well as about how we use the words "cat" and "animal". This knowledge could thus in principle be refuted by future evidence. The result is that neither philosophy nor mathematics can defend its assumptions by saying that they are true by definition – because nothing is true simply by definition. From this central point Quine has gone on to formulate a new way of understanding knowledge, and to describe a programme for making the philosophical theory of knowledge part of psychology and biology.

Quine uses this idea to argue in favour or an equally radical claim about the way beliefs are based on evidence. When the evidence conflicts with one or more of our beliefs, we have a choice about which to abandon – some may preserve the overall coherence of our beliefs better than others, by minimizing mysteries and anomalies and maximizing simplicity and explanatory force. For Quine, these are the factors that govern the acquisition of all our beliefs. We do not reason directly from evidence to theory; instead, we consider how to modify our whole body of beliefs to incorporate new evidence in a way that preserves or increases its overall coherence. This attitude, emphasizing the properties of whole bodies of beliefs, is known as "holism" or "coherentism" and dominates the contemporary theory of knowledge.

> *"The totality of our so-called knowledge or beliefs, from the most casual matters of geography and history to the profoundest laws of atomic physics … is a man-made fabric which impinges on experience only along the edges."*
>
> W.V.O. Quine, "Two dogmas of empiricism" in *From a Logical Point of View*

Willard Van Orman Quine 1908–2001

Quine showed that there is no simple distinction between what is true by virtue of the meaning of words and what is true by virtue of objective fact. Abandoning this classic philosophical distinction has radical consequences for how philosophy can be practised.

Quine uses his denial of the analytic-synthetic distinction to draw another far-reaching conclusion: philosophy is part of science. If philosophy cannot consist in discovering what is implicit in language, and if we have abandoned ideas of divine revelation and mystical insight, there seems to be no other way in which philosophy can give us any special kind of knowledge. Instead, philosophy must draw on, contribute to, and be judged by the same standards as the rest of science. Epistemology (the theory of knowledge) becomes part of biology and psychology. Metaphysics (philosophical theories about thr nature of reality) becomes part of physics. It is much less clear what happens to ethics and political philosophy.

Logic and reasoning

Logic reveals which patterns of reasoning are valid and which are not, and gives us tools to analyse complex inferences in terms of chains of simpler ones. However, the criteria of validity used in logic are too narrow to include every type of reasoning that we need in real life.

People often make mistakes in reasoning. If we know that people with meningitis have severe headaches and rashes on their skin, and we know that a particular child has these symptoms, we are tempted to conclude that the child has meningitis. But this is wrong: we know that if a person has meningitis then they will have these symptoms, but this allows that someone could have the symptoms without having the disease. This example illustrates two points. First, that we have standards we apply to reasoning: while some conclusions follow logically from the premises (the assumptions or starting points of the reasoning), others are derivable only by mistake or confusion. Second, that although we often violate these standards and make mistakes in reasoning, we can see where we have gone wrong when the reasoning is expressed differently or broken down into smaller steps.

So what is it for reasoning to be correct according to the rules of logic? A conclusion follows logically from some premises if there is no way that all the premises could be true without the conclusion being true too. For example, there is no way that the statements "all poodles are dogs" and "all dogs have teeth" can be true without the conclusion "all poodles have teeth" also being true. On the other hand, if the premises can be true without the conclusion being true, then the conclusion does not follow and the argument is said to be invalid. If "all poodles are dogs" and "some dogs have tails" are both true, the conclusion "some poodles have tails" does not follow – no matter how plausible it

Computer chip circuitry is based on logic, as the conducting paths form "logic gates". For example, current will pass through an "OR" gate if there is any current from either of two incoming paths, representing the statement "If A or B is true, then C is true".

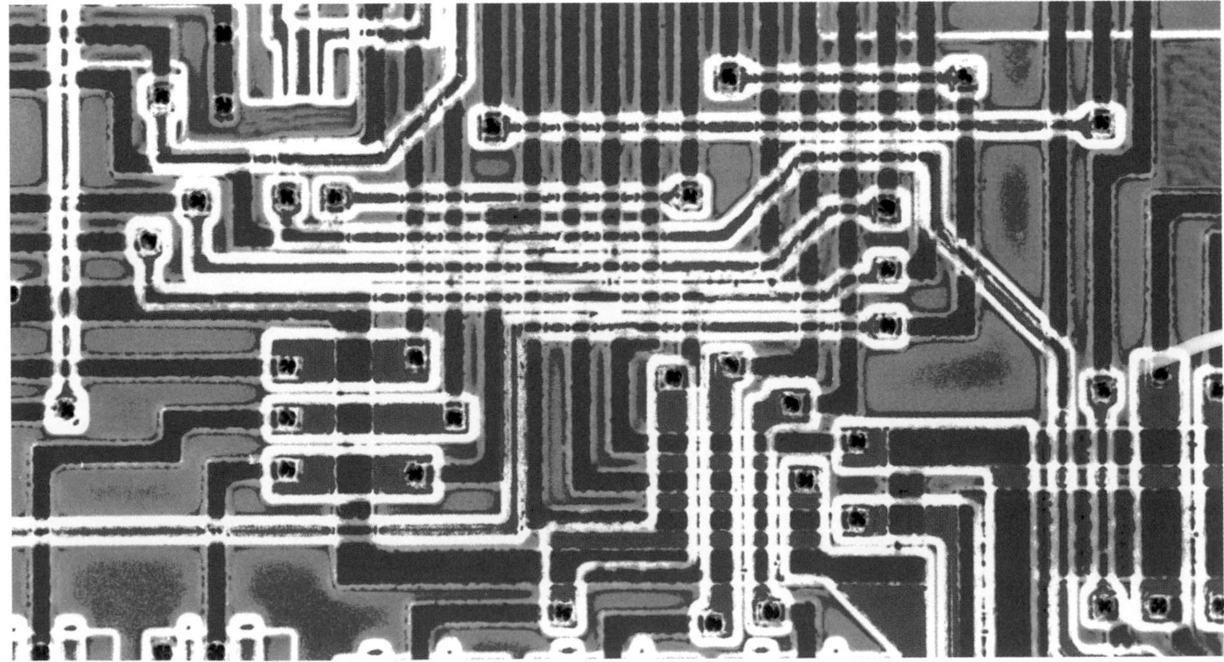

Fallacies of reasoning

Logicians have produced lists of fallacies, or traps that people can easily fall into when reasoning. The best-known such fallacy, called "affirming the consequent", consists in reasoning along these lines:

If a tyre were flat, the car would be pulling to the side
The car is pulling to the side
Therefore a tyre is flat.

It is easy to see that the conclusion (the last statement) does not follow logically. from the first two statements (the "premises"). The first premise does not say that a flat tyre is the only cause of pulling to the side, so there could be side-pulling with undamaged tyres. So why do we often take such reasoning to be persuasive?

First, the reasoning is near enough to a valid pattern of reasoning to be confused with it. The valid pattern would be: "If a tyre is flat, the car will pull to the side ; a tyre is flat; therefore, the car will pull to the side.". Second, in many cases the premises do provide evidence, though not a conclusive argument, for the conclusion. Your car's pulling to one side is evidence that you may have tyre problems: not enough to be sure of it, but enough to look for further evidence.

may seem – because, based on the premises alone, it could be that poodles are in fact a tail-less breed. Notice that, for an argument to be logically valid, we do not need to know whether in fact the assumptions actually hold in the real world – just whether, if true, they support the conclusion.

Patterns of logical reasoning

Logic, then, consists largely of finding ways of evaluating an argument by comparing it to a set of standard patterns in which it is easier to see what follows logically and what does not. The earliest set of patterns were Aristotle's syllogisms (see pp.13–15). Aristotle studied patterns of reasoning, like the examples above, that turn on words such as "all" or "some". Later, philosophers studied reasoning involving words such as "if", "not" and "or", as in "the keys are in my pocket or in my bag or in the door; they are not in my pocket or in my bag; therefore they are in the door." And 20th-century philosophers studied more complex patterns that required them to invent a new symbolic language, often called symbolic logic, that is one of the origins of programming languages for computing.

However, even with a variety of logical patterns to choose from, we very often find reasoning that does not conform to any of these patterns to be perfectly acceptable. Inductive reasoning (see pp.93–95), where we draw a general conclusion from seeing repeated instances, is a case in point. Intriguingly, we also sometimes find reasoning to be unacceptable even when it is deductively correct (that is, valid according to the rules of logic). For example, someone might believe from looking in her appointment book that she is in Boston on Monday, and believe from looking at the newspaper that it is Monday, and also believe, from looking out the window, that she is near the Eiffel tower. From these premises she can infer deductively that the Eiffel tower is in Boston. But that would be silly: it would be much more reasonable to conclude that her appointment book is wrong.

> "*'Contrariwise,' continued Tweedledee, 'if it was so, it might be, and if it were so, it would be; but as it isn't, it ain't. That's logic!'*"
>
> Lewis Carroll, *Through the Looking Glass*

The conclusion we should draw from all this is that people who want to have true beliefs should try to violate patterns of correct deductive reasoning as little as possible. But doing this is far from a complete guide for intelligent reasoners: they will also need to be guided by common sense in knowing when it is safe to go along with reasoning that is not deductively valid, and when the conclusion of logically perfect reasoning is so implausible that they should doubt some of the premises from which it is derived.

Carnap

Carnap was born in Germany in 1891. In 1935, he left Germany to escape the Nazis, moving to the United States where he worked up to his death in 1970. He played a dominant role in the Vienna Circle, a group of philosophers, mathematicians and scientists who brought to philosophy the idea – known as logical positivism – that some apparently intelligible questions are really nonsense, and that therefore there is no point looking for answers to them. For the logical positivists, most questions of religion and metaphysics were to fall on the nonsense side of the line and most scientific questions on the sense side. The pressing question, then, is how to draw the line.

Carnap's career can be seen as a search for a criterion for distinguishing sense from nonsense. In his early work in the 1920s, he built on the work of Frege, Russell and others to suggest a test along the following lines. Given any claim, we first try to translate it into symbolic logic, which uses symbols to represent sentences and reasoned arguments. If we cannot do this, then we know that it is nonsense. If the translation can be done, we then see whether there could be evidence that would refute or confirm the claim. If not, we consider it nonsense; but if evidence could confirm or refute it then we have transformed it into a scientific question to be resolved by empirical investigation. In *Pseudoproblems in Philosophy* (1928), Carnap argued on this basis that the problem of the existence of the external world and other classic philosophical worries are really non-problems.

> *The metaphysician believes that he travels in territory in which truth and falsehood are at stake. In reality, however, he has not asserted anything, but only expressed something, like an artist.*
>
> Rudolf Carnap, *The Elimination of Metaphysics through Logical Analysis of Language*

Rudolf Carnap 1891–1970

Rudolf Carnap was one of the founding fathers of 20th-century analytical philosophy. His work, which is focused on the distinction between sense and nonsense and how we can separate real disputes about the world from questions of terminology, demonstrates his life-long quest for a way of approaching philosophy that does not get bogged down in pointless or unresolvable debates.

Carnap further developed this idea in two directions. In *The Logical Structure of the World* (1928), he tried to explain how statements about the physical world can be reduced to statements based on perception; and in *The Logical Syntax of Language* (1934), he interpreted philosophical problems as questions about the choice of a language for science.

In the 1940s and 1950s the logical positivist program came under sustained criticism from philosophers who showed that the line between sense and nonsense could not be drawn in the way that the positivists intended. Carnap's reaction was to shift his attention to the concept of evidence. In a series of writings culminating in *The Logical Foundations of Probability* (1950), he described the relationship between scientific statements and the evidence that supports them. Subsequent writers have accepted few of Carnap's specific claims in these later works, but his ideas are at the origin of much current technical work in philosophy.

Carnap's influence lies in the idea that philosophical claims should be precise enough to be tested against evidence. Such claims will often fail the test, but, after Carnap, this seems a better fate than being too unclear to be tested.

Induction and deduction

When we generalize from repeated instances, we are reasoning by induction. Unlike deduction, where the conclusion follows logically, conclusions from induction are never certain. So what role can induction play in our attempts to gain reliable knowledge of the world?

From early in human history, people have noticed that the sea has two high tides every day. On most sea coasts, this regular pattern has been observed for thousands of years. As a result, people expect each day to bring two high tides. This is an example of reasoning by simple induction: people see many instances of a pattern and no exceptions to it, and they conclude that the pattern will continue. The reasoning is not indubitably valid: it is conceivable that tomorrow some divine or astronomical intervention will bring about three, one or no high tides where now there are two. But, intuitively, it is reasonable to feel fairly sure, given the evidence, that the tides will continue (and that there were regular tides in the past, before humans observed them). In fact, if we could not feel confident about conclusions we obtain through inductive argument, very many of our beliefs would be much less sure than we normally suppose.

Although induction seems to be a central element of rational thought, it is very hard to say what constitutes a correct pattern of inductive argument – in contrast to the deductively valid patterns of argument studied in logic. Here, if the premises (the assumptions used in the argument) are true, the conclusion must also be true. Inductive arguments, in contrast, merely give persuasive reasons for believing the conclusion – which could still be false, given the premises.

Hume (see pp.24–25) was the first philosopher to see these points clearly. He argued that, as induction does not give us conclusive reasons for

A paradox about evidence

Imagine you eat a Thai meal and it tastes good, so you take this as evidence that Thai food is tasty. And the more good Thai meals you have, the stronger the force of evidence for the idea that Thai food is tasty, because finding an A that is a B provides evidence for the statement "all As are Bs" (in this case, "all Thai meals are tasty"). But there is a problem. Suppose you are in your house and you sip some paint, which tastes terrible. Then you try some shoe polish, which tastes even worse. Then you reflect on the fact that both of these substances did not taste good and were not Thai food – so you have evidence for the general statement that anything that does not taste good is not Thai food. But in logic, this is the same as the statement that all Thai food tastes good – because "all As are Bs" is logically equivalent to "all non-Bs are not As". (Most people have to think about this step for a moment.) So without going near any Thai food, you can collect evidence that it tastes good. How can this be?

After C.G.Hempel discovered this paradox in the 1960s, using an example about ravens, some philosophers reacted by denying that when two statements are logically the same, evidence for one is evidence for the other. Others reacted by doubting that an A that is a B does always provide evidence that all As are Bs. A subtler reaction is that some "all As are Bs" hypotheses are more strongly supported by As that are Bs while some are more strongly supported by non-Bs that are non-As. For an example of the latter, suppose you have a deck of cards in which all but four cards have been marked. You want some indication of whether all the aces have been marked, so you draw a card at random. If it is an ace and it has been marked that doesn't tell you much, since almost all cards are marked. But if it is one of the unmarked cards and is not an ace, that tells you that only three of the unmarked cards remain as possible unmarked aces, so the chances that all the aces are marked goes up considerably.

"General laws may be laid down respecting the tides, predictions may be founded on those laws, and the results will in the main … correspond to the predictions."
John Stuart Mill, *A System of Logic*

believing its conclusions, we do not really know that there are two tides a day, that the sun will rise tomorrow, that bread is nourishing, and so on. In arguing this, he was taking deductive reasoning as the only way of reaching good grounds for our beliefs. Very few philosophers today would go along with this: most will say instead that inductive reasoning is simply a different way of providing reasons for beliefs, and that the lesson we must learn from Hume is that we cannot expect all our beliefs to be absolutely certain.

At the root of the lesser certainty of inductive reasoning is the fact that it is "non-monotonic". That is to say, if we add an additional premise to the reasoning, the conclusion may become less certain. If we add to the data about tides the additional premises that the tides are produced by the moon's gravitation and that the moon is about to collide with a giant asteroid, then the tide tables for tomorrow become very dubious. In contrast, if we add an additional premise to a deductively valid argument, the conclusion will still follow.

> *The man who has fed the chicken every day throughout its life at last wrings its neck instead, showing that more refined views as to the uniformity of nature would have been useful to the chicken.*
>
> Bertrand Russell, *The Problems of Philosophy*

Another deep difference is that, unlike with deductive reasoning, it does not seem to be possible to define a pattern of inductive reasoning that is always valid. It may seem that, whenever we see a large number of instances of a pattern and no counterexamples to it, we should expect the pattern to continue. However, this is not the case. Take the pattern described thus: "The number of high tides in day N after Christ's birth is two plus whichever is greater of zero and (N – 750,000)". This has been satisfied for two thousand years with no exceptions, but to expect it to continue would be to expect that in a few decades there will be many more than two tides a day. The example may seem contrived, but the problem is general. No one has managed to define a pattern of inductive reasoning that holds in all cases.

We take our knowledge of the ebb and flow of the tides as near-certainty. But does merely observing repeated instances of such a pattern allow us to expect it to continue?

Reasoning from understanding

Despite the familiarity of the simple pattern of inductive inference considered so far – some As have been observed to be Bs; so all As are B – it is not obvious that inductive reasoning is best understood this way. An alternative is to view it as "inference to the best explanation". The idea is that, instead of reasoning by supposing that observed patterns will continue, we simply try to figure out which explanation of what we observe best fits with everything else we know about the world. After all, we do not carry out inductive reasoning in a void: we do so against a background of well-tested beliefs that form an integrated understanding of the world. This is particularly the case for natural phenomena, where science gives us reasons for expecting things to behave in particular way. For example, we do not expect the sun to rise tomorrow morning simply because it has risen every day of our lives so far. We do so because we understand that the earth is rotating in space, which makes the sun appear to rise. More scientifically, we may also reason that the earth is unlikely to stop rotating because this would defy the law of conservation of angular momentum. In all these cases, we integrate what we have observed with what we already believe to acquire a more comprehensive set of beliefs.

Some philosophers see inference to the best explanation as replacing simple induction. Others think that we have a very varied toolkit of ways of reasoning, including deduction, simple induction, inference to the best explanation and others, all of which have their limitations but yet are necessary for understanding the complex world around us.

Bacon

Francis Bacon was the original philosopher of science, the first to describe not only the intellectual ambitions characteristic of modern science but also the organizations by which science is practised. A brilliant, socially ambitious, arrogant man, in his long career in public life Bacon held high administrative offices and wrote copiously about the public benefits of what we would now call applied science.

Francis Bacon 1561–1626

Elizabethan social climber and thinker Francis Bacon broke with tradition in asserting that the proper method of science should be based on the careful collection of evidence and the role of experiment, much as we still think today. He also saw science as a cooperative activity, anticipating the need for complex and expensive scientific organisations.

Like his approximate contemporary Descartes (see pp.48–49), Bacon proposed a scientific method that suspended most traditional belief in favour of a project of establishing a comprehensive new understanding of the world. Unlike Descartes', Bacon's science would be based on meticulously gathered observations and experiments, and would involve the organized cooperation of numbers of scientists. The first stage of Bacon's project wold consist of gathering large amounts of data by direct, unprejudiced observation on all manner of topics. The data would be gently filtered to remove errors and absurdities, but left in a fairly raw state. The next stage would formulate plausible candidates for general laws pulling together the data. Bacon thought we should look for a limited number of basic characteristics so that the candidate laws would cover all the ways these characteristics may be combined. At this stage there is a great danger that we will be influenced by irrational beliefs, so we must guard against them. Bacon summarizes these influences as the four classes of idols: idols of the tribe (mistakes and illusions natural to humans); idols of the den (overemphasis on one's own experience); idols of the market place (assuming that different people use the same words to mean the same); and idols of the theatre (misleading ideas that result from systems of philosophy). Once we have our candidate laws, we test them against the data. If evidence to discriminate between the candidate laws cannot be found in the existing data, we produce it by performing a "crucial experiment". This will allow the implications of competing candidate laws to be tested directly and hence to indicate which is right.

Many elements of this methodology fit the pattern of the biological and physical sciences, as they later developed, very well. In particular, the idea of manipulating nature to produce evidence which one will not obtain just by looking and waiting is crucial to scientific method. Other elements now seem rather naïve, particularly the idea that one can formulate a set of candidate laws that is rich enough to cover all the possible actual laws, yet simple enough that one can discover the truth simply by eliminating those laws from this set that do not fit the data.

Possibly the most prescient of Bacon's suggestions was that, to understand nature, we need to coordinate the work of many researchers, some gathering information and some systematizing it. He realized that this would be an expensive business, and he tried to interest the authorities of his day in founding what we would now consider scientific associations and research institutes. When he failed in this, he tried to fund research himself. When he died in 1626, Bacon was in disgrace for having taken a bribe in his position as a judge – thus, even early on in the history of science, the need for financial support was leading its practitioners to adopt desperate measures.

Diderot

The thinkers of the 18th-century enlightenment were convinced that human reason – when not hampered by religious and traditional dogmas – is capable of solving most of the problems of mankind. Denis Diderot was the most radical and outspoken of them, and the least willing to disguise what he thought in terms that would make it acceptable to the authorities. Consequently, many of his books were banned and he was occasionally imprisoned. A quirky, individualistic thinker, Diderot did not always have the opinions expected of him. When Catherine the Great invited him to Russia, she anticipated that Diderot would support her forced modernization of her country. Instead, Diderot advocated a slow evolution paced to the education of its citizens.

> *What has never been questioned has never been proven.*
>
> Denis Diderot, *Pensées Philosophiques*

Among Diderot's uncomfortable views were that there may be no purpose to the universe or to human life; that the will is not free; that there is no god; and that everything in the universe – including human minds – is material. For none of these did Diderot express a definite dogmatic opinion: his view was always that we must see where the available evidence leads us, allowing that future evidence may change our opinions. But this undogmatic attitude is, in a subtle way, even more subversive of authority than an outright assertion of an unpopular view, since it suggests an alternative method of thinking, which potentially threatens any number of opinions. Thus Diderot's open-mindedness had the effect of making his works even less acceptable. In particular, he held that religious and moral matters should be decided on empirical grounds, saying that a deist – who believes that God creates the universe and then lets it run without interference – is someone who has not lived long enough to be an atheist. His moral opinions were stoic and hedonistic, emphasizing both the value of self-control and the ultimate goal of seeking pleasure. Just as his views about the evolution of species anticipated Darwin, he anticipated Freud in holding that sexual repression tends to result in misery or perversion.

Denis Diderot 1731–1784

Started in 1750, the *Encyclopédie* was meant to survey all of human knowledge, separating out real knowledge from superstition and pointing the way for future research. It is to its chief editor, Denis Diderot, that we owe many of the ideas that we associate with the 18th-century enlightenment.

Diderot's main means for presenting his subversive point of view was the *Encyclopédie*, of which he became the chief editor. This enormous and ambitious work, which eventually filled 35 volumes, was intended to cover the state of knowledge the the time on all subjects. Diderot wrote a large number of the articles himself. It had enormous prestige as the work of the best minds in France at the time, with Voltaire, Rousseau and D'Alembert among its main contributors. Within the articles empiricist philosophers such as Locke and Bacon were cited as models, civil liberties were defended and biblical criticism was encouraged. Although the project was eventually banned, the *Encyclopédie* was influential in its advocacy of an undogmatic attitude to religion, an optimistic attitude to the possibility of scientific knowledge of all things, and the expectation that thought and evidence could lead humanity to better ways of carrying out its affairs.

Science

Science combines theory and evidence, requiring a division of labour between scientists. Individual scientists are motivated by many factors, and the development of science is not a direct march to the truth. But these facts do not undermine the power of scientific thought.

If asked to give a central example of human knowledge, many people would cite some well-established piece of scientific doctrine. So what is special about our knowledge of the law of gravitation, or of the role of DNA in heredity? The uniqueness of scientific knowledge seems to derive from two factors. First, scientific theories are not wild speculations. Unlike theological or metaphysical claims, they are grounded in careful observation and controlled experiment. Second, scientific theories are often very abstract. They use concepts that are not found in common sense and explain familiar events in terms of things we cannot see. This combination of the observable and the theoretical is unprecedented in human thought. While it is hard to think our way back to a time before we thought in scientific terms, it is still amazing that we can get so far from experience in relation to the concepts involved and yet stay connected to it in terms of the applications of this knowledge.

Through the work of modern philosophers of science such as C.G. Hempel and Karl Popper (see opposite), one can see two basic ways in which science combines these apparently contradictory elements. First, there is the link between hypothesis and test. A new scientific hypothesis usually arises in a situation in which a standard scientific view has run into trouble. Conjectures – variations on or alternatives to the standard view – are then proposed and tested by experiment and data-gathering. As a result, some conjectures survive to become accepted as new standard doctrines. The second basic feature of science is the precise, usually quantitative, formulation of theories. Precisely formulated theories will have precise consequences. Small discrepancies with the observed facts will then greatly increase the chance that false theories can be identified and refuted.

To describe science in this way is to see it as a heroic and largely successful enterprise of discovering nature's secrets. And that is science's own

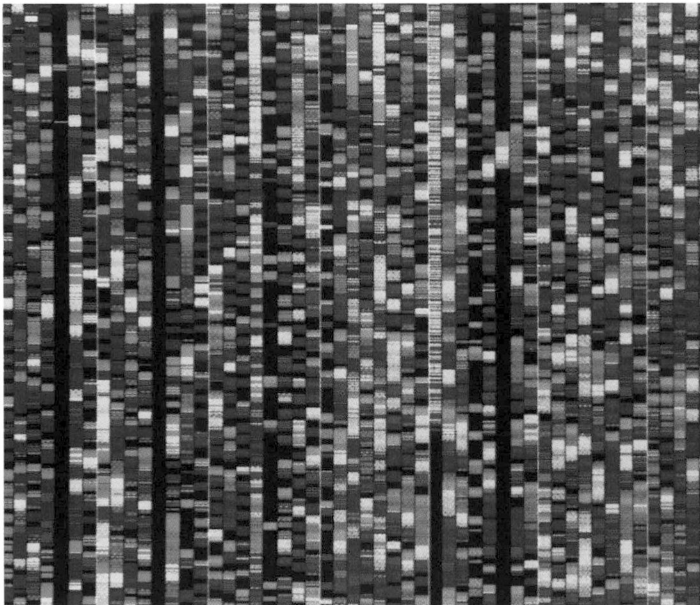

Each coloured band here reveals one of the three billion "base pairs" in the human genome. Unravelling this huge complexity required a similarly complex collaboration between scientists.

> *Bold ideas, unjustified anticipations, and speculative thought are our only means for interpreting nature… Those among us who are unwilling to expose their ideas to the hazard of refutation do not take part in the scientific game.*
>
> Karl Popper, *The Logic of Scientific Discovery*

view of itself. Many philosophers, however, are wary of this triumphalist image. Most scientific theories are eventually rejected and replaced with alternatives, and in retrospect the reasons given for their adoption often do not look very impressive. A theory may be replaced with a radically different one that, rather than solving the unsolved problems of the earlier theory, instead addresses quite different problems. Historian of science Thomas Kuhn has argued that, as a result, science can be said to change rather than to progress in a straightforward way, and the transition from one scientific position to another is as much a matter of sociological and psychological forces as of logic.

The social structure of science

But these two points of view need not conflict. We can see the power of science as coming from its marriage of daring conjecture and experimental evidence, and still see the processes that drive scientists in their work as being more complex than a simple determination to uncover the truth. One of the factors that allows these two views to be reconciled is the social structure of science. Consider, for example, an experimentalist whose work is well received if it succeeds in uncovering evidence that is uncomfortable for fashionable theories and distinguishes between the consequences of rival conjectures. The experimentalist may be motivated by a desire to succeed in this way, and may also want to see some conjectures refuted for personal reasons. But as long as the result is that problems in current theories are revealed and new conjectures are subjected to rigorous scrutiny, the experimentalist's work will indeed contribute to the discovery of truths.

The model of science presented so far is largely based on the biological and physical sciences, particularly physics. But contemporary science is a large and rambling structure, incorporating many different disciplines from theoretical astronomy to sociology and psychology. In some disciplines, theories are not formulated mathematically, or (as in areas of medical science) controlled experiments are difficult. Within most disciplines, scientists are engaged in many different kinds of activities, with a social structure coordinating the activities of theoreticians, experimentalists (or other data-gathering people) and others. It is a difficult and important question, though, whether there is anything like a single "scientific method" that applies across the sciences. We can accept that in scientific ways of thinking we have found our most effective tools for understanding the world without being forced to the further conclusion that these tools must all be used together, or that there is a single set of instructions on how best to use them.

Science and pseudo-science

Many ideas are presented as "scientific" in order to receive a share of the authority that science has in our culture. But how can we tell if a theory, such as astrology or acupuncture, really is scientific? One answer was defended by the influential philosopher of science Karl Popper (1902–94). For Popper, scientific theories are marked by their refutability. Imagine finding evidence that would show that astrology is false. Astrologers would probably respond by claiming that the evidence did not really refute their theory. According to Popper, this is a fundamentally unscientific attitude: the scientific spirit reacts to refuting evidence by saying "OK, the theory's wrong; let's try to make a better one". On this basis, not only fringe doctrines such as astrology can be criticized, but also psychoanalysis and the Marxist account of history. In these and other cases, a theory is held in such a way that it cannot be refuted. So, for Popper, irrefutability is not a sign that a theory is true, but rather that there is something intellectually substandard about it.

Rationality

A rational person is one who makes the best use of the information at his or her disposal. But this reasoning is ambiguous: what is "best" depends on our aims and the limits of our reasoning ability. How should we distinguish between rational and irrational ways of thinking?

Rationality is an ideal. To formulate standards of rationality is to describe ways in which we would think and act if we could choose the way our minds work. A rational way of acquiring beliefs would give the maximum chance of reaching true, useful and explanatory beliefs, and would minimize illusions, mistakes and fallacies. But the ideal of rational beliefs is a fairly ambiguous one: is it most important to be correct, or to understand, or to achieve practical results? Given a limited amount of evidence, is it most rational to draw the conclusions that are safest, and so are least likely to be false; or those that are most enlightening in explaining things that puzzle us; or those that are most useful? It is most plausible to say that we should go for a combination of these, and that there are different combinations that a person could rationally choose.

There are additional constraints on our belief choices if we wish to be regarded as rational thinkers. One basic aspect of rationality is coherence. We all have some degree of incoherence in our beliefs, but a rational person should try to move towards a more coherent body of beliefs. When beliefs are coherent, they do not contradict one another. So if a person believes that all men are monsters and also that her three sons are perfect human beings, there is a degree of incoherence in

Failure to understand the nature of random processes results in people standing in thunderstorms under trees that have earlier been hit by lightning, on the grounds that lightning rarely strikes twice in the same spot.

The gambler's fallacy

If a coin has landed heads five times in a row, how do you expect it to land the sixth time? Many people think that tails is likely, as "by the law of averages", a run of six heads seems even more unlikely than five heads followed by one tail. But this reasoning is mistaken. Either a coin is fair, in which case it is equally likely to land heads or tails the next time; or it is biased, in which case a run of five heads suggests that it is more likely to land heads again.

The tendency to believe that a random process is likely to continue so as to counteract its deviations from the expected average is called "the gambler's fallacy". The mistake is to overlook the fact that, in a random process, each toss of the coin or spin of the roulette wheel is an independent event, and the outcome is not influenced by what has gone before. Interestingly, this fallacy is so persuasive that some versions of it will fool even experts in reasoning.

her beliefs. A set of beliefs can also be incoherent because it fails to hang together in subtler ways. For example, one might believe in some general principle and have an arbitrary way of explaining away the exceptions. Someone who believes that all fish have fins, and that cuttlefish and shellfish are fish, might explain away the discrepancy just by saying that the arms of cuttlefish and the shells of shellfish are like fins. This move would result in a loss of explanatory coherence: we would no longer be able to state general principles about the evolution of fish, or the ways in which fish use their fins.

However, no person can live up to the ideal of perfect rationality, because we are all operating within the limitations of our memories and attention spans. Given our limited abilities, there are problems that are too hard for humans to solve, and we are best off not wasting time on them. One important example of this concerns probability. There is a mass of evidence now that humans are subject to a large number of systematic errors when dealing with probability. For example, we may ask what a patient's probability of having a disease is, given a positive result from a reliable test (one that usually detects the disease, but occasionally also indicates its presence in healthy subjects). Most doctors will say that the patient has a high chance of having the disease. But this is often a mistake: in fact, the probability depends on the prevalence of the disease in the population. If it is very rare, the patient is quite likely not to have the disease, even after the worrying test result. (If the vast majority of the population does not have the disease, and the test gives a positive result for even a small proportion of them, then few of the people who test positive will actually have the disease.) Doctors, it seems, consistently fail to understand this – not because they are stupid, but because they are human, and human beings have great difficult with probability.

So what is the most rational response to the fact that our rationality is limited? In most circumstances, it is to work within these limitations. For example, we should generally avoid thinking probabilistically – particularly in thinking about risks, when the dangers of getting confused add to rather than manage the dangers we face.This may seem very simple advice, but in fact it is very hard to follow since it requires an exact understanding of one's limitations, and this is a kind of self-knowledge that is very hard to gain.

> *"Man is a rational animal – so at least I have been told. Throughout a long life, I have looked diligently for evidence in favour of this statement, but so far I have not had the good fortune to come across it."*
>
> Bertrand Russell, *Autobiography*

Common sense

The skills that keep us in touch with our environment, allow us to deal with one another socially and provide our common-sense knowledge, are generally reliable. More surprisingly perhaps, science and other activities that go beyond common sense rely on these same skills. So how does common sense relate to other, more sophisticated forms of knowledge?

We are well equipped for everyday life with senses that give us information about many aspects of the world that directly impinge on us. We can see the tiger lurking in the grass, and hear its tail swishing. Above all, we can transmit information by language: we can call out to let others know where the tiger is hiding and we can tell our children where tigers tend to hide. These capacities evolved to allow animals like us to survive, and if they were not roughly reliable our species would not have managed to do so. Of course, there are many aspects of danger that are less noticeable to us: we do not perceive ionizing radiation that threatens us with cancer, and we rarely study the statistics that would allow dangers to be compared. But still, many human cultures have persisted for centuries without finding any need to modify what they know of the world.

> *"Common sense is the most widely distributed commodity in the world, for everyone thinks himself so well endowed with it that the hardest to please in all other respects do not want more of it than they have."*
>
> René Descartes, *Discourse on Method*

Common sense is the composite of knowledge-gathering and decision-making capacities, together with accepted beliefs, that allows people to negotiate their everyday lives. It obviously varies to some extent from one time and place to another, but perhaps much less than we usually suppose, because there is a large background of knowledge that we are all predisposed to discover through normal human psychology. In this category belongs much of what is termed "folk psychology", the capacities and beliefs with which human beings understand one another's actions and motives. It is central to common sense, in that an ability to interpret others allows communities to grow up and information to be transmitted and preserved within them, providing a basis for common knowledge. Without this ability, each human being would effectively be alone, able to acquire knowledge only through his or her own experience.

Philosophers have often been reluctant to call common-sense beliefs "knowledge" unless they are backed up by a sophisticated intellectual justification. But our highest intellectual achievements, such as those of physical science, do not depend only on our capacity to reason critically and reflectively. Physics would be impossible if physicists could not rely on innate human perceptual capacities to make observations, or could not pass on information to one another (relying on innate human linguistic capacities), and could not coordinate the efforts of many researchers, relying on normal human social capacities. All of these capacities need to be fine-tuned to fit into a scientific enterprise, and some of them (such as our powers of observation) need to be treated with some caution. But if we were not usually accurate in reporting what we see, and if we did not usually know when another person is sincere rather than joking or deceiving, then we would not have been able to acquire the sophisticated scientific knowledge we have. So, while scientific knowledge may be more painstakingly obtained than common-sense beliefs, its acquisition relies on many of the same fundamental human capacities.

Pragmatism

Pragmatists avoid metaphysical speculation by defining truth in terms of the outcome of inquiry. For all pragmatist thinkers, the important question in evaluating an idea is "what real difference would it make if we accepted it?"

Pragmatism arose at the beginning of the 20th century, among philosophers who wanted to accept much of the philosophical legacy of Immanuel Kant (see pp.141–143), who argued that our minds shape our experience to make it intelligible. However, Kant's account of exactly how the mind does this is completely mysterious, so pragmatist thinkers suggested a different story: for them, the mind makes truth by deciding what counts as true.

In this spirit, C.S. Peirce (1839–1914), the founding pragmatist, defined truth as whatever in the long run humanity comes to believe. One might object that humanity could be affected by a long-term delusion; the pragmatist's reply to this is that if truth is anything different from what our beliefs gravitate towards, it is of no practical importance. By this view, we can decide what we mean by "true", and the sensible decision is to apply the concept to what we can achieve and what there is some point to achieving. This leads to pragmatist William James's (1842–1910) variant definition of truth as whatever it is useful for us to believe.

While these definitions may lead to subtle debates about the nature of truth, their intention is to shift attention away from purely philosophical issues to questions about the ways in which it is in our interest to think. In the work of John Dewey (1859–1952), pragmatism simply assumes that the purpose of philosophy is to develop ideas that help us in practical ways. As applied to questions about knowledge, this means that we should no longer consider individual thinkers as having to find reasons for beliefs about the world that are essential to their lives; instead, such beliefs are simply part of the practical equipment of each individual.

Such problem-solving thinking proceeds by posing and then testing hypotheses. To pass such tests, a hypothesis must cohere with experience and also have practical applicability. If the hypothesis is coherent and applicable, then it should count as knowledge. This knowledge then becomes part of the experience of those who have acquired it, leading to new hypotheses and tests. So the process continues, with the content of experience and of knowledge always changing. Later philosophies of science, such as those of Popper and Hempel, have taken on board this two-way play between experience and theory. The close connection between enquiry and practice was also the basis of Dewey's philosophy of education, whose slogan was "learn by doing".

Louis Pasteur in his laboratory. According to pragmatism, the important issues are not subtle questions about whether Pasteur's discoveries were "true", but rather whether they worked.

Wisdom

We can all identify people we think of as wise, without being quite clear about what wisdom is. This many-sided concept seems to have elements of both intellectual and personal qualities, but its relation to knowledge is not straightforward.

Imagine you are in an intellectual tight spot. You have just discovered a contradiction among your beliefs, or are trying to find an argument for a position you want to defend, or are trying to see what might be wrong with evidence that suggests an unlikely conclusion. To think your way through the situation, you will have to try out various possible lines of investigation, follow them only as long as they seem promising and evaluate the tentative conclusions you arrive at. A person can be more or less skilful at this: being intelligent and good with argument does not guarantee that a person will be able to find a way through a maze of conflicting considerations and arrive at a satisfactory outcome. So what, in addition to sheer mental ability, is required to deal effectively with such situations?

> *Everything that the human spirit undertakes or suffers will lead to happiness when it is guided by wisdom, but to the opposite, when guided by folly.*
>
> Plato, *Meno*

What it seems are required for reaching a satisfactory conclusion are personal characteristics akin to those that guide us through practical and social situations. As well as being intelligent, a person must be inquisitive but not credulous, courageous but not foolhardy, energetic but not exhausting. In recent philosophy, such characteristics, as applied to a person's struggle for true, consistent and useful beliefs, have been called "epistemic virtues".

The importance of the idea of an epistemic virtue is that it focuses on the fact that the capacity to derive conclusions and assess the force of evidence is not enough for acquiring satisfactory beliefs: one also needs a variety of traits of character. We might include among the purely intellectual epistemic virtues those of knowing what topics to investigate, and when an investigation has arrived at a satisfactory answer. A person exemplifying this type of epistemic virtue to a high degree would therefore be wise – in the acquisition of knowledge, at any rate. And it seems likely, as a matter of intuitive psychology, that intellectual and other virtues are to some extent connected. A person who is brave or even-handed in intellectual matters is likely to show these qualities to some extent in the rest of his or her life. Building a moral element into the definition of an epistemic virtue will also go some way towards putting knowledge and wisdom back together: an epistemically virtuous person would know, for example, whether investigations into nuclear weapons or on the best ways of extracting confessions from others were good uses of his or her intellectual energies.

Beyond epistemic virtues, there are two other ways in which knowledge and wisdom meet. One is understanding answers to esoteric questions about life and the nature of the universe. "Understanding" as used here is something that goes beyond simple factual knowledge, though knowledge is usually required for it. For example, one might know that matter is made of quarks (perhaps from being told this as an isolated fact by someone whom one had reason to trust), but this is not the same as understanding why matter is so composed or what it means that it is. When one has understanding, one is also better placed to acquire further knowledge. If a person understands many things about important topics, then we consider them to have a kind of wisdom – especially if the topics include human motivation and the ways people can deal with one another. The second meeting point of knowledge and wisdom is the possession of knowledge that allows one to lead a good life. The right kind of understanding of one's own motives and those of others, and of ways in which one's desires can be managed, can allow a person to lead a satisfying and valuable life.

The life of reason

Plausible though these different connections between knowledge and wisdom seem, they have to be taken as somewhat loose and general. One might find epistemic virtues used on trivial subject matter and understanding exploited for courses of action that lead to bad lives, while a satisfying and valuable life can be based on very little appreciation of deep facts about the universe or any other areas of profound understanding. However, many philosophers have denied that the connections between knowledge and wisdom are in fact so fragile and see these two concepts as intimately linked. This view has often stemmed from a commitment to the life of reason, whereby through cultivating the intellect one will gain an understanding of human nature and human life, which will in turn lead to a good life. At the same time, the development of reason itself is seen as an essential part of the good life. This idea is common in ancient Greek philosophy, from Plato (see pp.76–79) to Stoicism (see p.138), and is one of the central ideals of Western culture. But, for all that, most contemporary thinkers have serious doubts about its truth. Religious thinkers have long questioned whether the cultivation of the intellect for its own sake is part of the good life as they conceive it. And today's secular philosophers, while valuing the development of the intellect, will usually accept as a sad fact that it is possible to have deep knowledge of important things and yet be a morally and personally very imperfect person.

Is there such a thing as wisdom, then, and is it intrinsically linked with knowledge? Although wisdom itself does not seem to be a single thing, there is a coherent ideal of a person whose thoughts and actions are well constituted through the application of what we could call virtues of intelligent activity. Following this ideal is one way, at least, in which one can try to achieve a life in society that one can, on reflection, judge to be good.

Real-life decisions require both knowledge and judgment: the decision to use nuclear weapons at the end of World War II combined the feats of intellect needed to develop these weapons with an assessment of the political and moral consequences of such action.

Chapter 4

FAITH

Is there a God?

There is a long history of arguments to prove there is a God. More recently, philosophers have questioned the nature of the statement that God exists. Is this a factual claim, like a scientific statement? Or does it signal some more basic response to the kind of reality we inhabit?

Faith in God is generally acquired as a result of growing up in a certain culture, rather than through philosophical argument. Nonetheless, there is a long tradition of "natural theology", which attempts to prove the existence of God by strictly rational means. Although in our contemporary culture there is a fundamental question mark over the existence of God, for the medieval thinkers who laid the foundations of philosophical theology, God was securely at the centre of their world view. To them, the role of rational debate was to enhance understanding of God's existence and nature, not to question it. In his *Proslogion*, the 11th-century Benedictine monk Anselm of Canterbury began by defining God as "that than which nothing greater can be thought", and reasoned that a being so defined could not exist only in thought. To exist in reality, Anselm maintained, is greater than to exist merely in the mind, so if God were merely a construct of the mind he would not be the greatest being we could think of: such a supreme being must necessarily exist in reality.

Anselm's argument has come to be known as the ontological argument (from the Greek root *ont-*, from *ontos* or "being"). Fundamentally, the argument is that God's essence or nature is such that he cannot but exist. Although versions of this argument have been defended by other philosophers – for example, Descartes (see pp.48–49) – the consensus is that it does not work. Even if we concede that the label "God" carries the implication of such unsurpassing greatness as to imply real existence, it still remains to be shown whether there really is anything that qualifies for such a label.

While the ontological argument proceeds *a priori* (from concepts alone), most arguments for God's existence start from observations about very general features of the world, or from the fact that it exists in the first place. These are known as "cosmological" arguments, and their best-known exponent is Thomas Aquinas (see p.112). Developing some earlier ideas of Aristotle, Aquinas reasoned that the chain of causes in the world depends on a first or ultimate cause that is not caused by anything else. This first cause Aquinas identifies as God. Critics have asked why there should not be a chain of causation stretching back infinitely far into the past. Aquinas in some of his writings allowed that reason alone cannot show that the universe has not existed from eternity, but he main-

The rational universe

The spacious firmament on high
With all the blue ethereal sky
And spangled heavens, a shining frame
Their great original proclaim…

In reason's ear they all rejoice
And utter forth a glorious voice
For ever singing as they shine
"The hand that made us is Divine!"

The rousing words of this 18th-century hymn by Joseph Addison encapsulate a view that continues to appeal to many today: that the universe, in its intricately ordered structure, provides evidence of a rational creative power, with God seen as the great cosmic mathematician. Thus the French philosopher-scientist Descartes attempted to derive mechanical conservation laws from God's immutable nature. Today, quantum physics posits a universe in which (at the subatomic level at least) exact mathematical prediction is impossible. Nonetheless, science still regards the universe as in some sense orderly, and some scientists see this as evidence of divine origins.

A 15th-century miniature by Guyart de Moulins that shows God as the creator-architect of heaven and earth.

tained that an independent creative cause of the whole ensemble would still be needed.

In addition to his argument from causality, Aquinas argued more generally that, since the things around us might not have existed, in order to explain why there is now anything at all we must eventually posit something that is "necessary in its own right" – and this, he says, everyone calls God. A version of this argument was propounded by the Islamic philosopher Ibn Sina, or Avicenna (980-1037), who argued that "contingent beings must end in a necessary being". Much later, the German philosopher G.W. Leibniz (see pp.38–39) argued that everything must have a "sufficient reason" for its existence, and that in the case of the world as a whole, this reason must lie in something outside the world.

Such arguments reflect the ancient question "why should there be something rather than nothing?" But could not the universe be (in Bertrand Russell's phrase) just *there*? Philosophical opinion remains divided on this issue. Some find it unacceptable to suppose that the existence of the universe could be an unintelligible brute fact, while atheist thinkers have countered that any explanation of things, even a religious one, must ultimately invoke some fact (for example, the existence of God) that will itself not be further explained.

Design arguments

Perhaps the most popular reason for positing the existence of God derives from a sense that the universe manifests some kind of order, design or purpose. Aquinas observed that goal-directed behaviour is common in the world around us (roots seek water, leaves open out to the light), and he reasoned that "things lacking knowledge do not tend towards a goal unless they are directed by something intelligent, as an arrow is by the archer". Purpose certainly seems rife in nature; moreover, even inanimate things seem to many to possess a kind of inherent harmony or order. Isaac Newton (1642–1727) wrote that "the most beautiful system of the sun, planets and comets could only proceed from the counsel and dominion of an intelligent and powerful Being".

The most famous version of the design argument was put forward by the archdeacon William Paley in his *Natural Theology* (1802). Paley notes that, if we found a watch lying upon the ground, we would notice at once "that its several parts are framed and put together for a purpose". The inference is inevitable, argued Paley, that the watch must have had a maker. However, the celebrated

> *"There cannot be design without a designer, contrivance without a contriver, order without choice… , subservience and relation to a purpose without that which could intend a purpose."*
>
> William Paley, *Natural Theology*

Scottish philosopher David Hume (see pp.24–25) was highly sceptical about design arguments. The analogy between the universe and a human artefact, he observed, is "very weak and liable to error and uncertainty". In any case, how do we know that matter does contain a principle of order within itself? Moreover, the likely cause of any given phenomenon (such as order) can properly be established only by observation of previous instances; yet the universe is something that is single, individual and without parallel. In *Dialogues Concerning Natural Religion* (*c*.1755), Hume argues that, since we have never observed worlds being formed, we are in no position to pronounce on whether the order found in our world must have a divine mind as its cause. A further serious blow to design arguments was dealt by the success of Darwin's theory of natural selection, which proposed that complex and intricate life forms could arise simply from the blind processes of random variation plus the struggle for survival, without the need to posit any guiding intelligence.

Many thinkers have viewed the physically ordered nature of the universe as evidence that it has a creator – just as the complex inner workings of a watch require a watchmaker.

Religious and moral experience

For many people, the main reason for believing in God is evidence from religious experience – either their own or that of others, as reported (for example) in sacred scriptures and the writings of saints and mystics. Accounts of such experience often describe it as having an utterly compelling quality. Nevertheless, its status as evidence for the truth of religious claims is hard to evaluate, partly because such experience often occurs in the context of emotionally heightened states, which may cast doubt on the objectivity of the subjects' testimony. In addition, the sceptic may find it easy to suggest alternative, non-religious, explanations for the occurrences in question – for example, what Hume called the "strong propensity of mankind to [gullible acceptance of] the extraordinary and the marvellous". More recently, our growing knowledge of the functioning of the brain has led to claims that there may be a neurological basis for much religious experience, and that we may even be able to induce the relevant states artificially (for example, by drugs). However, it has long been known that chemical changes (such as those caused by fasting) may facilitate religious experience; such discoveries cannot in themselves settle either way the question of whether there is any objective reality behind what the subjects think they perceive.

A more widespread aspect of human experience is the phenomenon of morality, often thought to provide important grounds for belief in God. Cardinal Newman (1801–90) was one of many defenders of religion to argue that the authoritative deliverances of conscience provide good grounds for belief in a supreme moral lawgiver. Following the work of Sigmund Freud, this type of argument has subsequently come under pressure from those who see the voice of conscience as merely an internalized "superego" – the enduring influence on the young child's psyche of the controlling voice of the parent. However, the tradition of invoking the existence of objective moral values as evidence for God's existence continues: the British scholar and writer C.S. Lewis (1898–1963) was a celebrated defender of this approach. If there are genuine moral truths (for example, that compassion is good), truths that transcend the personal psychological desires or fears of the subject, then it may seem hard to find a place for them within the natural world. If so, this may appear to support the notion of a supernatural or divine realm from which they spring. Much modern moral philosophy has, however, aimed to explain morality in other ways – either along subjectivist lines (that moral judgments are merely projections of our desires or those of society), or as reducible to natural properties (for example, that the good is what maximizes happiness). Nevertheless, those who believe in objective and eternal moral truths, which retain their validity irrespective of whether they are acknowledged or not, may still be drawn to invoke God as the source of such ideas.

> *I do not seek to understand in order that I may believe, but I believe in order that I may understand.*
>
> Anselm of Canterbury, *Proslogion*

Whatever the merits of the arguments discussed above, it seems unlikely that God's existence will ever be definitively established or refuted by means of rational or evidential considerations alone. Religious beliefs are not like ordinary factual beliefs, since they point beyond natural phenomena, beyond the observable universe that is the domain of factual inquiry. But as philosophers have been increasingly reluctant to try to make all types of discourse conform to a single template, so perhaps a religious believer may instead see his or her belief in God as a central organizing principle of life. In this view, the assertion of God's existence is not to be tested directly through experience, like the hypotheses of scientists, but should instead be understood as unifying and grounding the other areas of human inquiry – including the scientist's search for order in the cosmos and the individual's quest for enduring moral value.

Intelligent design and human life

Recent support for the design argument has come from modern cosmology, which suggests that the laws governing the universe may be "fine-tuned" in such a way as to permit or even encourage the emergence of human life. If the force of gravity were appreciably stronger than it is, stars would exhaust their hydrogen fuel much faster and human life would probably not have had time to evolve. Or again, the water necessary to life could not be formed in a universe in which the "strong" force binding the nuclei of atoms was marginally greater. Some have insisted that this means only that, if the laws of the universe were significantly different, there would be no humans to wonder why things are the way they are. But others have stressed the improbability that a purely random process could account for the precise physical values that permit human life to evolve. If this is correct (though we are in an area where the calculation of probabilities is notoriously problematic), then it may seem to favour the idea that the universe is the product of intelligent design. At the very least, philosophers and scientists are having to confront the question of whether there may be something about the universe that is itself favourable to the emergence of life and intelligence.

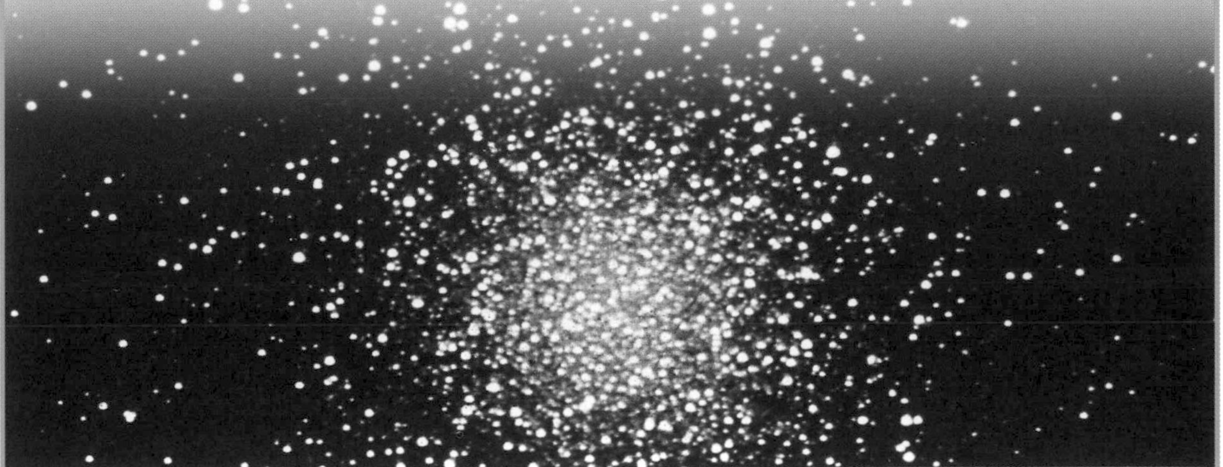

Aquinas

The son of a wealthy aristocratic family, Thomas Aquinas was born near Aquino in southern Italy. At the age of 20 he joined the Dominicans, the first religious order to make devotion to study one of its main objectives. After studying philosophy and theology in Paris and Cologne, in 1256 he became a professor at the University of Paris. During the 1260s he worked in Italy in papal service, but returned to Paris in 1269, until ill heath obliged him to abandon teaching. He died in 1274, aged just 49.

During the last two decades of his life, Aquinas produced a massive output of theological and philosophical work. His thinking is deeply imbued with the ideas of Aristotle, on whom he wrote many commentaries, developing and adapting Aristotle's ideas to the demands of Christian doctrine. For example, the Aristotelian account of virtue is enlarged by Aquinas to encompass Christian virtues such as chastity and poverty; and Aristotle's very secular account of happiness is changed to allow for the spiritual values connected with the believer's relationship to God.

Aquinas' most celebrated work is *Summa Theologiae* ("Summation of Theology"). Composed from 1266 to 1273, it runs to hundreds of articles, each debating a chosen proposition using objections and rejoinders. The importance given to the citing of authorities, whether Holy Scripture or the early Church fathers is striking to the modern reader. Despite this, much of Aquinas's style remains characteristically philosophical, in the sense that rational argument is the primary way of proceeding. Aquinas insisted that if theology aspires to make a genuine contribution to our knowledge or understanding (*scientia*), it cannot resolve issues on the basis of authority alone.

> “*Philosophy treats of existing things according to concepts derived from created objects … but there is another knowledge which considers existing things according to notions received by the inspiration of the divine light.*”
>
> Thomas Aquinas, *Commentary on Sentences*

Thomas Aquinas 1224–1274

The most influential philosopher-theologian of the Middle Ages, Thomas Aquinas was the chief architect of scholasticism – the synthesis of biblical doctrine and the classical Greek philosophy of Aristotle that dominated European thought until the Renaissance. In his extensive writings he developed what is arguably the most comprehensive philosophy of religion ever produced.

In *Summa Theologiae,* Aquinas expounds his famous "five ways", which aim to demonstrate God's existence from various features found in the world (*a posteriori*). These are the arguments from (1) motion; (2) causation; (3) contingency, or the mere existence of the world; (4) perfection; and (5) design. Aquinas takes these arguments merely to establish the existence of an original creative power: little can be inferred from them about God's nature. But Aquinas went on to argue that we can at least establish what God is not (for example, his nature cannot be limited by being bodily). As for other features ascribed to God in the religious tradition, for example his goodness and wisdom, these, according to Aquinas, are not applied to God literally but only by analogy with how we apply such terms as "good" and "wise" in ordinary human contexts. Here, as in many other areas of philosophical theology, Aquinas's intricate arguments and distinctions have laid the foundations for much subsequent discussion of the nature of religious language.

Faith and reason

Does religious belief depend on evidence – or is it a matter of faith? And does the success of science place religion under threat? The relation between religious faith and reason raises perennial questions that still perplex philosophers and theologians.

The classic account of the relationship between reason and faith was given by Thomas Aquinas in the 13th century, who maintained that the two are complementary. Some religious beliefs (for example, the existence of God) can, he argued, be established by "natural reason", while others (including the "revealed truths" of Christianity, such as the doctrine of the Trinity) require faith. For Aquinas, there is a harmony between reason and faith, since both types of truth are worthy of our belief. Moreover, he taught that even the truths of natural reason may sometimes be accepted on faith – for example, by those who do not have the time to follow the relevant arguments.

While the idea of a harmony between reason and faith probably represents the most coherent and satisfying position for a religious believer, many religiously inclined people have been unable to see religious truths as established by reason and evidence alone, and thus have been drawn to various forms of fideism (from the Latin *fides*, faith) – the view that, for the religious believer, faith must have priority over reason. At the extreme end of the spectrum, some fideists have even gloried in flying in the face of reason – as in the slogan taken from Tertullian at the end of the 2nd century CE: *certum est, quia impossibile* ("it is certain, because it is impossible"). Augustine (see pp.116–117), by contrast, thought that religious belief must start from faith but could be bolstered by rational understanding. For him, the religious quest was one of faith seeking understanding. For the 18th-century philosopher Immanuel Kant (see pp.141–143), faith takes over where reason fails. In *Critique of Pure*

In this painting by Paolo Morando (1486–1522), the risen Christ invites his disciple Thomas to touch his body as proof of his resurrection. Thomas's need for physical evidence was censured in the fourth gospel as a weakness in his religious commitment: faith alone should have been sufficient.

Reason (1787), he writes, "I have found it necessary to deny knowledge in order to make room for faith." Later, the Danish thinker Søren Kierkegaard (see p.128) adopted a particularly strong form of fideism, arguing that religion requires a resolute decision to trust, a "leap of faith" whose essential precondition is the lack of objective certainty.

> *The righteous man may say: 'I will that there be a God… I firmly abide by this, and will not let this faith be taken from me.'*
>
> Immanuel Kant, *Critique of Practical Reason*

Belief and evidence

In Christianity, faith is (with hope and love) one of the three great theological virtues. From at least the time of the gospel writings, those demanding proof before committing themselves have been held open to criticism. "Blessed are they that have not seen, and yet have believed", the risen Christ is reported as saying in an implicit rebuke to Thomas, the doubting disciple. Religious adherents, however, often claim their beliefs are supported by evidence – for example, that the divinity of Christ is established by miraculous occurrences reported in the Bible. Against this, the atheist philosopher David Hume (see pp.24–25) argued that, since the ordinary laws of nature are established on the basis of the overwhelming preponderance of past evidence, the balance of evidential probability must always count against reports of miraculous events. As he puts it in *An Enquiry Concerning Human Understanding* (1748): "A wise man proportions his belief to the evidence."

In contrast to the hard-headed approach that insists on matching belief to evidence, American philosopher William James (1842–1910) argued

Religion and science

Religion is often thought of as coming under threat from the progress of science. Galileo Galilei seemed to demote the earth from its privileged place under heaven by arguing that the earth moves about the sun rather than occupying a fixed central position, thus making it harder to see this planet as the special focus of the creator's concern. The condemnation of Galileo in 1633 inaugurated a long period of tension between the scientific and religious outlooks. Nevertheless, there were many who saw the new sun-centred cosmology as perfectly compatible with traditional religious views. The philosopher René Descartes (see pp.48–49) thought it was entirely appropriate that an infinite God should pour forth his power in an unimaginably vast creation with innumerable other worlds; and the great scientist Isaac Newton was able to provide a strictly mathematical account of planetary motion, while being "compelled to ascribe the frame [of the solar system] to an intelligent Agent".

Charles Darwin is widely supposed to have undermined religious faith with his theory of natural selection, which proposed that the entire variety of life forms arose by a process of random mutation overlaid by competition for survival. Those taking a crudely literalistic view of the creation story in Genesis may find the idea of evolution threatening, but in fact many Victorian clergymen were enthusiastic supporters of Darwin, and there seems nothing inherently contrary to divine creation in the idea of species emerging gradually, as opposed to arriving instantaneously and ready-made. Nevertheless, the apparent cruelty and wastefulness of the evolutionary process did (and does) seem disturbing from the religious perspective: would a benevolent and loving God chose such a seemingly ruthless mechanism as the instrument of his creativity?

The general relation between science and religion is harder to assess. Certainly, modern science has provided an increasingly comprehensive account of the entire universe. As the scope and explanatory power of science has increased, the idea of a "God of the gaps", invoked to account for what is unexplained by science, seems increasingly redundant. But as the cosmos appears to be ordered and accessible to human reason, scientists of a religious persuasion may still be able to see it as a manifestation of divine creative intelligence.

Ultimately, the religious outlook appears to be a way of seeing the significance of reality as a whole, rather than a claim about particular items located within that reality. From this perspective, there may indeed be no ultimate incompatibility between religion and science.

The emotions on the faces of these visitors to the shrine of Fatima in Portugal suggest a spiritual experience. Although such responses may explain why some people become religious believers, their value as evidence for the tenets of faith is less certain.

that in cases where the facts are not finally determined, "our passional nature not only may but must decide" what to believe. Moral and religious questions cannot be settled by the evidence, and in such cases we should consult our heart rather than suspending judgement. The highly influential 20th-century philosopher Ludwig Wittgenstein (see pp.59–61) also stressed the idea of commitment as central to the religious outlook, describing the religious view of the world as a "passionate seizing hold of a certain interpretation of life".

In order to assess such approaches, it is important to ask what exactly the religious believer is supposed to be committed to in terms of claims about reality. Wittgenstein thought that religious statements do not describe any kind of reality, but should rather be understood as constitutive of a certain way of living. But although passionate adherence to a way of life is an important part of what it is to be religious, critics have asked whether such commitment in fact presupposes belief in certain statements (for example, about the divine creation of the universe or the afterlife). More recently, the American philosopher Alvin Plantinga has argued that religious beliefs do indeed commit the holder to certain factual claims, but that such claims are not based on evidence but are simply basic to the believer's system of thought. Just as in the case of ordinary judgements of perception or memory, Plantinga argues, so with religious claims: there are always some basic beliefs that we just accept without argument, but this does not make them unreasonable.

Some critics have objected that this view could open the door to irrationality by allowing that all sorts of wild beliefs might be "basic" for a given group of people; but defenders of Plantinga have argued that it is quite possible to employ rational standards in deciding whether a belief is properly basic. The debate continues as to how far the believer in God is warranted in maintaining the reasonableness of this "basic" belief in the face of difficulties (such as the amount of suffering in the world) that appear to count against it.

Augustine

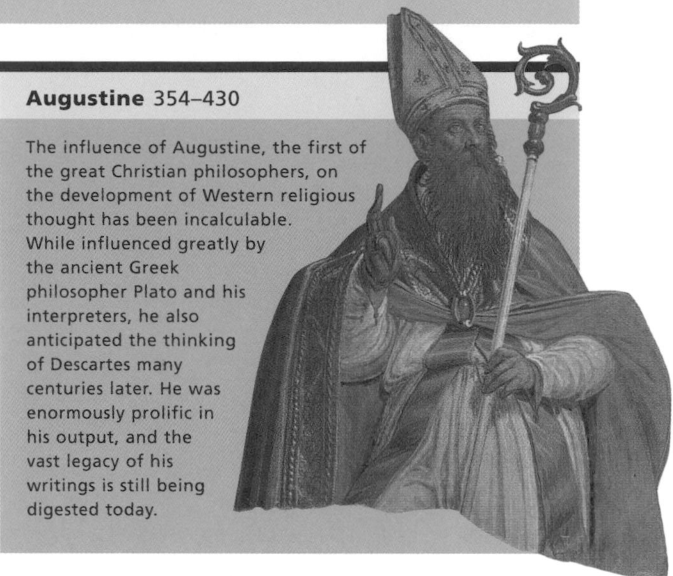

Augustine 354–430

The influence of Augustine, the first of the great Christian philosophers, on the development of Western religious thought has been incalculable. While influenced greatly by the ancient Greek philosopher Plato and his interpreters, he also anticipated the thinking of Descartes many centuries later. He was enormously prolific in his output, and the vast legacy of his writings is still being digested today.

Born at Tagaste in North Africa, Augustine was initially raised as a Christian by his mother, but during his teenage years he gradually abandoned his faith. He went on to study rhetoric in Carthage. There by his own account he strayed further from Christianity, both morally – becoming fascinated by the licentious atmosphere of the town – and also intellectually, when he became attracted to the Manichaean outlook. This view – that the cosmos is an eternal struggle between the forces of light and darkness – seemed to the young Augustine to provide a better explanation for the existence of evil and suffering in the world than the Christian position attributing all reality to God.

At the age of 29, Augustine moved to Italy and came under the influence of Ambrose, Bishop of Milan. He studied various thinkers influenced by the ideas of Plato, and after a prolonged moral struggle was converted to Christianity and baptized in 387. He left his partner (with whom he had by this time had a son), returned to North Africa, and in due course established a monastery at Hippo (modern Annaba, on the coast of Algeria), becoming Bishop of Hippo in 396. The closing years of Augustine's life were marked by increasing external instability as the collapse of the Roman empire gathered pace. He died in 430 at the age of 75, during the invasion of Hippo by the Vandals. Although the city was burned down, Augustine's library survived, and with it most of the voluminous corpus of his treatises and letters.

A 15th-century Italian edition of Augustine's *De Civitate Dei*, showing Rome as the city of God and Augustine writing.

The inward turn

"Do not go outside; return into yourself. In the inner human being dwells the truth." This celebrated quotation, found in his *De Vera Religione* ("On the True Religion"), indicates one of the most pervasive features of Augustine's philosophy – its understanding of spiritual and intellectual inquiry as a meditative inner journey, directed not outwards to the world around us but inwards towards our own reflective self-consciousness.

Anticipating Descartes's famous *cogito ergo sum* ("I think, therefore I am"), Augustine argued for the indubitable existence of the thinking subject: "even if I am being deceived, I must exist". By finding oneself, and reflecting on the nature of that self (so Augustine reasons), the soul is naturally led towards God.

Augustine inherited a philosophical framework derived from Plato, according to which ultimate reality is an objective, eternal and intelligible realm that transcends the human world of the five senses. Although meditative and reflective in character, Augustine's philosophy thus contrasts with the "subjectivist" accounts of later religious writers such as Kierkegaard. Fusing this Platonist view of reality with the Christian vision of divine grace descending to each individual soul, Augustine argued that salvation can come to all who do not turn from the light of God.

> *When someone says that eternal things are better than temporal things, or that seven plus three equals ten, no one says that it ought to be so. We simply recognize that it is so; we are like explorers who rejoice in what they have discovered, not like inspectors who have to put things right.*
>
> Augustine, *On Free Choice of the Will*

Augustine thus focuses on a problem that is fundamental to the religious outlook: the gap between the eternal and infinite goodness of God, and the weakness of human beings. Ideally, the soul should turn to God, for only there can true happiness be found; but it is the nature of a finite creature to be weak-willed, lacking some of the divine reality and perfection. In highlighting these issues, Augustine set the scene for a debate over the relationship between human freedom and divine goodness that was to last for many centuries.

The Augustinian corpus

"My eloquence does not match my loquacity", Augustine once declared. Aided by a team of secretaries to whom he constantly dictated his ideas, Augustine produced an almost unbelievably vast output. According to Augustine himself he produced some 230 works (not all have survived), and his biographer Possidius observed that "there is hardly a scholar with the capacity to read and know them all".

Augustine's most celebrated work is his *Confessions*, a long and intensely personal account of his life's spiritual journey. Written in his early 40s, it is addressed directly to God and contains in its opening chapter the striking lines "You have made us for Yourself, and our heart is restless until it finds repose in You." Another famous work, *De Civitate Dei* ("On the City of God"), produced in instalments during the period 416–422 and comprising 22 books in all, argues that the Kingdom of God is to be established in the next world; but it also advocates a more humane and forgiving earthly society (arguing, for example, against capital punishment and torture). Also influential are the *De Genesi ad litteram* ("Commentary on Genesis"), a detailed exposition of the first book of the Bible (arguing for a metaphorical interpretation of some of the language there), and the 15-volume *De Trinitate* ("On the Trinity"). This work provides a defence of the Christian doctrine of a God who is both one and three by deploying an analogy with the human soul as a triune entity – a single personality constituted by the three elements of being, knowing and willing.

Many of Augustine's writings are polemical in tone, directed against pagan religions, and particularly the Manichaean view. This saw the world as poised between equal rival forces of good and evil – a view that Augustine had himself once accepted. Other writings are aimed at rival interpretations of Christianity, which were later to be condemned as heretical, often as a result of Augustine's arguments. For example, a substantial series of treatises against the Pelagians insisted on the central importance of divine grace for the salvation of what Augustine saw as our inherently sinful human nature (contrary to Pelagius's view, which regarded human nature as in principle perfectible, and denied the doctrine of original sin).

Miracles

Many religions make reference to stories of miraculous occurrences, which the faithful take as signs of divine intervention in the world. Philosophical discussion of miracles has centred on whether there could ever be good evidence for such events.

The term "miracle" comes from the Latin *mirari* ("to wonder at"). Narratives of the lives of holy men often involve stories of "signs and wonders" that testify to their special status or powers. In the case of Christianity, the gospel accounts contain many reports of miracles by Jesus – for example, the changing of water into wine at the wedding feast at Cana (John, chapter 2). In addition, the miraculous events relating to Christ's birth and resurrection are central to the religion.

While some "miracles" (such as cases of so-called "faith healing") may be explicable in natural terms, most reported miracles are quite outside the course of normal natural events, and this has given rise to sustained philosophical scepticism about reports of their occurrence. David Hume (see pp.24–25) defined a miracle as a "transgression of a law of nature by a particular volition of the Deity", and pointed out that, since by definition a law of nature is something supported by the whole weight of our previous experience, we already have an argument against miracles that is "as entire as any argument from experience can possibly be imagined".

By this Hume does not mean that it is impossible that a law of nature should have miraculous exceptions; for he himself insisted that there is no logical or universal necessity about the so-called "laws", or generalizations, of science. His point is rather that the balance of probabilities must always be against the truth of a reported miracle. For example, since our entire uniform past experience informs us that human beings cannot walk on water, if someone claims to have witnessed such an event, it will always be more probable that he or she was deluded, or is trying to deceive, than that the occurrence actually took place.

A statue of the Virgin Mary apparently cries tears of blood. Hume argued against trusting the veracity of such "miracles".

In contemporary philosophical discussion, the consensus seems to be that the Humean line shows there could not be independent evidence for miracles based on the mere probability of the historical evidence. Yet this does not necessarily entail that those with a commitment to a religious outlook could not reasonably accept the truth of reported miracles. For many modern theologians, what is important about miracles is not the quasi-magical status of the reported events themselves, but the symbolic meaning of such accounts (thus the changing of water to wine may be seen as a symbol of spiritual renewal). By this view, a miracle may be understood, in the words of the 20th-century theologian Paul Tillich, as "an event which points to the mystery of being … an occurrence which is received as a sign". However, such interpretations raise the problem of whether one may talk of the significance of an event without confronting the question of whether that event actually took place.

The afterlife

Many religions offer their followers the prospect of a future existence after the earthly one. Philosophical problems about the "afterlife" centre on the question of how conscious experience could continue after the death and decay of the body.

The doctrine of the afterlife figures in many religions, and has played a particular role in the theology of Christianity, where one of the articles of faith is belief in the "life of the world to come". Christianity envisages a "Last Judgement" in which everyone who has ever lived will be held responsible for all they did on earth, and will be consigned either to heaven, the abode of the blessed, or hell, the "outer darkness" or the "furnace of fire" where, in the words of the gospels, there will be "wailing and gnashing of teeth".

Since our physical remains are destroyed when we die (by cremation or decay in the earth), it may be asked how such future judgement is conceivable. Many suppose that a non-physical part of us, the soul or spirit, can survive the death of the body. This corresponds to the view proposed by René Descartes (see pp.48–49) and hence known as "Cartesian dualism", namely that the mind (or soul) and the body are two separate and independent substances. Descartes did not distinguish between the terms "mind" and "soul", regarding both as labels for the conscious thinking self that in his view was entirely distinct from the body.

Although it is sometimes thought that belief in the afterlife requires one to be a Cartesian dualist, this is by no means clear. The traditional doctrine of the Christian church (expressed for example in

This 15th-century painting by an unknown Franco-Flemish painter depicts the Christian idea of the Last Judgement. On this day, souls are judged worthy of either eternal bliss or perpetual hell.

Compensation and retribution: heaven and hell

That so many good people experience terrible sufferings, while so many cruel and vicious people appear to "get away with it", often seems unendurable. The traditional doctrines of heaven and hell found in Christianity, Judaism and Islam envisage future states in which those who have "fought the good fight" will be eternally rewarded in the bliss of heaven, while the damned will be consigned to hell, a place of eternal torment without hope of redemption.

Some theologians have argued that the idea of an eventual heaven for the righteous is logically required by the believer, since without it, it would be impossible to "sustain belief in a providential God who watches over his chosen people" (Dan Cohn-Sherbok, *Jewish Faith and the Holocaust*). This view at least underlines the moral appropriateness of a future wiping-away of earthly suffering; but the converse doctrine of hell presents a special problem of its own, namely that eternal and unrelenting punishment seems incompatible with the idea of a supremely merciful redeemer. For this reason some contemporary theologians reject the finality of hell as traditionally conceived. Others, by contrast, maintain that if people are to have genuine freedom, God must logically allow them the possibility of finally and irrevocably cutting themselves off from his presence.

the ancient "Apostles' Creed") does not assert the survival of a disembodied spirit, but rather speaks of the "resurrection of the body". Some construe this resurrection as involving God's gathering together all the molecules from the bodies of those who have died; this might be a problem, however, since large numbers of those molecules may have been shared by several bodies – for example, if a corpse is eaten by worms, which are later eaten by a bird, which is later netted and eaten by a bird-catcher. Perhaps less problematic is the conception of the apostle Paul, who speaks of the resurrection involving a new incorruptible or "spiritual body", as opposed to the corruptible biological body. This idea has been taken up by recent writers, such as the philosopher John Hick, who has suggested that in the next world God might create new matter and re-activate it with the conscious memories and dispositions of the former person. Whether the existence of such a reconstituted body would logically count as the survival of the original person is a topic on which modern philosophers fiercely disagree.

Although the precise nature of any supposed post-mortem existence has been the subject of much debate, the notion of the afterlife is not perhaps as vital for a religious outlook as might at first appear. The great monotheistic religions (Judaism, Christianity and Islam) are all concerned to promote a fuller and more abundant life here on earth, one oriented towards moral and spiritual good as opposed to suspect materialistic values; and it is hard to see why this project of moral and spiritual growth should suddenly lose its value if death is the final end. But the philosopher Immanuel Kant (see pp.141–143) argued in *Critique of Practical Reason* (1788) that it is a rational human goal to aim for a state of perfection in which the mind is in perfect accord with the moral law; yet this implies unending moral improvement and progress, which is "only possible on the supposition of an endless duration of the existence and personality of the same rational being, which is called the immortality of the soul". Certainly the idea of a continuing possibility for moral growth is an attractive one; this of course does not establish its truth, though it does perhaps explain the appeal of doctrines such as the Catholic one of purgatory, a supposed future transitional state between death and afterlife in which our human weaknesses and imperfections will be gradually cleansed.

> *"This 'I', that is the soul, by which I am what I am, is entirely distinct from the body, and would not fail to be what it is even if the body did not exist."*
>
> René Descartes, *Discourse on the Method*

Pascal

A leading figure in the scientific revolution of the early modern period, Blaise Pascal achieved fame at a young age as a mathematical prodigy. During his comparatively short lifetime, he invented the first mathematical calculator, worked with Fermat on the foundations of probability theory, and conducted experiments with a barometer which refuted the prevailing view of the impossibility of a vacuum.

On November 23, 1654, there occurred what Pascal later called his *nuit de feu* ("night of fire"), a conversion experience of extraordinary spiritual intensity, which led to his abandoning his former life and entering the Jansenist monastery at Port Royal. After his death, a piece of parchment describing his conversion was found sewn into his clothing: it speaks of "certainty, heartfelt joy, peace", "total submission to Jesus Christ", and "everlasting joy in return for one day's labour on earth". Perhaps most significantly, it suggests a revolt against over-intellectual conceptions of religion: the God to whom Pascal was henceforth to devote himself was the God of a living tradition of faith and commitment, the "God of Abraham, Isaac and Jacob, not the God of the philosophers and scholars". A large collection of Pascal's notes, reflections, and other fragments, some intended as the basis for an unfinished *Defence of the Christian Religion*, were collected after his death and published as the *Pensées* ("Thoughts"), the first selection appearing in 1670.

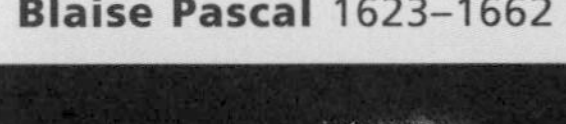

Blaise Pascal 1623–1662

The French scientist and mathematician Blaise Pascal was also an intensely spiritual thinker who combined passionate religious commitment with acute philosophical reflection on the relationship between faith and reason.

In the philosophy of religion, Pascal is most famous for his "wager" argument. Strictly speaking, this is not an argument for God's existence, Pascal's view being that we are incapable of establishing the existence or nature of God by rational means. But in the absence of rational proof, Pascal maintains, we simply have to decide whether to commit ourselves. And now the wager is brought in to encourage belief. If God exists, the religious believer can look forward to "an infinity of happy life"; however, if there is no God, then nothing has been sacrificed by becoming a believer ("what have you got to lose?", asks Pascal). The upshot is that "wagering" on the existence of God is a "sure thing" – a safe bet.

Critics of the wager have pointed out that even if Pascal is correct about the terms of the bet, one cannot simply decide to believe, just like that. But Pascal's argument is designed to encourage people to embark on the path of religious praxis (to start going to church, read the scriptures and so on). By starting out on this path, Pascal supposes, one may reasonably hope to acquire faith in due course, and thus secure its benefits.

Some have rejected the appeal to the rewards of the next world as dubious, but quite apart from any question about the afterlife Pascal himself clearly felt the religious path provided joy and tranquillity here and now; so from his perspective the religious choice is one that will bring genuine spiritual benefits, without risking the loss of anything except what he called "tainted pleasures". However that may be, Pascal's approach succeeds in highlighting the extent to which adopting a religious outlook often depends on the decision to make a personal commitment, rather than on the intellectual assessment of abstract arguments.

Atheism and agnosticism

Doubts about the existence of God encompass many shades of opinion, from the atheist's outright denial to the more cautious stance of the agnostic. Contemporary philosophy has been concerned to clarify the terms of debate, and to establish where the onus of proof lies.

For thousands of years, indeed perhaps for the whole previous history of humankind, the "default" position from which most people intuitively began was the assumption that some god or gods existed. Only in the last hundred years, or less, has the question become entirely open: the prevailing mindset of most educated people in the contemporary Western world no longer automatically includes a commitment to a religious outlook.

Atheism, however, is not just a recent phenomenon. In ancient Greece, Democritus put forward a wholly materialist world picture: worlds come in to being and pass away through random collisions of what we would now call atoms, without any guiding intelligence; and human consciousness arises from the arrangement of the material stuff out of which everything is composed. Epicurus (341–270BCE) developed a philosophy of life based on this radically physicalist outlook: human happiness lay in calmness of mind, and we should free ourselves from superstitious ideas of supernatural intervention in human affairs. In the words of the Epicurean motto, there is "nothing to fear in God, nothing to feel in death, good can be achieved, and evil can be endured".

The most celebrated atheist philosopher of the early modern period was David Hume (see pp.24–25), whose *Dialogues on Natural Religion* mounts a systematic attack on the standard arguments for God's existence. In *An Enquiry Concerning Human Understanding* he argues fiercely that alleged miracles do not provide evidence for the supernatural. The German philosopher Immanuel Kant (see pp.141–143) was influenced by Hume's sceptical approach, and argued that philosophical reason could never establish the existence of any supernatural reality. He pointed out, however, that this did not imply the non-existence of God, but merely that assertions about God – either his existence or his non-existence – were beyond the reach of rational knowledge. Hence, Kant regarded himself as leaving the door open for religious belief: saying in the *Critique of Pure Reason* that he "denied knowledge in order to make room for faith".

After Kant, many felt the need to distinguish between those who (as the British statesman William Gladstone put it) merely "held off from the affirmative", rather than "being driven to the negative assertion" regarding God's existence. In

Many people today dispense with any religious involvement in life's important events, as shown in this French civil wedding.

Theism, deism and humanism

Although atheism may be broadly understood as the denial of the existence of any god, a full grasp of the term comes from looking at the contrasting positions. Adherents of the great monotheistic religions (Christianity, Judaism and Islam) believe in a single creator God who is all-powerful, all-knowing, and also benevolent towards humankind. To adhere to such a view is to be a theist, and to deny it is to be an atheist.

In contemporary culture many people no longer subscribe to traditional religious institutions, but many maintain a belief in the existence of some kind of creative "power". Yet belief in such a supernatural power does not necessarily make you a theist, since you might think of that power as indifferent to the affairs of humankind. In the 18th century, the term "deism" was coined to refer to a belief in a non-interventionist creator who, having created and ordered the world, left it to its own devices to run according to its natural laws. Deists were thus often condemned by theists as taking the first step towards atheism.

A fairly popular modern position rejects the idea of any "ultimate power", even an impersonal one, behind the universe, and instead maintains that human beings have the ability to cope with the problems of existence entirely through their own resources. Such an outlook is referred to as "humanist" and takes various forms. Scientific humanism rejects any appeals to revelation or other supposed supernatural interventions, and maintains that the rational procedures of science are the key to understanding the cosmos and tackling the challenges of human life. Ethical humanism argues for a system of morality based entirely on natural human standards (such as the promotion of happiness). One of the key claims of humanists is that meaning and value in one's life can be realized without any reference to ideas of the divine or the supernatural, and that the so-called "spiritual" values (for example, those connected with our moral and aesthetic sensibilities) can be followed and fostered within an entirely human frame of reference.

1869, the biologist T.H. Huxley coined the term "agnostic" (from the Greek for "not-knowing") for one who holds that the existence of God is unknown and, so far as can be determined, unknowable.

Modern atheism takes several forms, but is best understood as the denial of a personal supernatural creator of the universe (that is, a being who transcends the natural material cosmos, and who is in some sense conscious). The strongest form of atheism maintains not just that God does not exist, but that God could not exist: that the idea of the existence of such a being is incoherent or self-contradictory. (For example, it may be asked how a being can be eternal and changeless, yet also capable of entering into a relationship with creatures in time.) Perhaps a more common atheist position is the view that God's existence, while not in itself impossible, is rendered extremely improbable by known facts about the world (for example the amount of suffering in it).

> *The Christian religion not only was at first attended with miracles, but even at this day cannot be believed by any reasonable person without one.*
>
> David Hume, *An Enquiry Concerning Human Understanding*

Recent discussion of atheism has focused in part on the question of who bears the onus of proof about God's existence. The British philosopher A.G.N. Flew has suggested that it is "up to believers in the existence and activities of God to provide good reason for believing, rather than to unbelievers to provide positive reasons for not believing."

Perhaps the most cogent modern statement of the case for atheism has been provided by John Mackie, who argues that none of the traditional arguments for the existence of God holds water, and that when considerations on the other side are taken into account (notably the problem of evil), then "the balance tips still further against theism". In this view, shared by many contemporary atheists, the idea of a divine personal creator is extremely improbable, and is also unnecessary. In the words of the great French scientist Pierre-Simon Laplace (1749–1827), we have "no need of that hypothesis".

> *A world in which there can be no pain or suffering would also be one in which there can be no moral choices and hence no possibility of moral growth and development.*
>
> John Hick, *Encountering Evil*

Pain and evil

The amount of suffering in the world, whether arising from natural causes or human action, has long been a serious obstacle to belief in an all-powerful and benevolent God. There is a correspondingly long tradition of debate on the "problem of evil" and its possible solutions.

If God exists, whence comes evil? So runs the old question that continues to trouble religious believers. "Evil" as traditionally used in discussions of the problem of suffering and pain in the world includes both physical evil (disease, earthquakes and so on) and moral evil (torture, oppression and so on). How can the existence of such evil be explained, if there is a (Judeo-Christian-Islamic type) God who must know it occurs (since he is omniscient); must be able to prevent it (since he is omnipotent); and must presumably want to prevent it (since he is benevolent)?

Some have claimed that the existence of evil proves God does not exist – that it is logically incompatible with the existence of an omniscient, omnipotent, benevolent being. More commonly, however, the claim is that the existence of evil at least makes God's existence very improbable. Typical is the argument in *Think* of contemporary philosopher Simon Blackburn, who compares the world in which we find ourselves to a dormitory in a grim boarding school: "The roof leaks, there are rats about, the food is almost inedible, some students in fact starve to death. There is a closed door, behind which is the management, but the management never comes out. You get to speculate what the management must be like. Can you infer from the dormitory as you find it that the management, first, knows exactly what conditions are like, second, cares intensely for your welfare, and third, possesses unlimited resources for fixing things? The inference is crazy. You would be almost certain to infer that either the management doesn't know, doesn't care, or cannot do anything about it."

Graves of US servicemen killed in World War II. How could a benevolent, omnipotent God allow such wars to happen?

The project of trying to explain the evil in the world is called theodicy (literally, "the vindication of God's justice"). Perhaps the oldest form of theodicy is the "free will defence", found in Augustine's thinking (see pp.116–117). Augustine argued that "Everything called 'evil' is either sin, or the penalty of sin"; God creates only what is good, but since human beings have free will, they may turn away from good and so be responsible for suffering. Certainly, human choice is responsible for enormous amounts of misery (consider the actions of a Hitler or Pol Pot), but this does not seem to explain physical evils such as cancer or devastation caused by earthquakes – unless these

Pain – an unmitigated evil?

Pain is often cited by moral philosophers as an example of something that is intrinsically bad, so the problem for a religious believer is to explain why a loving God would nonetheless allow it to occur.

One response is that since pain mechanisms are highly beneficial for an organism's health and survival, a species or individual that was not acutely distressed by serious damage to its body would quickly be eliminated. This type of consideration led Descartes to argue that the sensory systems of the body, though they may cause us pain on any given occasion, are none the less all evidence of the benevolence and goodness of God, since their proper working is indispensable to life and health.

One problem with this solution, however, is that when the body is diseased, acute pain may persist beyond the point where it seems to serve any useful purpose for the ultimate well-being of the individual. The theist may respond that God's creation operates in accordance with immutable causal laws; however, it may still be asked why God does not intervene to override such laws.

are regarded as a penalty for past sin, which seems to invoke a morally unacceptable conception of a God who allows the innocent to suffer for the guilty.

A second type of theodicy argues that suffering may be permitted by God as a means to greater good. Thus the Oxford philosopher Richard Swinburne has argued that this often painful world is, in the words of the poet Keats, a "vale of soul making" – its trials and tribulations promote moral growth. Yet while it is true that suffering does often enrich people's understanding and sympathy, there appears to be a residue of misery that is not linked to any chance of improvement (such as the suffering of starving children in Africa).

The 18th-century philosopher Leibniz (see pp.38–39) argued that the evil found on earth might be counterbalanced by blessedness found in the rest of the cosmos (an argument condemned by the atheist Bertrand Russell as like reasoning that since the visible layer of a crate of oranges is rotten, the layers below must be sound). In his *Theodicy* (1710), Leibniz reasoned that if God (being supremely perfect) is to create anything separate from himself, this creation must contain some residual imperfection: the created universe cannot be completely perfect or else it would not be distinct from God. This connects with an ancient idea (found in Augustine), that creation is a process of subtraction from the total perfection that is God. However, critics may ask if this explains the amount of pain and suffering in the world, which seems far more than is required by the mere fact of the cosmos necessarily lacking certain perfections.

The debate is still unresolved. Some, perhaps most, of the suffering that troubles us results from the fact that the stuff of which we and our world are composed is fragile, impermanent and subject to change and decay. That is our human lot. But why would a loving God not intervene to improve things? Some claim that he has intervened – hence the Christian view that God became incarnate as Christ to share our suffering and redeem the world. Whether or not this doctrine provides the materials for a complete solution to the problem of evil, it takes us into the realm of faith and so beyond philosophical reasoning alone.

A stack of human skulls found in Cambodia – the last remains of some of the victims of the Khmer Rouge. Man's inhumanity to man is often incomprehensible, but does the fact of it also make the idea of a benevolent, all-powerful God untenable?

Voltaire

One of the important transitional figures in the emergence of the modern age, François-Marie Arouet was born in 1694 and is generally known by the pen name under which he published his numerous pamphlets and essays – "Voltaire". Educated by the Jesuits, he was throughout his life fiercely hostile to the Catholic church and incurred strong criticism for his attacks on such religious thinkers as Blaise Pascal. In his youth Voltaire was attracted to the ideas of John Locke (see pp.82–83), and it is through Voltaire's work that these ideas first became known in France. The first collection of Voltaire's short essays and articles was published in 1734 as the *Lettres philosophiques*, and was banned in France for its criticism of the political establishment. This was followed in 1764 by the *Dictionnaire philosophique*. Expressly planned as a vehicle for liberal and anti-establishment ideas, this later work was widely condemned as subversive of religion.

In addition Voltaire wrote plays and poems, together with his most famous work, the novel *Candide* (1759). The message of the book is the vacuity of philosophical and religious dogma; especially targeted is the absurd Doctor Pangloss, a figure (based on the German philosopher Leibniz) who espouses a form of religious optimism under the slogan "All's for the best in the best of all possible worlds". Voltaire's serious point is to scrutinize the traditional belief in a benevolent providence overseeing the course of events: how can such a view cope with the problem of evil and suffering in the world? A telling episode in the novel is based on the terrible Lisbon earthquake of 1755 in which many thousands lost their lives; the pompous insistence of Pangloss that there must be a "sufficient reason" for such an event is exposed in all its vacuous insensitivity.

Francois-Marie Arouet 1694–1778

The most celebrated of the *philosophes*, the group of free-thinking writers and essayists of the French Enlightenment, Voltaire was a champion of religious and social toleration, and a sharp critic of religious authoritarianism. He nevertheless insisted on the importance of belief in God, famously observing that "if God did not exist, it would be necessary to invent him".

Voltaire's own view of these matters seems to have been that it was best to set aside metaphysical speculation (symbolized in Pangloss's name, which means "all talk") in favour of positive social action – a view encapsulated in *Candide* by the slogan that expresses his eventual conclusion: "We must cultivate our garden". Nevertheless, Voltaire retained his belief in God, the God whom human beings would be driven to "invent", even if he did not exist. God for Voltaire was a pragmatic necessity – a necessary bulwark against moral anarchy, and the ultimate support for the ideas of toleration and brotherly love in which he strongly believed.

> *Houses came crashing down. Roofs toppled on their foundations and the foundations crumbled. Thirty thousand men, women and children were crushed to death under the ruins … 'What can be the "sufficient reason" for this phenomenon?' said Pangloss.*
>
> Voltaire, *Candide*

Kierkegaard

Kierkegaard was a complex and often anguished figure, whose early life was marked by outward comfort and inner turmoil. He had a problematic relationship with his gloomy and pious father; moreover, his mother and five of his six siblings died before he reached the age of 21. His agonized decision to break off the engagement with his fiancée was a theme of his earliest writings. At 29 he published under pseudonyms what were to become among his most famous works, *Either/Or* and *Fear and Trembling*. In 1846 Kierkegaard admitted, in a brief appendix to his *Concluding Unscientific Postscript*, his authorship of this and the earlier works. Kierkegaard abandoned his plans to become a pastor, and founded a magazine that was highly critical of the Danish state church. He died after collapsing on the street at the age of 42.

Søren Kierkegaard 1813–1855

An opponent of dogmatic systems of philosophy and theology, the Danish philosopher Søren Kierkegaard saw religious experience as passionate personal confrontation with the problems of human existence and the demands of faith.

Fear and Trembling is a reflection on the story of the testing of Abraham in Genesis, in which God orders the patriarch to sacrifice his beloved only son, Isaac, as a burnt offering. What Kierkegaard succeeds in doing is to highlight in a particularly vivid way the situation of a religious adherent who believes that our human fulfilment lies in obedience to the will of God: total allegiance to a higher authority seems to involve a radical compromising of our autonomy as rational moral agents.

Though Kierkegaard exerted a strong influence on the subsequent philosophy of religion, he was in many ways unsympathetic to philosophy as an abstract intellectual discipline. His famous slogan "truth is subjectivity" implies that in matters of morality and religion, it is quite inappropriate to rely on the objective tools of academic scholarship or scientific method – the formal analysis of doctrines and evaluation of evidence. Kierkegaard contrasted mathematical propositions, in which there is objective certainty, with religious inquiry, where "I see much that disturbs my mind and excites anxiety". In the latter there is an "intense inwardness that embraces this objective uncertainty with the entire passion of the infinite".

Kierkegaard is often described as a precursor of the "existentialist" approach to philosophy. Though this label is hard to define precisely, some of the strands in existentialism include a distrust of formal systems claiming to present the "essential truth", a stress on the individual's response to the human predicament and a more intense and personal style of philosophizing. All these elements can be found in Kierkegaard's work, though his deep commitment to Christianity puts him at odds with such celebrated 20th-century atheist existentialists as Albert Camus and Jean-Paul Sartre. Kierkegaard's influence has perhaps been most important for the understanding of what it is to have a religious outlook, and of how the discourse of religion differs from that of science. His close attention to the emotions and passions, such as anxiety and guilt, highlights what is for many a vital part of the religious impulse: that sense of a gulf between the limitations we experience in ourselves and some power beyond ourselves that drives us forward to transcend those limitations.

The meaning of life

The search for meaning in our lives is one of our most powerful human propensities. While religious thinkers invoke God as the ultimate source of meaning, critics of this approach have questioned how the purposes of a supernatural being could affect the human struggle for a meaningful existence.

The phrase "the meaning of life" is a problematic one: some would argue that only linguistic items (for example, documents, poems, letters, sentences) have meaning, and that asking about the meaning of life in general is a confusion. People often speak of individual activities as "meaningful", in the sense that they consider them worthwhile and enriching; thus a scientist may say his work in the laboratory is meaningful, or a parent describe the project of raising a family as meaningful. But can our lives as a whole be said to have meaning? In an unstable and uncertain world, in which many of our projects end in failure, and death is the inevitable end, it may be hard at times to retain anything except a sense of futility.

Nietzsche and eternal recurrence

Nietzsche (see p.153) designed his myth of the "eternal recurrence" to highlight the problem of how human beings can find meaning in their lives. Are we willing, he asked, to say such a passionate "Yes!" to each single moment of our existence that we would make all the same choices again, even on condition of eternally repeating them? He wrote in *The Joyful Science* (1882): "The life as you now live it you will have to live once more and innumerable times more, and everything unutterably small or great in your life will have to return to you, all in the same succession or sequence. The eternal hourglass of existence is turned over, and you within it, a grain of dust."

The religious answer is that a human life has meaning in so far as it fulfils the purposes for which we were created by God. The 13th-century Franciscan thinker Bonaventure, encapsulating a common theme in Christian thought, observed that "the soul is born to perceive the infinite good that is God, and accordingly it must find its rest and contentment in him alone" (*Commentaries on Lombard*, 1250). The central idea here is that if we turn away from the values that God has ordained we will bring misery on ourselves (as in the story of the original disobedience of Adam in the Garden

Eve presents temptation to Adam in this detail from the 1528 painting *Adam and Eve* by Cranach the Elder. Keeping to the path God has set out for us – as Adam and Eve failed to do – is seen by many religious people as the road to fulfilment.

of Eden); but if we conform our will to God's we will find the true meaning of our existence ("In his will is our peace", as the poet Dante put it).

A common objection to this religious approach is that even if one grants that there is a God, it would still not be clear how his purposes could confer meaning on our lives. Submitting oneself wholly to the will of another does not seem consistent with our status as autonomous rational agents; and, conversely, for an all-powerful being to impose his purposes on his creatures might seem to be a violation of their freedom and dignity. However, the religious thinker may reply to this that God is not an arbitrary tyrant, but by his nature good and benevolent; so his purposes for us are those in which we will find our genuine fulfilment (God is the one "in whose service is perfect freedom", as the Anglican *Book of Common Prayer* of 1666 has it). There is, of course, a further question about how any given religion can justifiably claim to have identified what the purposes of God actually are.

Human meaning in human life

The German philosopher Friedrich Nietzsche (see p.153) is famous for his proclamation of the "death of God". Mankind, he maintained, will have to

Nuns working in the garden of their convent in the village of Asolo, Italy, For some, dedication to a religious way of life is a profound source of meaning and fulfilment. But does this mean substituting the will of God for our own will?

Meaning, futility and eternity

A powerful image of the human condition is the ancient Greek myth of Sisyphus, eternally condemned by the gods to push a rock to the top of a hill, only to see it roll to the bottom time and again. The story encapsulates the futility of many of our human endeavours: the lasting difference we can make to anything is often minimal.

The French existentialist Albert Camus famously declared that "we must imagine Sisyphus as happy"; the defiant heroism of the condemned man brings a type of contentment arising from his "refusal to hope and the unyielding evidence of a life without consolation" (*The Myth of Sisyphus*, 1942). However, this seems to involve abandoning the possibility that such a life could be truly meaningful; Camus himself used the term "the Absurd" to characterize the human predicament.

The Sisyphus story also raises the question of whether immortality would in itself confer any meaning on our activities. The British philosopher Bernard Williams has argued that immortality would make no difference – an eternal existence (even one much more pleasant that that of Sisyphus) would inevitably produce boredom and so be meaningless. On the other hand, some thinkers have maintained that there is often a systematic misunderstanding of what is intended in the religious tradition by the notion of eternal life. The philosopher of religion D.Z. Philips has suggested that religious talk of "eternal life" is best understood as proclaiming a new way of living, rather than a continued existence in the next world. In *Death and Immortality,* he argues that "eternity is not more life, but this life seen under certain moral and religious modes of thought". This suggestion implies that when we ask how a life can be meaningful, we should look at the quality of that life and its values, rather than its indefinite continuation.

learn to do without the comforts of religion, designed as consolations for the weak. Instead, we must in effect become like gods, and generate meaning from within ourselves: "Ultimately man finds in things nothing but what he himself has imported into them: the finding we call science, the importing, art, religion, love, pride" (*The Will to Power*, 1888). Only by our own heroic determination, our own resolute acts of will, can we make our lives meaningful, according to Nietzsche.

Though there may be something admirable in the resolute Nietzschean determination to accept that humankind is thrown entirely on its own resources, it is doubtful that our subjective desires and inclinations are enough on their own to generate meaning. Recently, philosophers have argued that something can only be valuable if we have reason to pursue it, and what we pursue is partly a matter for objective assessment. In the words of the American moral philosopher Susan Wolf: "Meaning arises when subjective attraction meets objective attractiveness" (*Happiness and Meaning*, 1997). In other words, when someone is drawn to pursue *x*, this is typically because of some feature of *x* that makes it objectively worthy of being pursued. There are many philosophers who support the idea of objective value without supposing that it requires any appeal to a supernatural (that is, religious) source, and debate continues as to how such value is best to be understood.

Chapter 5

ETHICS AND AESTHETICS

What is morality?

The basic concepts in which morality deals are good and bad, right and wrong, duty and obligation. Moral theories vary in the emphasis they put on these concepts and in the way they interpret them. This variation, however, does not necessarily preclude a common morality.

Morality is sometimes thought to be concerned just with personal behaviour, or even just with sexual behaviour. But this is a very narrow view, peculiar to modern times. When the earliest recorded discussions of morality in the Western tradition took place in Athens in the 5th century BCE, both Plato (see pp.76–79) and Aristotle (see pp.13–15) took it for granted that questions about the good person and the good society were inextricably linked. The central moral concepts emerged in their discussions: not only goodness itself, but also notions of right and wrong, justice and injustice, together with virtues and defects of character such as courage and cowardice. Since then, views of morality have expanded to cover not only personal behaviour but also global concerns.

Moral beginnings

So where does the human capacity to see issues in moral rather than purely practical terms originate? It begins, perhaps, with the first philosophical question that anybody asks – "what ought I to do?" For interaction with the world and other human beings starts even before the ability to walk or talk are acquired, and certainly before the ability to reason can play a role. When a human infant is first aware of itself as facing a situation of choice, it has, consciously or unconsciously, had its first encounter with the possibility of morality. It is to be expected that the grounds of that first choice will be the satisfaction of its own needs and wants. Later, the interest of others will be encountered as a constraint. Perhaps, later still, the awareness of a more distinctively moral ground for action will emerge. It is the search for the source of this potential moral life and the attempt to ground it on a secure theoretical basis that provides much of the substance of moral philosophy.

The first and most obvious way to understand morality is to equate it with an established code of behaviour – for example, the Ten Commandments, the Sermon on the Mount, or the Islamic Sunna.

Morality and religion

Can religion provide a basis for morality? The standard response of the modern secular philosopher to this question is "no", because religion must itself, in the end, depend on a prior moral judgement – that of the goodness of God, who is held to be the final authority for morality. In other words, religion cannot provide a moral system unless it can give some account of the goodness of God – but it cannot give an account of the goodness of God unless it first has a conception of morality. If this argument is correct, it means that the attempt to found morality on religion is essentially circular. But it is significant that the major present-day religions are closely associated with systems of morality, suggesting that this argument may be based on a misunderstanding of the nature of religious commitment. Religion is as much a matter of "following" as "believing", and its ethical codes are at least as important as intellectual assent to dogmas or creeds. The question, then, is not whether what is right, good or morally obligatory is so because it is commanded by God; but whether individuals should follow the precepts of faith in their own lives. However, in a world divided by religious differences, people may prefer to seek answers to moral questions that do not depend upon a particular religious perspective, but can cut across divisions of culture and religion.

In many societies,the prevailing moral codes can be traced back to traditions and social customs, including those of diet and hospitality. Here, a group of Muslim men in Marrakesh share a meal in traditional fashion, eating from a common dish.

Human communities formalized moral codes from the earliest times, and most of the world's great religions offer ethical systems to their followers. Etymology supplies some support for equating morality with a moral code of this kind, for both *ethos* (the Greek root of "ethics") and *mores* (the Latin root of "morals") are connected with customs and behaviour.

So should morality slavishly follow whatever tradition is dominant in a particular place at a particular time? It would seem not, for moral codes themselves may be open to moral criticism. At the same time, there are some certainties or convictions that stand the test of time as well as of place and culture. The search for morality is the search for something that has substance and standing in its own right.

One of the earliest recorded discussions of the nature of morality in the Western tradition is to be found in Plato's *Republic*, in which Socrates leads fictional debates about the ideal state (see pp.76–79). Thrasymachus, a participant in the dialogue, expresses a strong cynical viewpoint, arguing that what is just or right is what is in the interest of the strongest party, or at least what they believe to be in their interest and are able to enforce by law. This power-analysis of morality is not unlike the views of modern thinkers such as Marx (see pp.210–211), Nietzsche (see p.153) and their postmodernist followers. Socrates' interlocutors also suggest that everyone would like to be immoral (freely committing murder, theft and adultery) if it were not for the threat of punishment and unpopularity. Socrates' response is to question these assumptions about the true nature and desires of human beings, and to suggest that justice is not only a means to happiness but essential to it. Arguing that the common rules of morality accord with human nature – they are not artificial or external – Socrates tries to show that therefore people can never be placed in a position where they have to choose between morality and personal happiness.

This view of the nature and scope of morality, then, belongs to a long philosophical tradition. It

Calculating benefit: the greatest happiness principle

According to the late 18th-century philosopher Jeremy Bentham (see p.197), "The greatest happiness of the greatest number is the measure of right and wrong." As Bentham saw it, this principle offered a science of ethical decision-making, a means of resolving issues by testable practical methods that, at the extreme, may be quantitative and statistical. To this end, Bentham devised a "felicific calculus" with seven dimensions of pleasure and pain. These were: intensity (how intense is the pleasure or pain?), duration (how long does it last?), certainty (what are the chances of that type of sensation resulting?), propinquity (how soon will it result?), fecundity (if pleasurable, is it likely to be followed by sensations of the same kind?), purity (is it likely to be followed by sensations of the opposite kind?) and extent (how many people will it affect?). Someone contemplating taking up smoking or offered a hard drug at a party, may realistically go through a process of calculation like this in asking the question: "Is it worth it?" Formalized in the public sphere, it becomes the economist's strategy of cost-benefit analysis, by which, for example, the cost of new railway safety systems is weighed up against the likely number of lives saved.

gave place, however, first to the Stoic ethics of the Greek and Roman world (see p.138) and then, as Christianity became the dominant religion of Europe, to a theologically-based morality. In the modern period, however, the debate initiated by Socrates has developed along rather different lines.

Sense and reason

In 18th-century England the debate turned to the question of whether morality was based on "sentiment" or on "reason". British "moral sense" theorists, such as the Earl of Shaftesbury (1671–1713) and Francis Hutcheson (1694–1746), continued to support the principle of a natural harmony between virtue and self-interest. Resisting the idea that morality must be based on reason, they insisted that it must depend on whether an action was, in Hutcheson's words, "amiable or disagreeable" to one's moral sense. The case against reason and for sentiment was most tellingly put by the Scottish philosopher David Hume (see pp.24–25) when he said: "It is not contrary to Reason to prefer the destruction of the whole world to the scratching of my finger."

While these views might seem to turn ethical disagreement into a dispute about taste, they provided a foundation for another important conception of morality that developed in Britain in the late 18th and the 19th century, and which continues to dominate Western social and political thinking: utilitarianism. This is the theory that what is right is what produces the greatest balance of pleasure over pain. It combines the factual belief that people are entirely motivated by personal self-interest with the moral claim that they ought to pursue the general welfare. The reconciliation of these apparently incompatible principles was to be achieved, according to the first great exponent of the theory, Jeremy Bentham (see p.197), by law, that is, by using punishment and reward to make individual interest coincide with the public good. Utilitarianism can, however, be advocated simply as a normative theory, that is, as a recommendation that we *should* act so as to maximize happiness.

Classical utilitarianism speaks of the maximizing of pleasure – the greatest happiness of the greatest number – but contemporary utilitarians often prefer to talk of maximising the satisfaction of desires or preferences. In any case, critics of utilitarianism point to the impossibility of estimating all the possible consequences of an action, and the oddity of judging an act by its actual consequences as opposed to what was intended or what was probable or foreseeable at the time. Many opponents of utilitarianism challenge it, too, in the name of justice, since it seems that it might justify or even mandate the sacrifice of the few to the many, permitting atrocities in the name of a Utopian future and making thinkable what is and should be morally unthinkable.

Ethical principles

The alternative to utilitarianism seems to be to adopt a principle-based approach to ethics which ignores the consequences in particular cases. Deontological (duty-based) theories of morality, such as the one put forward by Kant (see pp.141–143), regard consequences as irrelevant to whether an action is right or wrong. But this approach is problematic, too, because it seems to mean allowing wholly unacceptable and avoidable disasters to result from an unbending commitment to justice or other rigid principles. Kant is often criticized for arguing that lying and promise-breaking are wrong in all circumstances, and that principles should never be qualified by appeal to the facts of particular situations, still less to their consequences for the happiness of those involved. Kant's approach is usually thought to be too stringent for everyday life, even if the sheer expediency of utilitarianism is recognized to be morally unsatisfactory.

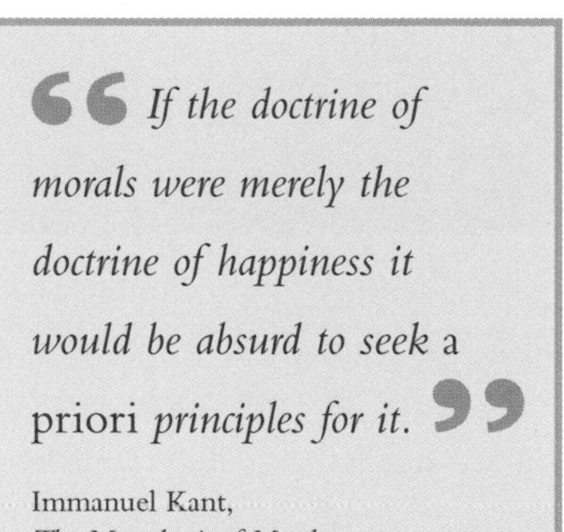

“*If the doctrine of morals were merely the doctrine of happiness it would be absurd to seek a* priori *principles for it.*”

Immanuel Kant, *The Metaphysic of Morals*

A contemporary solution to this problem was put forward by the Harvard philosopher John Rawls (see p.203) who, in *A Theory of Justice* (1971), developed an account of justice based on the idea of a hypothetical contract among free and equal individuals. Rawls's method was designed to arrive at basic principles of justice from an impartial perspective by means of a thought experiment. The potential members of a society work out, behind a "veil of ignorance", basic principles for organizing life in the community they are about to share. The people in this "original position" are assumed to be both rational and self-interested. The "veil of ignorance" protects them from knowledge of the particular social conditions in which they will live their own lives, and in this situation they will, according to Rawls, adopt what he called the "maximin principle", which means they will seek to protect themselves by selecting the best of the worst possible outcomes. That is, they will ensure that the worst off are not entirely destitute, lest they end up worst off themselves.

Rawls, then, sees certain moral principles as being derivable from the "original position". However, because it ultimately grounds rationality on considerations of self-interest, it is disputable whether this theory supplies the universality or stringency that morality requires. The idea of goodness and justice as moral absolutes seems likely to elude an approach which assumes nothing except individuals who think only of themselves.

It has become fashionable to dismiss the idea that there is a core of universal values that transcend cultures and other differences. This dismissal leads to a form of cultural relativism, according to which values are only meaningful within a particular culture. But the search for a common morality can be based on an awareness of what all human beings as a matter of fact have in common – at a minimum, what is necessary for the individual to survive a normal life-span and to raise offspring. Even a conception as simplified as this argues for a fundamental linkage between morality, human nature and personal happiness.

Stoicism

Stoic philosophy dominated the classical world for some six centuries from the late 4th century BCE. Stoics looked for peace of mind in a troubled world, advocating the pursuit of virtue rather than wealth or health as the route to harmony of the spirit under a common moral law.

Stoic philosophy is named after the porch or arcade (*stoa*) in Athens where the first Stoics met and discussed their ideas. The works of the founding Stoic, Zeno of Citium (334–262BCE), and his followers survive only as quoted fragments in later writings, but the Stoic school was also influential in the Roman world and original texts are known from this time. Stoicism was revived in the Renaissance and continues to influence ethical thought today.

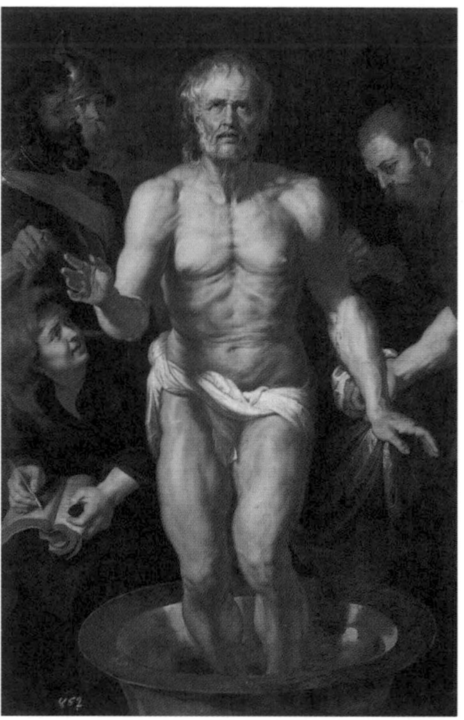

The Death of Seneca by Rubens depicts the dignified death of this Roman Stoic thinker, whose works are the most important body of Stoic literature to survive from antiquity.

Stoic philosophy included a theory of the natural world as well as ethics. Stoics believed in a cosmos formed and guided by a *logos*, or reason, that represents order, destiny and the law of nature. The Stoics' ethical system is based on a belief in the harmony of the universe. Pain and suffering exist because the dark is needed to give form to the light, as in a painting; the whole, though, is perfect and harmonious. As far as pain and evil beyond our control are concerned, they recommended *apatheia* (indifference, or freedom from intense feelings). Tranquillity is to be achieved, they taught, by suppressing irrational emotions – for example, regrets about the past – and bringing one's reason into line with the cosmic order by the acceptance of its inevitability.

The origins of Stoic ideas go back beyond the Greek philosophers to the religions and philosophies of the East. The conception of wisdom that came to the Greeks from these sources was one of pursuing inner peace, seeking finally to reach the state of "nothingness" that alone frees a human being from the pain and struggle of existence. This philosophy of acceptance and withdrawal from the "self" is to be found in Epicurus (341–270BCE) as well as in Stoic doctrines. It has also influenced certain modern philosophers such as Spinoza and Schopenhauer. The common thread is a conception of moral wisdom as a recognition of the inevitability of things, and a determination not to corrode one's soul with resentment at what is beyond reach.

Stoicism is not only concerned with looking inward and cultivating self-control and tranquillity – the qualities with which the term "stoical" is commonly linked today – but also looks outward, recommending social usefulness on the stage of the world, where all human beings meet as equals. Stoic philosophers were aware of the diversity of human views of truth and right, and this led them to distinguish between the laws that could rightly be regarded as varying from place to place, and universal law – the law of nature – which was not variable or relative in this way. Stoicism, then, was a cosmopolitan philosophy in the true sense of the word. Stoic duty is the duty of a citizen of the world, not of one particular country; it is a duty to promote the wellbeing of all those you can affect.

Mill

Britain's John Stuart Mill was the classic exponent of liberalism. His father, James Mill, (1773–1836) was a utilitarian and a close friend of Jeremy Bentham (see p.197). He educated his son himself, seeing to it that Mill had mastered both Greek and Latin by the age of seven. Mill described his rigorous education in his *Autobiography* (1873); in which he also describes the mental breakdown he suffered at the age of 20, which led him to turn towards poetry and literature. Mill worked as a colonial administrator for the East India Company in London until 1858. He was also a Member of Parliament for a short time (1865–68).

Despite society's disapproval, Mill had a long association with Harriet Taylor who, when they first met, was the married mother of young children. They shared intellectual interests and he claimed her as his philosophical inspiration. When they finally married, following the death of her husband, he formally renounced the rights vested in him as a husband by the laws of Victorian England. He was an early supporter of feminism, the theme of his *The Subjection of Women* (1869).

Mill's new utilitarianism

In *Utilitarianism* (1861), Mill defended the principle that actions are to be judged according to their tendency to promote happiness. Bentham was undoubtedly an influence and inspiration for Mill but, unlike Bentham, he believed that some forms of happiness are more worthwhile than others, and this worth applies especially to intellectual pleasures. As he said: "It is better to be Socrates dissatisfied than a fool satisfied." This is often regarded as a weakness in Mill's utilitarianism, but, as one commentator, John Gray, points out, Mill's more complex notion of pleasure or happiness echoes that of Aristotle (see pp13–16): according to Aristotle, humans flourish best when they can exercise their distinctive human capacities, especially reason. Mill, then, valued education and believed a certain cultural level necessary for the full realization of human potential. He rejected Bentham's conception of human nature and placed much more emphasis on the social and cultural context in which life was to be lived. For this reason, Mill also valued traditional moral principles, especially justice, freedom and toleration.

So was Mill an inconsistent utilitarian? Mill himself believed he had supplied the answer in the last chapter of *Utilitarianism*. In what has come to be called "rule utilitarianism", he argued that principles such as liberty and justice are themselves important social instruments for utility. This means that most of the widely recognized principles of moral behaviour, such as telling the truth, keeping promises, not stealing and so on, are best understood as rules-of-thumb, not as absolute rules. It means, too, that it is right to promote a social policy of encouraging people to follow such rules as a matter of habit. As Mill put it, there are

> *"The utilitarian doctrine is, that happiness is desirable, and the only thing desirable, as an end; all other things being desirable only as means to that end"*
>
> J.S. Mill, *Utilitarianism*

John Stuart Mill 1806–73

A many-sided thinker and philosopher, John Stuart Mill was interested in ethics, politics, social science and humanism, and also wrote significant works on logic and scientific method. Although strongly influenced in his early years by Bentham's utilitarianism, he went on to develop his own distinctive version of the utilitarian system.

The limits of tolerance: public and private morality

The principle of toleration as set out by Mill recommends minimizing interference by one person or group with the beliefs or conduct of another. It is especially associated with drawing a distinction between the public and the private spheres.

Mill's defence of individualism led to a long and continuing debate about the limits of tolerance. In 1957 an official report recommending changes in the laws on prostitution and homosexuality in Britain adopted principles that closely followed Mill by endorsing the idea of a private realm in which the law should not interfere. Its practical conclusion was that neither prostitution, nor homosexual acts between consenting adults in private, should be illegal.

Following this, one of England's most senior judges, Lord Devlin, challenged these liberal assumptions, claiming that there is a popular morality that the law should enforce. This "public morality" he saw as actually defining society. He wrote: "Without shared ideas on politics, morals, and ethics, no society can exist." While acknowledging that moral views might change, Devlin argued that the law should *follow* change, not attempt to lead it. Unlike Mill, he believed that law exists to protect society, not the individual.

Legal contemporaries, however, attacked these views, some insisting that it is not the function of law to enforce morality, and that immorality should not be a crime. This position agrees with Mill that the only justification for legal intervention is the prevention of harm to others.

The debate on tolerance initiated by Mill has moved on but it is far from having ended.

"certain classes of moral rules, which concern the essentials of human well-being more nearly, and are therefore of more absolute obligation, than any other rules for the guidance of life". These, he says, have tended over the course of millennia to be found to promote human happiness. Mill also regarded the conscious pursuit of happiness to be to some extent self-defeating, and believed that following well-established moral norms would probably, in the long run, and apart from in certain extreme cases, be more conducive to happiness than setting bare utility as the goal.

Mill and liberty

Mill believed that human happiness is closely bound up with freedom and the possibility of choice. In *On Liberty* (1859), Mill argues in favour of liberty of thought, speech and association; this includes freedom to choose one's own lifestyle, if this does not involve harming others or impinging on their freedom. The idea of a private realm where the state should not intrude is a fundamental theme of Mill's political philosophy (see box, above). He applied these principles in the field of education, too, arguing strongly against a state monopoly of education and for freedom of choice.

Mill's contribution to philosophy was that of an empiricist in the British tradition: he believed that truth was to be established by observation rather than reasoning from first principles. He extended his discussion to the social sciences and is regarded as a founder of modern sociology.

Mill's critics have suggested that his Victorian faith in progress blinded him to the possibility that liberty might not after all contribute to happiness. But Mill's primary concern was to leave room for the wide variety of human motivations.

Mill was in favour of compulsory education, but believed there should be competing systems rather than one state-run system.

Kant

Immanuel Kant was born in Königsberg in Prussia (now Kaliningrad, Russia) in 1724 and died in 1804. He never married, and he lived a simple and ascetic life; indeed, his lifestyle and working habits were so regular that people joked that you could set your clock by his routines.

Kant's earlier writings reflected the philosophical methods of his time and his most important philosophical and ethical works were published quite late in life. The start of this later phase, and of what is called Kant's critical period, was marked by the publication in 1781 of his most famous critical work, the *Critique of Pure Reason*. His most important ethical works followed: the short but pioneering *Groundwork of the Metaphysic of Morals* (1785) was published when Kant was 60, and his *Critique of Practical Reason* (1788) and *Metaphysic of Morals* (1797) still to follow.

Kant is one of the giants of philosophical history, but views on him are suprisingly varied. Bertrand Russell called him "a disaster", but C.D. Broad, another British philosopher and close contemporary of Russell, rather more fairly said: "When all criticisms have been made... Kant's failures are more important than most men's successes."

Morality as duty

Kant's ethical views are best understood in the context of his metaphysical theories. In *Critique of Pure Reason* he argued that we are confined within the world of our perceptions, with the realities that give rise to our perceptions forever beyond our grasp. We understand our world only by imposing on it our own broad conceptual categories: time, space and causality. These concepts provide an essential element for our understanding of the physical world. They are not derived from sense-experience or observation but are, in Kant's terminology, *a priori*. That is to say, they are fundamental requirements of reason. Kant argued that morality, too, must be grounded in *a priori* reasoning, rather than in any appeal to authority or religion.

> *"Two things fill the mind with ever new and increasing admiration and awe, the oftener and more steadily they are reflected on: the starry heavens above me and the moral law within me."*
>
> Immanuel Kant, *Critique of Practical Reason*

Immanuel Kant 1724–1804

The implacable enemy of utilitarianism, Kant is known as the philosopher of duty ethics. He argued that moral principles are to be followed unconditionally, and without regard for the consequences. In Kant's view, moral duties are thus "categorical imperatives" that admit no exceptions.

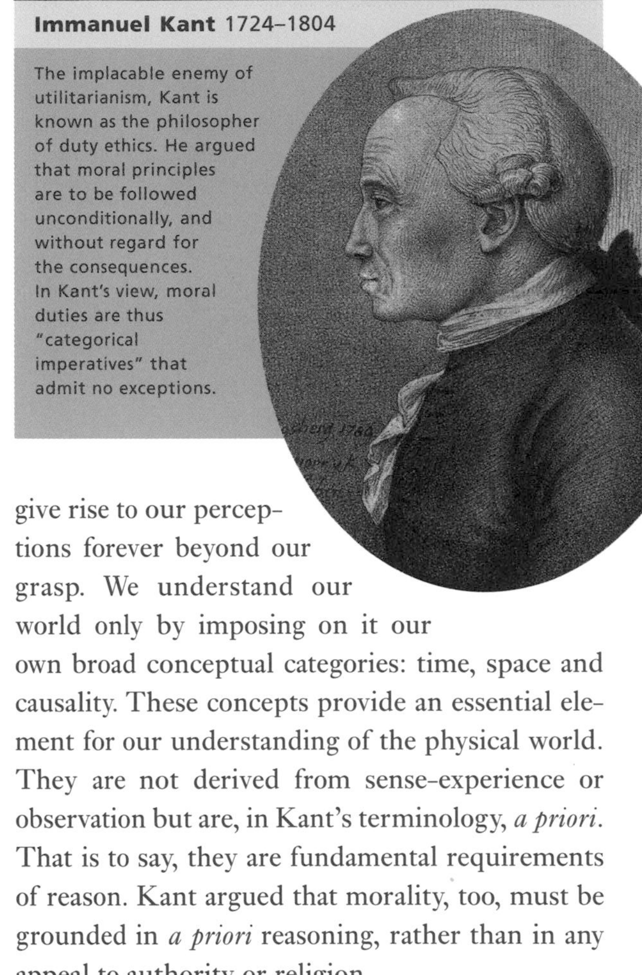

As a moral philosopher, Kant was the architect of deontology (duty-based ethics), often summed up as the principle of "duty for duty's sake". This was to reverse the tide of two millennia: where the ancient Greeks had identified virtue with happiness, Kant insisted that the two ideas were, and should be kept, separate and distinct. Happiness, he said, belongs in the empirical realm and to the sciences of human nature such as psychology and anthropology; but moral thinking involves only human reason, not human nature.

It was on this basis that Kant set out to find what he called the supreme principle of morality, uncontaminated by empirical observations. In *Groundwork of the Metaphysic of Morals*, he writes: "A law has to carry with it absolute necessity if it is

The Kantian heritage and the idea of human dignity

Kant emphasized the principle of respect for persons, writing: "So act as to use humanity, both in your own person and in the person of every other, always at the same time as an end, never simply as a means." Sometimes expressed as a principle of human dignity, this idea has played an important role in contemporary debates from issues of human rights to debates about abortion, euthanasia and stem-cell research.

For example, in Germany, where legal protection is extended to any "subject of human dignity", there was debate in relation to abortion about whether or not this applies to the fetus. The debate was rekindled in the light of the controversy surrounding embryo research, especially research using stem-cells taken from embryos. Against those who wished to ban such research, the German Chancellor, Gerhard Schroeder, used an argument that effectively set utilitarianism against the Kantian principle of "respect for persons" when he said that the ethic of respect had to be weighed against the ethics of healing and helping.

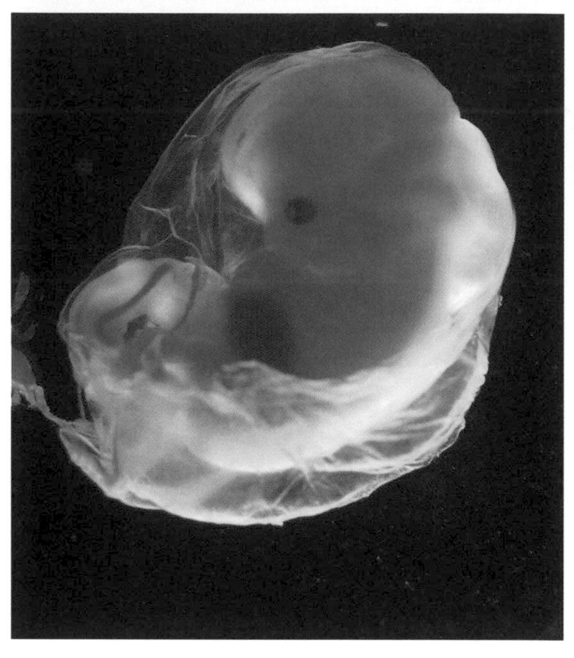

to be valued morally – valued, this is, as a ground of obligation ... the ground of obligation must be looked for, not in the nature of man, nor in the circumstances of the world in which he is placed, but solely *a priori* in the concepts of pure reason." His starting point for this claim is the observation that the value of the traditional virtues can be affected by context and consequences. For example – it is not Kant's example, of course, but he might well have used it – courage is usually regarded as a virtue, but not if it is used in pursuit of a murderous suicide hijacking. Similar arguments could be used in connection with the other virtues and so, Kant argued, there is only one thing that can be said to be good without any qualification at all and that is what he called "*ein guter Wille* (a good will) – that is, doing something from a moral motive, from the desire to do right just because it is right. In particular, consequences are irrelevant to the rightness or wrongness of an action. According to Kant, then, a shop-keeper's honesty can take on a moral aspect only if his motive is "because it is right" and not, for example, "because good ethics is good business".

The categorical imperative

Kant describes the obligation of duty as an imperative or command, and its absolute or unconditioned nature as categorical – hence the famous term associated with Kant, the "categorical imperative". In *Groundwork of the Metaphysic of Morals*, Kant presents the categorical imperative in a number of different formulations. The first and best-known of these is: "Act only on that maxim through which you can at the same time will that it should become a universal law."

Kant goes on to explain how this principle, which is itself more like a logical requirement than a purely moral principle, can generate duties or principles that are straightforwardly moral in the usual sense. By way of explanation, he provides examples that follow the classification common in his time into perfect and imperfect duties (Latin *perfectum*, "completed", and *imperfectum*, "incomplete" or "ongoing"). Perfect duties, such as paying a debt or keeping a promise, prescribe a single course of action, while imperfect duties, such as a duty to give to charity, can be variously carried out. Kant offers as examples of perfect duties the duty not to commit suicide and the duty to keep a promise. To endorse suicide would, he argues, be self-contradictory, since any justification would have to be based on self-love, and self-love is necessarily directed to self-preservation. His argument for seeing the duty to keep a promise as unconditional is that if you were to propose a universal principle – one to be followed by everyone all the time — of making a false promise whenever convenient, your thought-experiment would actually break down. In other words, the attempt to conceptualize such a rule would be impossible for it would destroy the very institution of promising. In the case of perfect duties, then, Kant argues that denial of the maxims concerned cannot be conceived without contradiction.

In the case of imperfect duties, on the other hand, it is possible to *conceive* of denying them, but not to *will* it. As examples of imperfect duties, Kant offers cultivating a natural talent and helping others. In both of these cases, Kant argues that, while no formal contradiction is involved in expressing maxims that deny these duties, it is impossible to *will* them. This is because, in the first case, we have a *desire* to nurture our talents for many useful purposes, and, in the second, we can conceive of situations in which we might ourselves want to be helped.

Through these arguments Kant presented, at a minimum, a strong case for impartiality as a necessary feature of moral judgements, which need to stand up to criticism as general maxims and not merely supply subjectively based conclusions fashioned for each instance. His refusal to allow for exceptions to moral principles has been criticized as too formal and legalistic, but it is an inevitable consequence of the idea of a categorical imperative. Further, Kant did not see principles as constraining people, but – on the contrary – as an expression of their freedom. They are what the rational person would want if it were not for the fact that human beings are not purely rational beings, but are also deeply affected by their desires and impulses. And this is the ground of humanity's uniqueness: whereas other animals are determined by their nature, humans can choose to follow their rational rather than their instinctive or emotional selves and to act in accordance with the moral law.

Found Drowned, by the 19th-century painter G.F. Watts. Suicide became something of a romantic notion in Victorian times, although Kant had argued that self-killing is always wrong, because it is contradictory – a self-interested act that is yet self-destructive.

Lying

The question of whether, and in what circumstances, lying may be justified is at least as old as Western philosophy. Are there situations in which it is acceptable to lie, or is it always our duty to speak the truth?

Truth is, along with reason, one of the pillars of Western thought. To discuss lying, however, there is no need to engage with the metaphysical question of the nature of truth. There is a widely accepted practical understanding that a lie has two features: first, it is factually inaccurate; second, there is an intention to deceive. A lie may be described, then, as an intentionally deceptive false statement.

Not all thinkers by any means have condemned lying as wrong. The Sophists of ancient Greece famously made their living by committing themselves to winning legal cases rather than to defending the truth. And Plato (see pp.76–79), despite Socrates' opposition to the Sophists, and despite his own decision to expel poets and playwrights from his ideal community as purveyors of fiction, recommended that politicians in his Republic should propagate a "noble lie", designed to keep people happy with their lot: that citizens were born with gold, silver or bronze in their make-up, and so innately destined for a particular role in society.

But while there have been special defences of lying in contexts such as these, it has more commonly and traditionally been regarded as morally wrong. So the question that has been widely discussed is not whether lying is wrong, but whether it is *always* wrong. Or can a duty to tell the truth be ranked against other duties? Many religious thinkers have taken an absolutist position on this, insisting that there can be no circumstances in which it is right to lie. In an early discussion of lying (*On Lying*, 395CE), Augustine (see pp.116–117) set out various kinds of lie, some less serious than others, and allowed that lies told with a good motive and with good effects might be easier to pardon, although they were still wrong. Thomas Aquinas (see p.112) reiterated that there is a permanent responsibility to tell the truth whatever the circumstances, difficult though they might be. He, too, drew a distinction between more and less morally serious lies, distinguishing helpful ("officious") and harmless ("jocose") lies, which are not mortal sins, from malicious lies, which are.

Others, however, sought ways to temper the impact of an absolute ban on lying and to avoid its rigorous consequences. One such means was equivocation or "mental reservation", in which a person might use ambiguous language that would lead to the hearer wrongly interpreting what was said. Another was a restriction depending upon whether the hearer had a right to the truth. So, for example, the legal philosopher Hugo Grotius (1583–1645) saw this as allowing exceptions in the case of lies to children, the insane and enemies.

In modern times, Kant (see pp.141–143) is the best known advocate of the absolute wrongness of lying. In a famous example, he argues that it would be wrong to tell a lie, even to save the life of someone fleeing from a would-be murderer. Kant has two main reasons for holding this absolutist position. One is a logical argument derived from his "categorical imperative". Kant's point is that the very possibility of lying presupposes the normality of truth.The second reason is that to lie to people is to fail to treat them as equals and as ends in themselves.

> *"It is not true that sometimes we ought to lie. And what is not true we should never try to persuade anyone to believe."*
>
> Thomas Aquinas, *Summa Theologiae*

Lying in public life

In some public contexts, lying is explicitly and uncompromisingly condemned. These include courts of law, where a commitment to tell the truth must be sworn on oath, and parliaments, whose right to the truth is held to be absolute – notwithstanding the idea of the political lie "for the public good" that has been a subject for debate since Plato's time.

If the political lie is widely denounced in democratic societies, lying is often thought to be practically indispensable in other areas of public life. In medicine, notably, there is an ancient tradition of telling lies for the good of the patient. More recently, however, this has tended to be seen as infringing patients' autonomy – their ability to make their own decisions.

Until the last few decades it was also thought acceptable to lie to the subjects of social scientific experiments. A famous example were the Milgram experiments in the 1960s to seek understanding of a person's willingness to obey orders. In these experiments, subjects were ordered by "scientists" to administer painful and dangerous electric shocks to "victims". The high level of compliance displayed by the subjects horrified people. But at the same time, many were outraged by the deception within the experiment, which was an elaborate set-up in which both "scientists" and "victims" were playing a part.

Kant has been much criticized for his position. Schopenhauer (see p.173) launched an extensive attack on him, arguing that, far from being a moral offence, lying is sometimes admirable. He observed that the English considered the accusation of telling lies the greatest insult and so, he claimed, told fewer lies than other nations. But then, he added, they also disliked impertinent and intrusive questions. In response to such questions, Schopenhauer says, you are entitled to lie as the only way to divert "inquisitive and suspicious curiosity". Schopenhauer's preferred maxim was: "Ask me no questions and I'll tell you no lies."

Many people would say that it is permissible to tell lies in extreme cases, such as in self-defence, but are there circumstances in which lying could even be a duty? There are indeed situations in which it seems this might be so – in wartime when pressed under torture to reveal your country's secrets, for example, or when a lie would protect the life of someone in your family.

While Kantians would allow no exceptions, not even benevolent lies in these extreme situations, utilitarianism is often thought to *mandate* lying for the greater good. However, utilitarians could, like John Stuart Mill (see pp.139–140), resist the pressure to allow exceptions by saying that it is better for everyone in the long run to be truthful, even if there are heavy costs to be paid in some individual cases. This is not incompatible with utilitarian Jeremy Bentham's dictum in *Principles of Morals and Legislation* that "falsehood, taken by itself, … can never, upon the principle of utility, constitute any offence at all", for a lie never can be taken by itself – it is always embedded in a social context. An argument that could be acceptable to both Kantians and utilitarians, then, is that lying destroys trust and erodes human relationships.

Conscience

Conscience is the name given to the inner sense by which people recognize right and wrong. "Liberty of conscience" is held to be a basic human right. But what exactly is conscience, and why should it be accorded such high status?

Opinions differ about right and wrong, and about good and bad. A possible response to this observation is to say that everyone ought to follow his or her own conscience. But whether it is in fact right to follow your conscience must, after all, depend on what your conscience tells you to do. The fallacy of assuming that conscience must always be followed lies in conflating two views: that "the dictates of conscience are always right" and that "no one should be forced to act against conscience". Following one's conscience does not exonerate a person from moral responsibility. Conscience can make mistakes; it can also be too carelessly consulted. Sometimes it should be followed against the opinion of the crowd, or even against the law. But it cannot be an excuse for evil.

The nature of conscience

The early Christian Church saw conscience as an inner illumination on good and evil that was given to us by God. But because Greek philosophers, five centuries before the advent of Christianity, had reached sound conclusions on practical wisdom and moral virtue, Christian thinkers reasoned that there must be a way other than revelation or authority to arrive at this insight. There must be, it was thought, an innate faculty, whether of reason or intuition, common to all human beings. In the pre-scholastic period, intuition was favoured. Augustine (see pp.116–117) taught that God had given us conscience as a direct way of knowing the moral law. Later, however, the role of reason was given a greater emphasis, and Thomas Aquinas (see

In medieval Europe the price of conscience was high, from wars of religion to the torture and burning of heretics, as seen here in Florence c.1400. Only in 1965 did the Catholic Church finally assert that individuals must not be forced to act against conscience.

p.112) thought that, while it is self-evident that we should do good and avoid evil, conscience is a more complex faculty that helps us to reason about the rightness or wrongness of specific actions.

In the 17th and 18th centuries, too, philosophers thought in terms of a moral faculty, either a "moral sense" or conscience. Shaftesbury (*An Enquiry Concerning Virtue or Merit*, 1699), and Hutcheson (*An Inquiry into the Original of Our Ideas of Beauty and Virtue*, 1725) saw our moral sense as essentially a matter of feeling – repugnance at evil, and approval of good. Others saw such reactions as based on something closer to reason than to sentiment. Bishop Joseph Butler (1692–1752) criticized Shaftesbury for making morality dependent on feelingand for relating it only to human happiness. In contrast, Butler saw human nature as constituting a hierarchy with conscience at its peak. Self-love and benevolence had an intermediate position as important but lesser principles; while at the bottom of the hierarchy came the particular passions and appetites.

Kant's account of the part played by reason in moral decision-making was more abstract and complex than this simple appeal to conscience. Nevertheless, he gave a special place to "conscientiousness" in his moral theory. Indeed, he believed it offered the only moral motive. For Kant, conscientiousness was the desire to follow the moral law simply because it *is* the moral law – the principle of duty for duty's sake .

In the 20th century, the intuitionist philosopher H.A. Prichard (see p.151) attributed to all earlier moral philosophy the mistake of looking for a motive or reason for following duty. If in doubt about our duty – if we are wondering, for example, whether we should pay a debt – the only thing to do is to get into a situation where the principle in question is involved, or at least to imagine ourselves in such a situation and "let our moral capacities of thinking do their work".

> *Conscience and self-love, if we understand our true happiness, always lead us the same way. Duty and interest are perfectly coincident.*
>
> Joseph Butler, *Fifteen Sermons*

Moral relativism

It is a common presumption that conscience is to be obeyed. But there are a number of difficulties with this simple notion. Many moral issues are complex and need unravelling in ways that a simple appeal to conscience cannot settle. Also, there seem to be legitimate exceptions even to generally agreed principles, such as the principle that one should not lie. Finally, it appears that the dictates of conscience can vary between cultures. This was recognized in ancient times, as a story from the Greek historian Herodotus demonstrates.

Herodotus tells how King Darius of Persia asked some Greek visitors what he would have to give them to persuade them to eat the dead bodies of their fathers. Horrified, they said that no money in the world could persuade them to do such a thing. He then brought in members of a tribe called the Callatians, who considered it a sacred duty to consume the dead bodies of their parents, and he asked them what he would have to give them to persuade them to burn the bodies instead. They were equally horrified.

Beliefs today vary just as widely as in Herodotus's time. For example, some believe that capital punishment is the right way to deal with people who commit murder, while others are repelled by the idea of deliberately taking any human life. And some societies will accept polygamy, while others insist on monogamy.

Some will seek to draw sceptical conclusions from all this about the nature of conscience. But is such scepticism justified? Every culture, it seems, has a concept of murder, as distinct from judicial execution or killing in war; while the regulation of sexual behaviour, although it may vary in specifics, is probably universal, as are obligations between parents and children. Differences, then, can be exaggerated, but even where they exist, the idea of conscience as a source of shared values can find a foothold in the commonality of human needs.

Altruism and egoism

Altruism – acting not in your own interest, but for the good of others – is commonly urged upon people as the moral way to behave. But, as philosophers have long debated, is true altruism possible, or do we – consciously or not – always act from self-interested motives?

Philosophers have held very different views about human motivation. Rousseau (see pp.188–189) and Hume (see pp.24–25) believed that humans have an innate concern for others, and such concern has featured in the ethical systems of many philosophers. However, there are those who believe that human nature is essentially egotistical – that people are concerned only for their own interests. This view was certainly held by Jeremy Bentham (see p.197). Egoism should be distinguished from hedonism: while the hedonist identifies self-interest with pleasure, an egoist can recognize broader personal interests, such as honour or even virtue.

Egoism itself divides into psychological and ethical egoism. While psychological egoism holds that human nature is so constituted that people *can* only act in their own interest, ethical egoism holds that looking after your own interest is the morally *correct* thing to do. Psychological egoism may seem implausible at first sight, but at least two 18th-century philosophers, Joseph Butler and Adam Smith, have argued in favour of it, and Plato and Aristotle believed that doing the right thing, or behaving morally, is at least consistent with a person's own best interest. But both forms of egoism are perhaps better recognized by what they exclude: the possibility of altruism. For both reject any claim that altruism is an essential component of a satisfying human life.

Initiating a long line of economic thought, Adam Smith argued that people are probably better at judging what they want, than they are at judging what other people want. So egoism is, on the whole, more efficient than altruism. Smith presented this practical, economic and political argument in *The Wealth of Nations* (1776), in which he argued that if individuals pursue their own interest in the commercial sphere, in doing so they will be acting in the best interest of everybody through a natural mechanism or "hidden hand".

Supporters of ethical egoism also base their case on several more specific arguments. One is that ethical egoism provides people with a powerful motive for morality: for most people, their own happiness is a convincing consideration. Secondly, they point out that ethical egoism can include more worthy goals than narrowly materialistic pleasures. And finally, its demands, consistently obeyed, may well coincide with what is normally thought of as good moral conduct.

On the other hand, whether or not the last point is true will depend on the society in which a person is living. Also, there could be circumstances in

Gyges' ring

In his *Republic*, Plato's dialogue about the nature of justice, a story is told about a shepherd called Gyges who finds a magic ring with which he is able to become invisible at will. He uses this power to embark on a career of seduction, pillage and murder, pursuing his own pleasure whatever the cost to others. Socrates is asked to say why Gyges should not act in this way – indeed, why anyone in such a situation, where he is able to escape the unpleasant consequences of his actions, should not behave like Gyges. Socrates is also asked to accept that anyone who had the chance *would* behave like this – that it is human nature. His answer, in the end, is that morality or justice fits harmoniously with the nature of man; it is not something artificial or externally imposed. Vice or moral wickedness, on the other hand, is alien and discordant – a disease of the soul analogous to disease of the body.

The New York stock exchange in action. While Adam Smith's theory of rational egoism is often extended to defend the operation of the market and the modern consumer society, Smith himself took care not to equate material success with personal happiness.

which ethical egoism would seem to justify bad actions – for example, a suicidally inclined egoist could satisfy some vindictive whim, safe in the knowledge that it could have no personal repercussions. And finally, egoism provides an unethical motive, even if it results in moral acts.

For all these reasons, there are very few people who would hold the ethical view that promotes the pursuit of self-interest if they were not subconsciously assuming the psychological claim. In other words, it is usually because they believe people *do* act selfishly that they are inclined to build selfish action into a guiding principle.

Unlike ethical egoism, though, the psychological theory makes altruism not merely undesirable but logically impossible. This, however, is the theory's weakness. For it is either a tautology – that is, it simply reiterates the empty truism that "what I want is what I want"; or else it is the implausible factual claim that no one ever does anything for anybody else. The factual claim is refutable by counter-examples, probably the most convincing of which are provided by situations in which people have shown a willingness to die for others. For, whatever the egoist claims, the pleasure of a moment's satisfaction at duty done cannot outweigh the potential pleasures of a longer life.

> “*It is not from the benevolence of the butcher, the brewer, or the baker, that we expect our dinner, but from their regard to their own interest.*”
>
> Adam Smith, *The Wealth of Nations*

Is altruism possible?

Psychological egoism therefore seems fatally flawed as a theory because it can be refuted by a single case of unselfish action. Examples such as the donation of blood or bone marrow by public-spirited individuals, for example, would seem for many a sufficient refutation. What egoism does get right, however, is the motivating force of concepts such as pleasure, satisfaction, personal fulfilment and happiness: most people will certainly be influenced by the argument that something will make them happy. But one of the grounds on which they might well reject their *own* happiness as a decisive factor is consideration for the happiness of other people. The variety and richness of human motivation remain, therefore, extensive enough to provide ethical choice based on a wide range of possibilities, including the possibility of altruism.

Responsibility

The idea of moral responsibility for our actions is closely linked to the belief that human beings are free agents. It is the ground on which we are held to deserve praise, blame, reward and punishment.

Some people believe that human beings are trapped within a causal nexus that leaves no place for the concepts of freedom, choice and responsibility. In their view, all our actions are determined by past circumstances, and this leaves no room for freedom. However, most humans have a deep psychological reluctance to accept that their actions are not free. Whatever the underlying metaphysical reality, they remain convinced that their actions flow freely from their motives, including their moral motives – such as their sense of duty, of having a moral obligation to do something – perhaps even in spite of an inclination to do the opposite. Thus in practice humans cannot help but see themselves as responsible for their actions, whatever the scientific evidence about the ultimate causes of their behaviour may suggest.

One way to by-pass the issue of freedom and determinism is to ask a more limited question – not to seek a general understanding of human nature, but simply to ask whether some particular kind of behaviour can be influenced or changed by praise, blame, reward or punishment. For these purposes, we clearly need to distinguish between situations in which an agent has been physically compelled, threatened or hypnotized, and situations in which none of these things apply: for example, we distinguish between a case of kleptomania and a case of stealing; or, more generally, between an action that is constrained (physically or mentally) and one that is not. Normally we do not hold people responsible when their actions have been constrained. This fits with the fact that praise, blame, reward or punishment would seem inappropriate in such cases – precisely because there seems to be no room to change or influence the behaviour of constrained agents.

Responsibility and the care ethic

Recently, some feminist approaches to ethics have emphasized the importance of the notion of responsibility in real-life moral issues. Orthodox moral analysis focuses on abstract values such as rights and justice. In this view, the correct course of action should respect the abstract rights of all concerned, and conform to abstract principles of justice. However, recent feminist thinking suggests that there is room to replace this impersonal approach with a theory that places weight on the responsibilities inherent in personal relationships.

The theory arose from a critique of research into moral development by the psychologist Carol Gilligan. When questioning women about situations in which they had personally confronted the issue of abortion, Gilligan noticed that, instead of replying in abstract terms and referring to the rights of the parties involved or the fetus, these women spoke of their responsibility for particular others – an unemployed husband, a sick or dying relative, existing children in the family with special needs. Where other researchers had placed responses of this type low down the hierarchy of moral development, Gilligan detected a different and distinctive "voice" in the responses of female subjects to moral questions. Putting forward what has come to be called the "care ethic", she concluded that women are more responsive to their own responsibilities to particular others – often as a result of their position as carers – whereas men are more willing to take abstract principles of justice as moral determinants.

While this critique is undoubtedly valuable in presenting a broader picture of competent moral decision-making, whether it reveals a distinctive "female morality" is more open to question.

Moral absolutes

An absolute moral demand, whether based on principle, duty, right or obligation, is one to which there can be no exceptions. It is completely unconditional. A belief in moral absolutes is often linked with the view that such principles are intuitive or self-evident.

Discussion of moral absolutes raises two questions. One of these concerns our moral knowledge; the other is whether a moral demand is the something to which there can be no exceptions.

As far as the first issue is concerned, many philosophers support the idea that we simply know there are certain things we ought or ought not to do. For example, we ought not to commit murder, lie, steal and so on. Some recognize only negative prohibitions such as these, since they are more clear-cut than positive injunctions such as "be honest", or "tell the truth"; others speak of absolute good and evil.

H.A. Prichard (1871–1947; see also p.147) held that moral judgements are a special type of intuition. He believed that moral philosophers before him had made the mistake of trying to find grounds for doing your duty – something that people already know they ought to do without any argument. Moral truths, Prichard maintained, can either be known directly or not at all: "The sense of obligation to do, or of the rightness of, an action of a particular kind is absolutely underivative or immediate."

An ethic of intuited absolute principles, however, poses certain problems. To begin with, there is the problem of moral disagreement. If moral duty is so clear, why do different people have incompatible views?

Shakespeare's Hamlet is a man struggling between a desire to preserve his moral integrity and avenge his father's murder.

> *I am not sure whether what the philosophers call 'ethical absolutes' exist, but I am sure we have to act as if they existed.*
>
> Arthur Koestler, "The dilemma of our times - noble ends and ignoble means" (1946)

It is easy to assume that if there really are any intuited moral absolutes, then there would be little, if any, ethical disagreement. Yet it certainly seems that there is disagreement about morality, not only among different cultural groups and communities, but also among individuals (see pp.146–147). However, the extent of the differences can be exaggerated. They may be more apparent than real, a product of ignorance, self-deception or poor communication.

The second question raised by moral absolutes is whether some moral principles admit no exception. In an influential essay, "Modern moral philosophy", the Cambridge philosopher G.E.M. Anscombe (1919–2001) denounced the tendency of modern philosophy to adopt the utilitarian view that any principle can be qualified in the light of circumstance. According to the Judeo-Christian ethic, she claimed, certain things are forbidden whatever the consequences.

Are there different levels of principles?

A possible solution to this problem is to be found in the notion of prima facie duties – a concept introduced by the philosopher Sir David Ross (1877–1971). In *The Right and the Good* (1930), Ross sought to avoid the more unacceptable consequences of asserting, as Kant (see pp.141–143) and Prichard had done, that fundamental moral duties hold in all circumstances. To illustrate his views, he considers a situation in which someone has made a promise to one person, but can save someone else from serious harm only by breaking that promise. Ross points out that two duties are indeed involved here: a duty to keep a promise; and a duty to relieve distress. And in the circumstances, the second of these may be the greater. What Kant and others took to be absolute duties, then, are described by Ross as prima facie duties. By this Ross meant duties that are the result of looking at only part of a situation; what is actually a duty depends on looking at the whole situation. All the same, these duties are self-evident in the sense that they do not need any further proof or evidence.

Ross's theory offers hope of compromise between authoritative moral principles and the desire to allow for exceptions in extreme cases – an enterprise taken further in the work of the Oxford philosopher R.M. Hare (1919–2002), who recognized both a need for simple principles of duty in ordinary life and a need to consider consequences in some complex situations. The danger of an over-hasty dismissal of exceptionless moral principles is that it may be thought to reflect an impatience with the whole idea of morality and perhaps, too, a generalized reluctance to take it seriously.

Absolute moral requirements – Antigone's appeal to heaven

The idea that there can be a higher court of appeal than the rules made by human beings, a stronger and absolute notion of duty, is eloquently expressed by the Greek dramatist Sophocles in his play *Antigone*, written in the 5th century BCE. The eponymous heroine is commanded by the ruler Creon, her uncle, to leave her slain brother's body unburied because he is considered a traitor to the state. She decides, however, that she has an absolute and unconditional duty, at whatever cost, to disobey the command and obey a higher law, which obliges a sister to see that her brother is buried with due rites and respect. As Antigone puts it subsequently:

"Nor did I deem
Your ordinance of so much binding force
As that a mortal man could overbear
The unchangeable unwritten code of Heaven;
This is not of today and yesterday,
But lives forever having origin
Whence no man knows."

Later, after Antigone has been tried and imprisoned for her disobedience, Creon is prevailed upon by the prophet Tiresias to relent – too late, however, because by the time soldiers come to release her, Antigone has killed herself. Creon's repentance and the tragic ending suggests that Sophocles and his Greek audience would have understood and endorsed Antigone's appeal to an absolute moral law transcending that of human rulers.

Nietzsche

Friedrich Nietzsche was born in rural Prussia, the son and grandson of Lutheran pastors. He became Professor of Classical Philology at Basle University in Switzerland at the early age of 24, but his first book, *The Birth of Tragedy* (1872), which he dedicated to the composer Richard Wagner, had a disappointing reception. However, he went on to write a number of unusual and iconoclastic philosophical works, frequently ambiguous, often written in the form of aphorisms, that attacked the assumptions of Western intellectual traditions. The objects of his attack included God, morality, truth and democracy. In his own self-assessment, *Ecce Homo*, he described himself as "the first immoralist". His philosophical career came to an end with a mental breakdown in 1889, from which he never recovered.

Friedrich Nietzsche 1844–1900

Nietzsche challenged the accepted philosophical and ethical approaches of his time, and many of his ideas, especially his relativistic account of truth and moral values, set a direction for later existentialist thinkers. Key theories include the will to power, the concept of the superman, and the doctrine of eternal recurrence.

Nietzsche was greatly influenced by Schopenhauer (see p.173), endorsing his atheism, but rejecting his emphasis on pity. The question of where our moral ideas may have come from is addressed in *The Genealogy of Morals* (1887). Here Nietzsche sets out to challenge our most basic moral assumptions, especially our notions of good and evil. He describes the altruistic virtues of the Christian tradition – pity, self-denial and self-sacrifice – as simply the response of the inferior masses to their position. Jews and Christians had known slavery, so the values they espoused were, Nietzsche says, both in their source and in their nature, a "slave morality". He regrets that these values supplanted the "master morality" and warrior values of ancient Greece. So in a complete reversal of valuation, Nietzsche sees the conception of "good" in Europe's Christian culture as evil, and evil as good. "What is good?" he asks in *The Anti-Christ* (1888), and answers: "All that heightens the feeling of power, the will to power, power itself in man. What is bad? All that proceeds from weakness." Hope lies, he says, in the possible emergence of "free spirits" – people who have succeeded in "overcoming morality" and who will pave the way for the person Nietzsche calls the *Übermensch* or "superman".

The chances are that such a person would have a taste for war. In *Thus Spake Zarathustra* Nietzsche writes: "Man should be trained for war and woman for the recreation of the warrior: all else is folly". He puts into the mouth of his "wise woman" Zarathustra the advice: "You should love peace as a means to new wars. And the short peace more than the long."

The doctrine of eternal recurrence, as Nietzsche presents it, is the idea that the history of the world is cyclical. In our lives, we come back to the beginning over and over again – condemned to live forever with the circumstances of our lives, whatever they were. The hero, according to Nietzsche, will find this a joyful thought; a "loser" will despair.

After his death, Nietzsche's talk of a superman, his repudiation of Christian concern for the weak and powerless and his doctrine of the will to power, all fed into the Nazis' search for philosophical foundations for their own aspirations. But whether in fact Nietzsche's work provided a philosophical prompt for the Nazis' militarist ambitions is a matter of controversy.

Existentialism

Existentialism has its roots in Danish, German and French philosophy. According to existentialist reasoning, humans are individual, solitary and free, but this freedom of choice generates a deep sense of dread in the face of a universe completely lacking in order and direction.

Existentialism is a philosophical movement of the 19th and 20th centuries. It focuses on the notion of particularity; that is to say, it rejects any universal moral principles. It can take either a religious or a secular form.

The Danish theologian and philosopher Søren Kierkegaard (1813–55), often described as the first existentialist, grounded his ideas in the Christian tradition (see p.128). Reacting against the great philosophical system-builders, in particular Hegel and Kant, Kierkegaard insisted that, instead of seeking laws of morality, we should accept the fact that decisions are individual and particular; they are reached by inner conflict, accompanied by the agony and anxiety he called a "sickness unto death". His approach to religious belief, described in *Fear and Trembling* (1843), recommended replacing theological argument with a simple "leap of faith". In existentialist terms, this was to renounce the path of reason and instead to embrace deliberately the irrational or "absurd". Kierkegaard held that people should make radical, independent decisions in relation to their lives. We are free agents, responsible for our own character and ultimately our fate.

Existentialism and feminism: Simone de Beauvoir

Simone de Beauvoir (1908–86) was an existentialist and a feminist. Noting that most women's lives were defined by a male relationship – a father, or a husband – she chose an independent and unconventional lifestyle. She never married or had children, but like Sartre (with whom she had a long-term relationship) engaged in diverse and open sexual relationships.

An intellectual and professional writer, her first novel was *She Came to Stay* (*L'Invitée)*, published in 1943. This was followed in 1947 by *The Ethics of Ambiguity*, an explicitly existentialist ethical work that expressed the existentialist ideal of free will and the libertarian concept of the open future. It recommends the principle of authenticity (see next page) and condemns the "spirit of seriousness" that takes over when people allow their identity to be expressed in fixed values, qualities and prejudices. In a pioneering feminist work, *The Second Sex* (1949), de Beauvoir applied this analysis to the role and position of women. She compares a woman's passive acceptance of her role ("immanence") with the existentialist ideal of free choice. Her own life and experience convinced her that the separation of male and female roles is a matter of cultural conditioning, rather than biological necessity.

Les Deux Magots café, which still flourishes in Paris on the Left Bank of the Seine. A favourite haunt of writers and intellectuals since the 19th century, many existentialist thinkers including Sartre, Gide and de Beauvoir often met and wrote here.

The other strand of existentialist thought is independent of religious commitment. Influenced by the ideas of German philosophers such as Nietzsche, Martin Heidegger (1889–1976) and Karl Jaspers (1883–1969), it flourished in the years immediately following World War II, its most famous exponent being Jean-Paul Sartre (see pp.156–157). The key idea of existentialism is that individuals find themselves in situations that are concrete and particular; they are not to be generalized or used to make moral rules with universal application. In this context of absolute particularity, people must create their own identity. In *Being and Time* (1927), Heidegger saw the recognition of the ultimate meaninglessness of life as the source of human *Angst,* and suggests that this *Angst* may be overcome by using one's individual existence to build circumstances that can supply the meaning that phenomena themselves lack.

The existentialist view, then, is that we create our own ethical values; morality is not a matter of following rules, whether God-given or socially imposed. Indeed, to follow rules, to conform unreflectingly to convention, is to fail to be authentic. For this reason, existentialists attach value to what is termed an *acte gratuit* ("free action") – an action that cannot be explained as the end of some chain of motives and influences. In its ultimate form, as presented by some existentialist authors, it is a wholly arbitrary and pointless action.

> *The thing is to find a truth which is true for me, to find the idea for which I can live and die.*
>
> Søren Kierkegaard, *Journals*

Some of these ideas are better presented in novels and plays, as these cast individual people in individual situations, in contrast to philosophy's search for universal principles. While Sartre is known both as an author and philosopher, other French existentialists known principally as novelists or dramatists rather than philosophers include Gabriel Marcel, Albert Camus and André Gide.

Existentialist thought in the 20th century reflects many of the intellectual themes of the period: the notion of indeterminism in science; the renunciation of metaphysical system-building in philosophy; and, perhaps most of all, ideas of subjectivity and freedom, in which existentialism gives philosophical substance to the relativist concept of "right for me".

Sartre

Born in Paris in 1905, Sartre studied philosophy in his home city and went on to teach philosophy in Le Havre, returning to Paris in 1937. His lifelong relationship with the author and existentialist Simone de Beauvoir began in their student days, although they never married, in keeping with the existentialist philosophy of personal freedom. He was in prison for a year during the occupation of Paris in World War II. By the 1960s, he was an eminent figure on the world stage and in 1964 he was offered, but declined, the Nobel Prize for Literature. During the 1968 student uprising, he addressed student protesters at the Sorbonne. When he died in 1980, an icon of French intellectual life, 50,000 people flocked to his funeral.

The German philosophers Husserl and Heidegger played a key role in shaping Sartre's philosophy, which was summed up in a brief lecture given in 1946, *Existentialism and Humanism*. This optimistic defence of freedom inspired a generation. His existentialist philosophy was also given form and shape in his novels and plays, especially *Nausea* (1938). But the most substantial statement of his philosophy was in *Being and Nothingness* (1943), regarded as a classic of existentialism.

Like other French philosophers before him, Sartre takes Descartes's *cogito ergo sum* – "I think, therefore I am" – as his philosophical point of departure. However, where Descartes had taken his consciousness as a guarantee of his own reality, Sartre believed that consciousness presents us with the reality of external things. It is proof that there is an object of consciousness. To other people, however, each of us appears to be just an object. This point is explained by reference to "the look" — being caught in someone else's gaze. It leads to a feeling of alienation and separateness from others that we would like to overcome but cannot. Each of us is ultimately alone in the world. This means, too, that we can never recognize each other's freedom; the Kantian principle that others must be treated with respect as ends in themselves (see p.142) cannot be followed, and we must live with the conflict that entails. As a characters in Sartre's play *Huis Clos* (*No Exit*, 1943) puts it: "Hell is other people."

> *In life a man commits himself, draws his own portrait, and there is nothing but that portrait.*
>
> Jean-Paul Sartre, *Existentialism and Humanism*

Jean-Paul Sartre 1905–1980

Jean-Paul Sartre was a French philosopher, novelist and dramatist whose name has become almost synonymous with existentialism. His philosophical theories were given life in a series of remarkable literary works.

But if our perspective on others is limited and constrained, our concept of self is intoxicatingly untrammelled. To the *subject* of consciousness, Sartre attributes the unlimited freedom of self-creation. In contrast to the Aristotelian view that, for example, before there is a knife, there is somebody's idea of a knife, the opposite is true of man. Hence, Sartre's famous phrase "existence precedes essence". In other words, there is no initial blueprint for an individual human being. True, there are certain constants that we are unable to change – sex, age, race and so on – but, these apart, we can take our own social context and make of it what we will. As far as morality is concerned, it is wrong, according to Sartre, not to take advantage of this freedom, but to follow the crowd – to conform. Such conformity, together with belief in coherence – that we live in a tidy universe in which things will ultimately make sense – was what he called *mauvaise foi* (bad faith), and its reverse is authenticity. Recognition of the incoherence of reality, called by Sartre "the absurd", produces disgust or "nausea". It is the source of our *Angst* – our anxiety or existential guilt in the face of choice. We have, he said, "no excuses behind us and no justification before us". We are "condemned to be free".

These ideas belong to what is usually seen as Sartre's "classical" period - the years from the mid 1930s to the late 1940s, when he was preoccupied with reflections on the emotions and the imagination, and with questions of personal ethics. From the 1950s onwards, Sartre's work entered a more political phase in which he was willing to give more weight to the Marxist thesis that social and economic conditions, together with historical forces, affect the choices of both individuals and groups. It was in this later phase that Sartre wrote the *Critique of Dialectical Reason* (1960), which sought to reconcile Marxism with existentialism.

Popular attacks on existentialism caricature it as claiming that life is meaningless, and that the world is a nauseous mess of unpredictability in which the bourgeoisie play the role of villains. Sartre sought to defend himself against such attacks, although a dispassionate appraisal can detect some grounds for them. His admirers, on the other hand, projected a greatly enhanced image of him as a defender of political and moral freedom, a fearless anti-Nazi and hero of the French Resistance, for which there is little evidence. However, there is no doubt that Sartre was a revered writer and thinker and one of the seminal influences of his generation.

The waiter and the loss of individuality

Most of Sartre's writing was done in cafés, so it is perhaps not surprising that one of his most famous philosophical illustrations concerns a waiter. The example is intended to show how unwilling people are to be themselves. Instead, they take on a role, losing awareness of their own individuality. In *Being and Nothingness*, Sartre writes: "His movement is quick and forward, a little too precise, a little too rapid. He comes towards the patrons with a step a little too quick. He bends forward a little too eagerly; his voice, his eyes express an interest a little too solicitous for the order of the customer. Finally, he returns, trying to imitate in his walk the inflexible stiffness of some kind of automaton while carrying his tray with the recklessness of a tightrope walker by putting it in a perpetually unstable, perpetually unbroken equilibrium, which he perpetually re-establishes by a light movement of the arm and hand. All his behaviour seems to us a game, but what is he playing? We need not watch long before we can explain it: he is playing at being a waiter in a cafe."

This waiter, says Sartre, is not in the mode of *being in himself*. He is in the mode of *being what he is not*; he is trying to sustain a role from which he is essentially alienated. It is an example of inauthenticity, of what Sartre calls "bad faith".

Goodness

The question of what goodness is has been discussed since ancient times, when it centred on the issue of virtue and the virtues. Plato and Aristotle related these to the notion of self-fulfilment. Contemporary writers focus on the issue of character.

In his *Republic*, Plato (see pp.76–79) tells a story about chained prisoners living their lives in a darkened cave, a metaphor for the physical world of our sense experiences. The story carries a metaphysical, if not a mystical, message. It suggests that life is a struggle to escape from the darkness and constriction of the cave to reach the light of the sun. The sun represents the idea of the good; it is the source of light, revealing things as they really are, where the darkness of the cave obscured that reality.

Plato's immediate successor, Aristotle (see pp.13–15), offered a more down-to-earth account of the good, which related it to human needs and to the virtues. What has since come to be called virtue theory involves a focus on character and on seeing an individual human life as a whole – seeing it, too, under the broad moral categories of good and bad.

For both Plato and Aristotle, goodness and virtue were closely connected. For Plato, happiness is bound to coincide with virtue, for both are a type of knowledge: a wise assessment of what is truly in a person's interest. Plato paints a portrait of happiness as a consequence of harmonious self-fulfilment. It is a matter of achieving a well-balanced personality in which emotions such as courage are harnessed in support of reason, and reason has achieved control over instinct and sensual desire.

This doctrine is refined by Aristotle in his discussion of the notion of a *telos*. Aristotle believed, like Plato, that everything has a *telos* – an aim or point to its existence. The *telos* of human beings is something that follows from their essential nature. Only when that nature is fulfilled is happiness to be found. The Greek term for happiness, *eudaimonia*, also means well-being or flourishing. It is something a virtuous person is more likely to achieve than someone who is self-indulgent or wicked.

In his famous doctrine of the "Golden Mean" Aristotle provides an account of the virtues themselves. According to this doctrine, right or virtuous actions are those which are in accordance with the correct course of conduct, which is a matter of balance. Aristotle sees vices as existing in pairs, one of which is the result of too much of a quality, the

"Goodness by proxy": the moral philosophy of Iris Murdoch

The work of the Dublin-born Oxford philosopher and novelist Iris Murdoch (1919–99) has been described as "philosophy dragged from the cloister, dusted down and made freshly relevant to suffering and egoism, death and religious ecstasy...". Her non-fiction works include *The Sovereignty of Good* (1970) and *Metaphysics as a Guide to Morals* (1992), as well as books on Plato and Sartre. Her many novels, starting with *Under the Net* (1954) and ending with *Jackson's Dilemma* (1995) continue to explore, via a different medium, moral struggle, human weakness, and good and evil. Murdoch believed that the imagination can be used to penetrate the veil that our own selfish concerns usually place between us and moral illumination. The task is one of looking hard enough and carefully enough at situations: in Murdoch's own words, "really *looking*". She believed that literature, like art and music, could present a truthful image of the human condition in a form that allows this type of attention. In transcending a selfish obsession with personality, it could, she claimed, enlarge the sensibility of its consumer: "It is a kind of goodness by proxy."

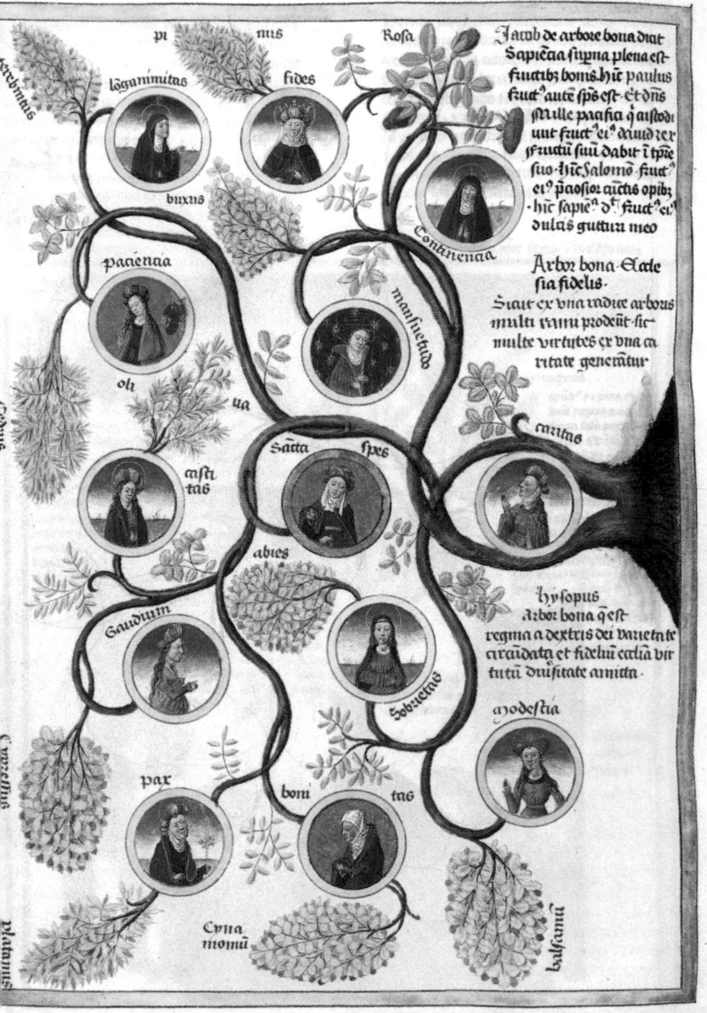

This 15th-century Flemish manuscript depicts a "Tree of Good" bearing medallions, each representing a different virtue.

other the result of too little; in between lie the virtues. So, for example, courage is the mean between rashness and cowardice, self-respect the mean between vanity and humility (a trait not considered a virtue by the ancient Greeks).

Virtue theory today

In the late 20th and early 21st century, there has been a return to the idea that moral questions should be approached by focusing on virtue, character and integrity. But contemporary theory differs from classical virtue theory in relating virtue more closely to its social and temporal setting. Both Plato and Aristotle offered a universalistic account of human good. They believed in a *summum bonum* ("highest good") common to all human beings, based on a conception of human nature not bound to time and place. The version of virtue theory now favoured by a number of writers reverses these underlying assumptions, seeking to locate morality in a tradition. For example, in *After Virtue* (1981) and subsequent publications, the Scottish-born philosopher Alistair MacIntyre attacks Kantian and utilitarian traditions for placing individual preferences above substantial social and moral traditions. MacIntyre turns instead to virtues based in culture and tradition. He attributes to Western societies a "rootless cosmopolitanism" in which those whose goal is to be at home anywhere become instead "citizens of nowhere". Their need, he says, is to relocate themselves within a tradition that defines virtues and vices, supplies norms of conformity and deviance, offers educational goals, and provides what MacIntyre calls "narratives of possible types of human life".

The work of the American philosopher Martha Nussbaum, too, is inspired by the literary and philosophical heritage of antiquity. In *The Fragility of Goodness* (1986), she focuses on the notions of justice, goodness and virtue. Here and elsewhere, she seeks to give substance to the notion of human potential and flourishing, specifying that it includes life itself, as well as health, and perhaps also capacities for sensual experience, imagination and thought.

The topics that modern virtue theorists explore include: how far are individuals responsible for their own character? Is there just one main virtue or several irreducible ones? And how are such notions as friendship, integrity, forgiveness, loyalty, shame and remorse to be understood? Modern virtue theory, then, focuses on the personal question: how should I live my life? It is concern with this practical and personal question that bridges the gap of millennia between Aristotle's virtue ethics and the present-day interest in the subject.

> *Goodness is connected with the attempt to see the unself, to see and to respond to the real world in the light of a virtuous consciousness.*
>
> Iris Murdoch, *The Sovereignty of Good*

Love and friendship

Both love and friendship are forms of human relationship. But is love simply a more intense form of friendship, or – as both literature and life suggest – are they very different ways of relating to others? If so, do different moral rules apply to each?

Philosophers, as well as poets, have been drawn to discussion of love since ancient times. The strength and often undisciplined nature of love is depicted by Plato in *Phaedrus* as the struggle of a charioteer to control two horses, one representing physical desire and uncontrollable passion, the other a love that expresses itself in a more intellectual and companionable way.

Friendship, in contrast, is often seen as a more manageable, less exclusive relation. As the ancient Stoic philosopher Epictetus observed: "The world is full of friends." He thought there was no reason to become too attached to those closest to you, for no one can be guaranteed for ever. There is also a sense in which we can choose our friends, and how long a friendship lasts can depend on the friend continuing to demonstrate those qualities that led to the friendship in the first place.

Love and friendship have distinct natures but are often experienced together, which can be comfortable, or confusing.

In the *Nicomachean Ethics*, Aristotle considers various definitions of friendship. One of these is in terms of wanting good for a friend; another is the suggestion that friendship might be simply valuing someone's company and sharing each other's joys and sorrows. Undoubtedly, friendship also provides a route from loneliness. The German philosopher Kant describes friendship as providing release from the prison of the self – a prison from which we have a duty to escape. These remarks suggest that Kant was a more convivial man than he is usually given credit for.

Compared to friendship, love in all its forms is less conditional and less easy to walk away from. In its most virulent form – the form the Greeks called *eros*, the word that has given us the concept of the erotic – it comes out of the blue to strike its unsuspecting victim, like the dart of a playful god.

Of course, romantic love is only one aspect of the wider concept of love, in which exclusivity is not always of the essence: parents may feel equally loving to more than one child, for example. And, moving to the outer boundaries of human love, there is the possibility of a still more all-encompassing emotion. One contemporary philosopher, Raimond Gaita, sees the love of persons – especially those who are the most difficult for us to love – as the foundation of universal human rights. In *A Common Humanity* (1999), he writes: "Were it not for the many ways human beings genuinely love one another – from sexual love to the impartial love of saints – I do not believe we would have a sense of the sacredness of individuals, or of their inalienable rights or dignity."

Sex

Is sex a moral matter? Many people in Western societies today would confidently assert that it is not. But should sexual behaviour really be free from any rules, or even consideration of its consequences? And what if those consequences affect the wider society, not just the individual?

In many parts of today's world, sex is regarded, as it was in the Western world in the past, as a matter of morals. Severe punishments may be imposed for sex outside the legally and ethically sanctioned area of formal marriage – although the way offenders are treated often depends on whether they are male or female. But within the Western world in the last few decades the pendulum has swung in the opposite direction, and the philosopher Peter Singer speaks for many when he writes: "Sex raises no unique moral issues at all." Politicians have pursued legislative change in ways that reflect this judgement, uncoupling the economic and legal connections between sex and the raising of families.

Religion and natural law

The contrary view, that sex is ethically significant, is often linked with a religious stance. However, it would be wrong to see ethical opinion about sexual matters as strictly divided between a repressive religious perspective and a secular position that sees sex as an ethical non-issue. For example, the natural law tradition in philosophy, which is older by some centuries than Christianity, is often appealed to by the Roman Catholic Church when advocating moral constraints on sex. This tradition relies on reason and nature rather than scriptural sources to supply a sexual ethic, and is especially identified with the teaching of Thomas Aquinas (see p.112). Starting from the fact that individual animals, including humans, are complete and self-sufficient in every natural function other than reproduction, it sees the physical coming together of two people as creating a special type of union. In the main religious traditions, this conception of union is embodied in the idea of marriage as an exclusive and permanent relationship. In its strongest form, this position cannot accommodate any kind of sex, inside or outside marriage, that is not open to fulfilling procreative purposes. But this is a very narrow interpretation of the "natural": procreation is a relatively rare event in a marriage, so it would be reasonable at least to extend the concept to non-procreative sex within

Sex and the philosophers

Many of the most famous philosophers, including Descartes, Spinoza, Leibniz, Kant and Schopenhauer, never married, and some have held very unconventional views on sex and marriage:

- The anarchist political philosopher William Godwin and the pioneer feminist Mary Wollstonecraft ridiculed the idea that anyone might need a "companion for life". They maintained the principle of separate residences, living apart until Mary's unexpected pregnancy and their marriage in 1797. This was tragically short-lived, because she died in childbirth later the same year.
- John Stuart Mill sought to renounce the privileges that 19th-century English law gave him over his wife Harriet Taylor when, after a friendship lasting 18 years, he was finally able to marry her. (Shocking to Victorian England, she was already a wife and mother when they met and formed their life-long bond.)
- Jean-Paul Sartre and Simone de Beauvoir expressed in both their life and work a mid-20th century libertarian philosophy of sexual relations. Lifelong companions, they detailed their separate sexual encounters in their letters to each other, lived apart, and never contracted a formal marriage.

marriage as this continues to serve the needs of procreation by reinforcing the bond between parents during the long process of child-rearing. A broader idea of the natural can perhaps also accommodate attachments between same-sex couples. On the other hand, the claims of nature cannot be stretched indefinitely, and where sexual exploitation in its many forms – child abuse, forced prostitution, de-personalized promiscuity – is involved, they will be trumped by the ethical requirement that people should not be used simply as means for someone else's satisfaction.

The Kiss, Gustav Klimt's famous painting of 1908, depicts the fusion of affection and desire in a loving sexual union.

Philosophical theories

A more purely philosophical tradition that implies moral constraints on sexual behaviour is utilitarianism – a practical ethical system that advocates maximizing the welfare of all those affected by a choice. As such, it might be expected to shun specific rules that censor the behaviour of individuals. But this need not be the case if a broad view is taken of the social and emotional consequences for the wider community, including children. For example, if sexual encounters become stripped of any long-term significance, and this has detrimental consequences for many of those involved, then the long-term utilitarian view might well support a more traditional moral perspective on sex.

In addition, there are ethical viewpoints that, unlike utilitarianism, do not rely solely on pragmatic considerations. One of these is a modern version of the ancient "virtue ethics" of Plato and Aristotle. This ethical position involves reflecting on what is most fulfilling for a human being. Taking into account physical, emotional and intellectual needs from the perspective of a whole lifetime, this, too, may well favour a moral framework for sex over arbitrary or egotistical behaviour.

Finally, there is a prominent philosophical position derived from the ideas of Kant (see pp.141–143) that emphasizes principles – in particular, promise-keeping. Kant himself, like Hegel and Locke, saw marriage as a relationship that placed sexual relations in a contractual framework. Kant had a strange view of this contract as establishing each partner's ownership of the other's "sexual attributes" – to the extent that a runaway spouse could rightly be brought back by force. At the same time, it was Kant who articulated the fundamental principle of respect for each human person and the view that no one should be used simply as a means for someone else's ends. This last principle is a version of Kant's famous "categorical imperative". In more recent times, the American philosopher George Santayana (1863–1952) used this famous phrase to challenge the opinion that sex and an exclusive and permanent relationship are necessary ethical companions: "Sex," he said, "is "nature's categorical imperative." In contemporary moral philosophy, discussion of sex has come to be dominated by views closer to those of Santayana than those of his predecessors.

> “*To be omnivorous is one pole of true love: to be exclusive is the other.*”
>
> George Santayana, *The Life of Reason*

Reproduction

The closing years of the 20th century brought a revolution in the means and modes of human reproduction. Social patterns have changed too, prompting the question: how should we respond, ethically and practically, to these changes?

Human reproduction has, until very recently, been linked to two apparent immovables: one, the dependence of conception on sexual intercourse; and the other, the idea of the family as the basic building block of human society. In the 1960s, however, the possibility emerged of creating human embryos in the laboratory. At first, it seemed that the moral objections would be insuperable, and scientists themselves speculated that what they were contemplating was an ethical impossibility. To quote the "test-tube baby" pioneer Robert Edwards, speaking in 1966: "If rabbit and pig eggs can be fertilized in culture, presumably human eggs grown in culture could also be fertilized, although obviously it would not be permissible to implant them in a human recipient."

But little more than a decade later, such ethical objections had been overtaken by demand for the

The abortion debate

Abortion can be looked at as the termination of an unwelcome condition; or as the snuffing out of an independent life rich in possibilities. So the abortion debate turns on the question of the moral status of the unborn. Some philosophers describe the embryo or fetus as a *potential* human being and argue that a merely potential being cannot have *actual* rights and interests. However, it also makes sense to say that the mere potential to become a complex entity such as a human being is itself important.

Beyond the issue of potentiality, the question of when an actual human life begins must be addressed. The most widely defended suggestions are at conception, at quickening (when the fetus's movements are perceptible to the mother) and at viability (when the fetus would survive outside the womb). But many philosophers attach moral importance only to a much later stage – the point when the fetus becomes a person. In order to be a "person" in this sense, certain essential conditions must be met, such as consciousness, a sense of self, rationality, memory and the capacity to want to continue living. Those who accept this account hold that only persons in this sense have either interests or rights. This can lead to some surprising consequences: for example, Peter Singer (one of the main architects of the personhood argument) believes that animal lives may be more valuable than the life of a human fetus, which is not yet a person. On this basis, Singer argues that, unless you are a vegetarian, it is inconsistent to object to abortion, and writes "Even an abortion late in pregnancy for the most trivial reasons is hard to condemn unless we also condemn the slaughter of far more developed forms of life for the taste of their flesh."

But despite its widespread deployment in philosophical discussions of abortion, the role of "personhood" in the abortion debate is of doubtful importance. For one thing, the requirements for being a person will not be met by the fetus at any stage or even by young infants – who, it would seem to most people, have as much right to life as an adult.

However, even if the fetus were a person, might not a woman's interests nevertheless override its interests? The view that gives priority to a woman's claims is part of a broad feminist position that emphasizes women's rights. It is a demand for women to have control of their own bodies, and involves the moral judgment that no one has an obligation to support another life at serious cost to themselves. Simply conceding that another life – that of the fetus – is involved is not, then, the end of the matter and the argument that has gained most ground politically and practically is that abortion may be, in some circumstances, the lesser of two evils.

Nobody's child – the Buzzanca case

As the transfer of human eggs, sperm and embryos becomes more widespread, and forms of surrogacy arrangements are legalized, the consequences for the resulting children can be bizarre and not always welcome. One real-life case in the USA provides a striking illustration of the more extreme possibilities.

In 1998, a divorced couple, John and Luanne Buzzanca, sought a legal ruling about their status and responsibilities in relation to a child, Jaycee. Her history was remarkable. A woman had donated eggs to a couple, Mr and Mrs X, which were fertilized by Mr X's sperm. Some remaining embryos were frozen and the Xs had agreed to donate one to the Buzzancas. They agreed a surrogacy arrangement with a fourth woman, who became pregnant using the donated embryo. But some weeks before the child, Jaycee, was born, John filed for divorce, claiming that the marriage had produced no children. Luanne contested this, but the court ruled that John did not have responsibility for Jaycee because he was not her biological father; nor was he her legal father, since she was not born to Luanne during their marriage. Furthermore, the court made the unexpected decision that Luanne was also not the legal mother; and nor was the surrogate the legal mother. The gamete donors (the original egg donor and Mr X) could also not be considered legal parents of Jaycee, since their donation had been made on the basis that they would not incur legal responsibilities. Jaycee was thus left with no parents at all.

An appeal was allowed against this ruling. In the end, the appeals court did provide Jaycee with legal parents: John and Luanne. The court ruled that, if a couple initiate and consent to medical procedures with intent to raise the child, they enter into a parental relationship with that child, even when they are not genetically related to it. The fact remains that these legal parents did not coincide either with the genetic parents (the gamete donors) or with the birth parent (the surrogate mother).

new technology. The first test tube baby was born in 1978 and following that widely publicized event *in vitro* fertilization (IVF) gradually gained acceptance as a treatment for infertility. At the start of this reproduction revolution, the emphasis was on helping couples to have their own (biological) children, but the novelty of the new developments was that it was now possible to transfer not just sperm, but eggs and embryos, from person to person without the need for sexual intercourse. So just as reliable contraception had made sex without the risk of reproduction possible, embryology had now made reproduction possible without sex. And in time, this powerful new technology may allow further intervention in the reproductive process by providing ways to manipulate human genetic material that no one could have imagined a century ago.

> “*Birth and procreation, the inheritance of genetic material, the developmental stages through which a child progresses – these are [regarded as] naturally immutable.*”
>
> Marilyn Strathern, *Reproducing the Future*

The changing family

Each step in reproductive technology has brought new ethical dilemmas, which in turn have had inevitable impacts on the notion of the biological family. Fatherhood can now be specified as genetic, social or legal; motherhood as birthing or biological. Children can be born years after fertilization and even after the death of their progenitors, while the transfer of eggs, sperm and embryos can produce generous numbers of half- and full siblings, possibly unknown to the others.

All this raises a question as to whether parenthood should now be seen as a purely social concept. But just as the social view has gained ground legally and politically, individuals are becoming increasingly concerned to know and understand their personal history, family connections and their own complex genetic inheritance.

The new developments, then, make possible new kinds of families: those founded by single parents, lesbians, gay men, groups and people older than the normal reproductive years. Some welcome this

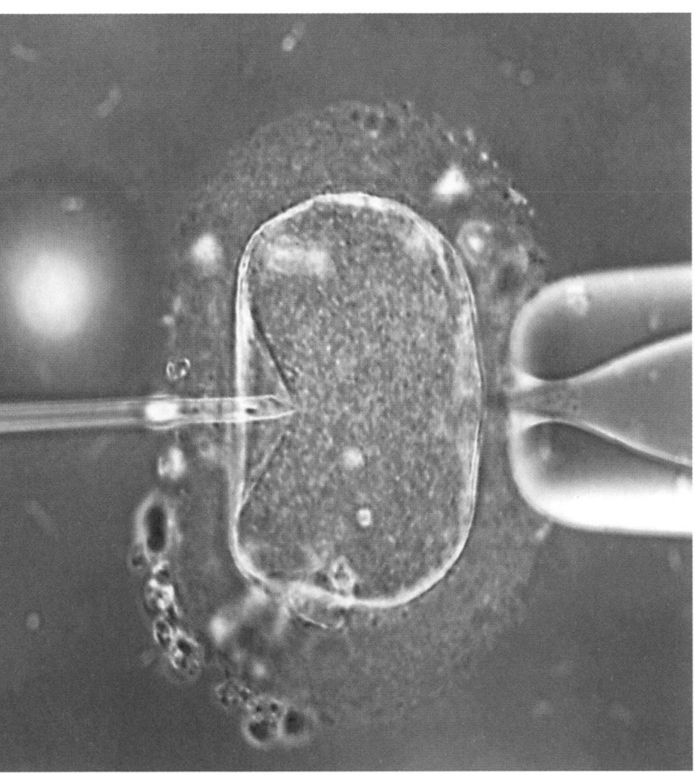

A fine needle injects a single sperm into a human egg. At one time "high-tech", such forms of IVF are becoming more routine.

expansion of choice, citing a human right to privacy, the right to found a family and a claim for procreative liberty. For example, a 1989 report for the European Commission, chaired by philosopher Jonathan Glover, suggests that the future shape of the family should be allowed to evolve experimentally.

But there are other points of view. One, derived from social anthropology, looks at matters from the perspective of the children concerned and their right to be part of a known kinship network. The social anthropologist Marilyn Strathern writes: "Until now, it has been part of most of the indigenous cultural repertoires in Europe to see the domain of kinship, and its biological base in procreation, as an area of relationships that provided a given baseline to human existence ... It is an extraordinarily impoverished view of culture to imagine that how we conceive of parents and children only affects parents and children." In other words, while reproductive practices operate at the level of individuals, changes at this level have consequences for the whole of society.

While this view from social anthropology emphasizes the importance of traditional kinship relationships, a contrasting sociological view largely discounts these connections. The influential sociologist Anthony Giddens argues that the law, taxation and welfare payments should be used as policy instruments for supporting non-standard family formation. In practice this means easy separation and change of partners, and "co-parenting" of offspring from separate homes.

Rights and interests

However, there is also an ethical viewpoint based on the principle of keeping law and morality apart. In this view, the state should not intervene in what are essentially private matters, including matters of sex and reproduction. After all, we may personally think that some situation or behaviour is wrong, but still not think it appropriate to enact a law against it. On the other hand, while reproduction is indeed an intimate and private area of life, it involves the interests of individuals at the most vulnerable stage of human life who, it may be argued, need protection from some source.

Finally, then, we may ask whose moral rights should count in matters of reproduction – and in particular, what role should the child's viewpoint play? For example, does the right to found a family apply only to adults who want to raise children, or should it take into account the interests of the children themselves? Those who hold that only the potential parents' interests matter tend to argue that however a child is conceived it would not otherwise have existed at all, and life is always to be preferred to non-existence. This view is seldom challenged in relation to IVF, but at the same time it is noteworthy that it is often questioned by advocates of abortion – particularly in cases of physical or mental handicap, where quality-of-life issues then become part of the debate.

So, given such controversies, who should decide what is acceptable in matters of reproduction? Whatever the answer to this question, it is clear that there is a need to take into account wide ethical and philosophical considerations, as well as the real consequences for individuals and for society at large.

Animals

Is morality entirely human-centred, or can it be extended to include non-human animals? If so, is this a simply matter of giving animals due care and compassion, or should they be accorded rights of their own, which may compete with those of humans?

There are two pictures of the relation between humans and other animals. One is of human dominance, often linked to the biblical account of creation in *Genesis*, which depicts animals as made for man's "dominion". The other is one of human stewardship that involves some duty of care, and a justification for this, too, can be found elsewhere in the Bible. For example, in Exodus 20, an image is painted of domestic life in which animals, while expected to work for their owners, are also allowed to share the sabbath rest. If we choose this latter picture, and recognize ourselves as having obligations to animals, there is still the question of whether these are a matter of justice and rights, or simply of compassion and kindness.

As far as justice is concerned, there is a long philosophical tradition, going back to Aristotle, that holds that duties apply only between equals and hence not to animals. Kant argued that humans have no direct duties to animals, merely indirect duties towards associated humans. To ill treat a dog, for example, would matter morally only because this may lead the perpetrator to ill-treat humans, too. In more recent times, the American philosopher John Rawls (see p.203), too, placed animals outside the scope of his theory of justice, which was based on the idea of a contract between free and rational equals.

Others, though, claim that if we have duties to animals, it is because animals matter in their own right. Today's animal rights theorists regard animals as having inherent value simply by virtue of being "the subject-of-a-life", and hold that anything having life has rights. But does it in fact make sense to say that animals have rights, or make the same moral claims on us as other human beings? A number of philosophers believe that the answer to this question turns on the issue of how far, if at all, animals share important human characteristics.

The idea that animals share many of the same feelings and impulses as humans has been mooted since ancient times. Pythagoreans (*c.*5th century

Animal experimentation

Descartes's description of animals as mere "animal machines" was seized on by scientific experimenters anxious to pursue investigations into the biology of mammals. The picture of animals as machines quelled objections both to the experiments themselves and to public demonstrations of the discoveries on conscious, living animals. Nevertheless, in his *Philosophical Dictionary,* the French philosopher and writer Voltaire (see p.127) protested in the strongest terms: "Barbarians seize this dog which in friendship surpasses man so prodigiously; they nail it on a table, and they dissect it alive in order to show the mesenteric veins. You discover in it all the same organs of feeling that are in yourself. Answer me, machinist, has nature arranged all the means of feeling in this animal, so that it may not feel?"

However, the practice of vivisection continued to go hand in hand with scientific enquiry, and the apparent pain responses of animals were often taken as reflexes involving no real sensations of pain or distress. In more recent times, while many experimenters still take a view of this type, other prominent scientists, including Charles Darwin (1809–82) and the medical missionary and theologian Albert Schweitzer (1875–1965), have accepted the reality of animal suffering and urged limitations and controls on animal experimentation.

Whether animals have rights similar to those of humans is a matter of current philosophical debate. However, the suffering involved in bullfighting and some other blood sports can be seen as morally offensive, whatever the moral status of animals.

BCE) in ancient Greece were aware of the sensibilities of animals and it led them to advocate vegetarianism. The most influential philosophical voice on this issue, however, was that of Descartes (see pp.48–49), who held that animals were mere automata. In *Discourse on Method*, he gave as a reason for this belief that "they cannot speak as we do, that is, so as to give evidence that they think of what they say". Utilitarian Jeremy Bentham (see p.197) explicitly repudiated this type of reasoning. Rejecting speech and reason as criteria, he said about animals: "the question is not, *Can they reason*? nor, *Can they talk*? but, *Can they suffer*?"

> *Wherever any animal is forced into the service of man, the sufferings which it has to bear on that account are the concern of every one of us.*
>
> Albert Schweitzer, *Philosophy of Religion*

Speciesism and personhood

According to Bentham's present-day successors, it is "speciesism" to deny that their capacity to suffer brings animals within the moral fold. In this view, "person" and "human being" are radically different notions and the line of demarcation should be drawn, not between humans and animals, but between "persons" and non-persons. So animals can be "persons", and humans, particularly at the margins of life, may not be. This means that there can be circumstances in which an animal's life may be more important morally than a human's, and some, such as the Australian philosopher Peter Singer, are willing to accept this conclusion.

But the argument that animals are moral persons in the same way as humans may be too strong for its purpose. Few, for example, would hesitate to sacrifice a dog or a snake that was attacking a child. And there are more moderate anti-speciesist claims that portray the debate less starkly than as one of *either* humans *or* animals – for example, that while it might be justifiable to cause modest discomfort to an animal for a major human good, it would be wrong to inflict agony on an animal for trivial human advantage.

There is, however, another and more plausible way to debate the issue. Instead of arguing that animals are persons, it may be better to emphasize that human persons are animals. This would lead to a shift from a purely anthropocentric view to a deeper ecological understanding that ties human interests firmly in with those of other animals.

Technology and nature

Technology involves the application of scientific knowledge to practical problems, and the creation of devices capable of solving them. Technology is also a means of manipulating the environment for our desired ends, and so presents us with moral choices about its use.

Today, the world is dominated by feats of engineering, the result of human creativity, planning and design. But these achievements may need to be considered alongside a willingness to set the aims and limits of technology in a moral framework. Explicit recognition of this need is a relatively recent development, following in particular the development of nuclear technologies in the mid-20th century. But the issue was implicitly present much earlier, when it became clear that wars were not always to be won by the courage of human beings, but by superior technology, whether siege engines, crossbows or cannons. In the case of technological innovations such as these, it is their uses that present a moral challenge; in other cases, the product is, inherently, morally bad. There could be no moral justification, for example, for the ingenuity humans have applied to developing the technology of torture.

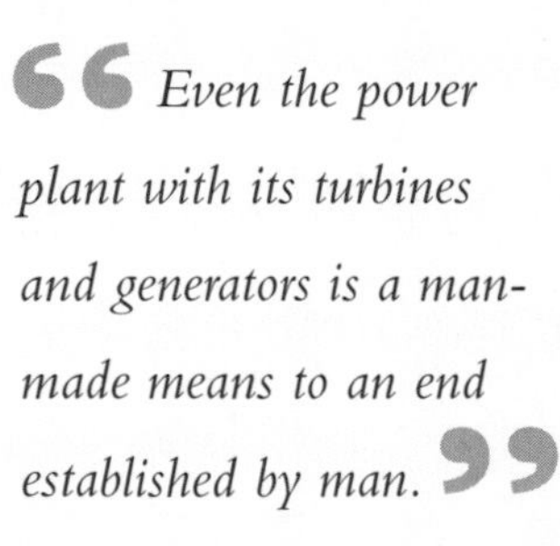

“Even the power plant with its turbines and generators is a man-made means to an end established by man.”

Martin Heidegger, *The Question Concerning Technology*

In general, however, the contemporary world owes a heavy debt to technological creativity. The English scientist and empiricist philosopher Francis Bacon (see p.96) saw the purpose of science as “the betterment of mankind”. And scientific and technological progress has brought machines to replace the drudgery of labour – while conversely the treadmill is now a fashionable health aid, not a life-destroying means of generating power. Technology has also brought increased mobility, heat in winter, cold in summer, space exploration, expanding food production and many medical gains, including diminishing infant mortality, vaccination and cures for many diseases.

But alongside these gains have come some unintended and less acceptable effects. These include pollution of the atmosphere and oceans, depletion of resources and the extinction of species. Critics paint a picture of humanity too dependent on its own machines; of concrete wastelands at the heart of cities; of factory-farming and the proliferation of harmful pesticides and chemicals. They warn, too, of the unpredictable results of genetic experimentation in the plant and animal world – an enormously accelerated copy of evolutionary change.

Those sceptical about the benign motivation of scientific advance, such as the German philosopher Martin Heidegger (1889–1976), emphasize the part played by the profit motive and commercial competition as driving forces of technological progress. They also point out that, in satisfying observed needs and wants, technology creates new ones. Heidegger’s view is that, in the promotion of efficiency, flexibility and control, humans become the tools of their own technology, and the human body itself becomes a resource. Once passenger planes have been invented, for example, people are needed to fill them, and products, once available, require consumers. Behind all this, these critics say, is a technological understanding of the world – humans are seen as over nature, not part of nature.

Science and its application

Science is in one sense as old as Western philosophy. The early philosophers who flourished in Greece in the 6th and 5th centuries BCE

“A thing is right when it tends to preserve the integrity, stability and beauty of the biotic community. It is wrong when it tends otherwise.”

Aldo Leopold, *A Sand County Almanac*

constructed theories about the constitution of the world, astronomy and weather, mathematics and geometry. Greek mathematicians knew how to measure the distance of a ship at sea from, say, a clifftop lookout, while in Egypt the know-how needed to build the ancient pyramids was already two millennia old. What was lacking in ancient times, however, and what dates only from Bacon and the dawn of the Enlightenment (see p.96), was the conscious scientific method of hypothesis and testing that has accelerated the pace of discovery and invention in the last few hundred years. Discoveries have been made at both the microscopic and the telescopic levels, but the newest technologies, in particular nanotechnology and gigatechnology, which deal with objects a billion times smaller or larger than their inventors, are set to expand those frontiers still further.

Scientific discoveries, of course, seldom remain in the area of theory; they find application from microchips to test-tube babies. Along with some scientists and lay people, there are moral philosophers who view the new possibilities as good, and would wish to see them pursued vigorously without undue legal restraints. Others have less confidence in humanity's ability to use its technical advances wisely. But what kind of dangers does science raise? Hard-headed empiricists and policy-oriented politicians see questions about scientific progress as largely practical rather than ethical, and so restrict their concern to the question of risk. As a result, they will want to see decisions made by assessing relative costs and benefits.

> “*We will master it. The will to mastery [of technology] becomes all the more urgent the more technology threatens to slip from human control.*”
>
> Martin Heidegger, *The Question Concerning Technology*

Risk and the "Frankenstein fear"

Closer inspection, however, suggests that the question of risk cannot be dealt with so simply. For cost-benefit analysis cannot answer the question:

The Chernobyl nuclear disaster caused such widespread contamination that whole towns were permanently abandoned, creating thousands of refugees. With hindsight, were the benefits of nuclear power worth the risk of such an accident?

what is an *acceptable* risk? How, for example, are we to evaluate a risk of a failure or malfunction that might in itself be minute, but which, if it did happen, would have extremely dangerous, widespread and enduring effects? The Chernobyl disaster of 1986, when a Soviet nuclear reactor malfunctioned, was near-global in its impact, and residual contamination from that incident may stretch into the indefinite future. How is one to set the sheer magnitude and persistence of such adverse consequences against their extreme improbability? This involves asking the question: does a risk that is infinitesimal or vanishingly small become significant when its scope is unprecedentedly extensive?

Such considerations may well lead to a cautionary approach that controls developments either directly by regulation or indirectly by taxation ("the polluter pays" principle). Developments in technologies affecting the especially sensitive area of human life are already subject to ethical and legal constraints: in many countries, curbs are set on developments such as embryo research, cloning and human genetic alteration. Where plants and animals are concerned, regulation is rather more limited and genetic modification is widely practised for commercial, agricultural and biomedical research purposes. Much of this work promises important benefits: superplants to feed the developing world; "green" fuels to replace petrol; microbes to purify water or clear up oil spills from the ocean. But there are clear signs of a more cautionary approach being applied in these areas too, with growing awareness of some of the risks involved. At the most extreme, there is the risk of our novel creations taking over irreversibly – the dreaded "Frankenstein" phenomenon.

However, ethical concerns about the manipulation and patenting of life are not confined to the question of risk. They also involve our conception of a species and the view we take of our own position in the universe. Such considerations set moral boundaries to what can be achieved in the name of expediency. To begin with, the idea that it is wrong for individuals to make an exception of themselves – "do as you would be done by" – can easily be extended to the principle that it would be wrong for one generation to privilege itself, leaving nothing for future generations. It follows from this that it would be wrong to close down options for future generations by making irreversible changes, such as the elimination of species or the exhaustion of scarce resources.

Secondly, the principle of autonomy, familiar from Kant (see pp.141–143) and libertarian philosophy (see pp.139–140), means, in practical terms, that where risk is concerned it is pertinent to ask: who is entitled to choose to take that risk? Is there not a right to make one's own decisions, including decisions about what risks one is prepared to accept, and not to have that right pre-empted by others? So libertarian considerations about rights, choice and freedom have a role to play in any debate about the direction technology should take.

Technology, then, has the potential to be used or abused. It is not in itself a moral issue, but moral issues arise if people fail to reflect on the ends and purposes of human scientific creativity.

Technology and the end of life

New technologies have changed the process of dying and its likely setting. In the rich countries of the developed world, the majority of people die from long-term diseases and in hospitals, not at home. This new technological way of death started with the discovery of antibiotics, while the availability of respirators, artificial feeding and hydration, together with the possibility of tissue and organ transplants, have added to its impact. In addition, a new understanding of disease has led to individualized and more effective drug treatments.

Through the use of such technological interventions we can expect lifespans to be prolonged even further. However, the assumption that it is better in all cases to prolong life belongs to an earlier, pre-technological age. Already today there are pressing moral questions about the quantity versus the quality of life: whether in each case treatment should be extended or curtailed; and whether euthanasia and assisted suicide should be among the choices available to the individual whose life is in question.

Beauty

How is beauty to be defined and how is it to be judged? Is it a matter of the response it produces in us, or is it, as philosophers have argued since the time of Plato, an eternal quality of the object itself?

What is beauty? Is it, as the old saying has it, "in the eye of the beholder" and thus a matter of personal taste? Or are there objective criteria for judging an object, a person or a work of art to be beautiful? The debate has a long history. The hallmarks of beauty, from classical times, were held to be harmony, proportion and unity. Kant (see pp.141–143) said that, unlike moral judgements, which are universal imperatives based on reason, aesthetic judgements are judgements of taste, and not based on principles. Nevertheless, he said, aesthetic judgements have "subjective universality and necessity". That is to say, they are not just an expression of personal likes or dislikes; it is reasonable to expect that other people will agree with them. Kant's contemporary, the British empiricist philosopher David Hume (see p.24), saw judgements of beauty in a way not so different from this. He saw them as arising from sentiment, but still deserving, on the whole, of universal acceptance.

The dress and posture of modern society's icons reflect current fashion. But can some aspect of their beauty transcend fashion?

So what is it to respond to an object as beautiful? Is it just a feeling of pleasure or satisfaction, or is there a special "aesthetic response" that results from the disinterested contemplation of a beautiful object? Francis Hutcheson, a leading influence in the Scottish Enlightenment, argued in his *Enquiry Concerning Beauty, Order, Harmony, Design* (1725), that recognizing an object as beautiful was a matter of distinguishing between its special aesthetic qualities and factual or empirical ones. The beauty of an object was essentially a matter of its capacity to affect an observer in some particular way. But different artistic genres produce different responses: comedy and tragedy, art, music and so on. This suggests that a person's emotional or aesthetic response will depend not only on the object itself, but on what aspect of it the observer is looking at or focussing on. Those who take this view would say that there is a special way of viewing an object – that there is something unique and distinctive about the aesthetic experience. Schopenhauer (see opposite) believed that there was such a distinctive experience. He said that viewing a beautiful object means "distancing" ourselves – forgetting our will and our individuality. We have to lose ourselves in pure contemplation, becoming a mirror of the object contemplated; or indeed even identical with it.

The debate about beauty – what it is and how to evaluate it – can be described in contemporary terms as a debate about art criticism. The art critic is centrally concerned with evaluation, and the point of art criticism is to help people understand art. In the older and more traditional language, this is to say that discussions of beauty educate our sensibilities, inform our interpretation and clarify our appreciation.

Schopenhauer

Schopenhauer was born in Danzig, Prussia (modern Gdansk, Poland). His father, a merchant, died when he was only seven and his novelist mother moved with him to Weimar in Saxony, where her soirées were attended by some of the great literary figures of the time. Schopenhauer went on to receive an excellent education, earning a doctorate from the University of Jena.

Schopenhauer belonged to the German idealist school of philosophy but he was unusual among Western thinkers of the time in the deep interest he took in Buddhist and Hindu ideas. The philosophers in the Western tradition who most influenced his thinking about metaphysics and art were Plato and Kant, and he accepted from both the philosophical notion of two worlds, one the perceived world of the senses the other a hidden reality.

Unlike Kant, however, Schopenhauer gave a special interpretation to the one aspect of reality we experience directly: the will. This is not "free will" in the sense that we as individuals control our world. Schopenhauer's "will" is a more impersonal force that controls *us* and everything else in the universe. As the philosopher Anthony Kenny describes it: "Will is the force which lives in the plant, the force by which crystal is formed and by which the magnet turns to the North Pole."

Art, especially music, is one of two ways to counter the pessimism induced by the thought that we have little, if any, control of our lives. The other way is through the type of asceticism displayed by saints and mystics. This is an idea to be found in some ancient Eastern philosophy and religion, as well as in the philosophy of the Stoics.

Arthur Schopenhauer 1788–1860

The German philosopher Arthur Schopenhauer (1788–1860) has been described as the philosopher of pessimism. He saw humans as being driven, not by reason, but by a cosmic will. He held that we come closest to understanding this metaphysical truth when we enter the world of art.

In *The World as Will and Idea* (1819), Schopenhauer gives art a supreme role in helping us understand the world and our own part in it. This is because it picks out the essentials – objects or items conceived in their purest form, stripped of their day-to-day variations – from the random variety of our perceptions. Art is also, according to Schopenhauer, a disinterested pursuit. The true artist is not trying to evoke some desire on the part of the observer – not, as Schopenhauer puts it, trying to create some fruit so temptingly depicted that you would want to eat it – but rather trying simply to present the naked beauty of the object.

Schopenhauer opposed art to science and technology; unlike these, it has no practical function. Indeed, the arts themselves can be ranked, in his view, according to their distance from material elements. At the base of this ascending scale is architecture, followed by painting and sculpture, since these arts necessarily take some specific physical form; literature and poetry come next, since they are not dependent on the specific physical matter in which we encounter them but can be presented in other ways, including speech; and, last, music, the most abstract and least material of all the arts, which is pure form. Schopenhauer writes: "Music is the unconscious exercise in metaphysics in which the mind does not know that it is philosophizing."

Schopenhauer has had many admirers from the ranks of composers, authors and dramatists, including Tolstoy and Samuel Beckett; and the German composer Richard Wagner described him as "the greatest philosopher since Kant".

Art

Art involves creativity and imagination. It can represent the world as we receive it through our senses, or present it symbolically or metaphorically. It can aim to express or evoke varying emotions and responses to that world. But beyond this, art is notoriously difficult to define.

What is a work of art? Why, for example, are prehistoric cave paintings recognized as the work of artists, while other marks made by humans are judged to be no more than valueless graffiti? To begin with, it is generally agreed that a work of art is indeed the product of a human being: while a natural object or landscape can evoke appreciation – an aesthetic response – it is not itself a work of art. However, human beings are productive in many different ways, so, while a work of art is necessarily an artefact, an artefact is not necessarily art.

The reasons that have been given for not acknowledging something as a work of art may offer a clue as to what conditions something needs to fulfil to count as art. Some people, for example, would refuse to call most architectural works or ceramic products art, since these usually have a practical use. Already we have here an implied assumption that art must not fulfil some utilitarian purpose – it must not be primarily designed for practical use. This suggests a view of art as something that is valued for itself and not for its practical utility. This is not to deny that, as both Hume in the 18th century and Santayana in the 20th pointed out, every art form has a distinctive purpose and point. Nevertheless, this ground seems to create a contrast between what are traditionally known as the fine arts – painting, poetry, sculpture, music and dance – and the applied arts, or crafts, in which the design of a product is strongly influenced by the practical use to which it is to be put.

> “*Move me, astonish me, rend me; make me shudder, weep, tremble; fill me with indignation.*”
>
> Denis Diderot, *Essays on Painting*

Philosophers on art

Many of the great philosophers of the Western tradition have discussed art. Both Plato and Aristotle viewed art as first and foremost reproduction – an attempt to copy reality. But Plato believed that the objects our senses reveal are themselves copies of some ideal form or type – a table made by a carpenter is a copy of an ideal concept of a table; the artist paints the carpenter's copy. So, since it is twice removed from ultimate reality, Plato regarded art as an inferior pursuit.

Plato also wanted to ban poets from his ideal republic and to allow only music with a moral message or purpose – as a citizen of Athens, one of the warring city-states of ancient Greece, he recommended uplifting, martial music. The view that art must be uplifting is, then, as old as the first philosophizing about the subject. It was a view shared, too, many centuries later by the French Enlightenment philosopher, essayist and editor-in-chief of the *Encyclopédie*, Denis Diderot (see p.97), who, like Plato, believed that art should serve a moral end. Diderot approved, for example, of the Rococo painter Jean-Baptiste Greuze for the moralistic subjects that he chose to paint.

This view can be contrasted with the German philosopher Nietzsche's view of art as that "in which precisely the *lie* is sanctified and the *will to deception* has a good conscience" (Nietzsche's italics in *On the Genealogy of Morals*). Nietzsche (see p.153) took from Schopenhauer the view that art can give meaning to existence. But he disliked the Platonic attempt to impose a moral purpose on art.

Dating from early in modern human prehistory, before any settled civilizations had emerged, these cave paintings in Lascaux, France, represent impressive artistic achievement. How this should be defined and recognized in our own time is more controversial.

Instead he understood it as combining the sense of cosmic disorder and passion associated with the Greek god Dionysus with the formal beauty inspired by Apollo. This, he held, was what characterized the great Greek tragedies and also great music, especially that of Wagner.

Recent and contemporary perspectives

Nietzsche's view was part of 19th-century Europe's Romantic movement which fostered the idea of art as expression. The expressive view of art may relate it either to the emotions and feelings of the artist or to the emotional response it is intended to evoke in the viewer.

There is also a view of art, based on a Marxist analysis of society, as fulfilling some social role or purpose, and a more recent view that sees it as closely linked to particular cultures or societies. Further possibilities arise when the notion of art or a work of art is extended to newer media such as film, video, photography, posters and computer art, to say nothing of objects made out of scrap material, or works such as the contemporary British artist Tracy Emin's unmade bed, which featured as a prize-winning exhibit in the Tate Gallery in London. Such examples have led some contemporary theorists to reaffirm the notion that art must have a moral purpose – a position countered by defenders of the autonomy of art: "art for art's sake" (a term coined by the 19th-century French philosopher Victor Cousin). Art can also be seen as embodying meaning – as a form of communication – as, for example, when political graffiti are presented as art. This comes close to another definition of art as symbol and metaphor.

Today, then, art is subjected both to conventional philosophical analysis and to a variety of more recent sophisticated critiques: it can also be seen as shaped by cultural attitudes and power relationships, with explanations offered in terms of psychoanalysis or psychological and cultural theory. Another contemporary opinion attempts to cut through this sea of contention by saying simply that art is what is exhibited in art galleries (the "context" theory) or – a related view – that anything that someone says is a work of art is a work of art. Such a statement is essentially the claim that it does not make sense to ask what art really is; the issue is only one of recognition by the shifting "Establishment" of the art world.

Taste and decency

Works of artistic expression have long been subject to censorship on grounds of taste or decency. In the mass-media societies of the West, there is continuing debate about good taste and decency as a balance is sought between libertarian claims for artistic freedom and a desire to preserve community values and to protect the young.

Many philosophers, from the Scotsman Francis Hutcheson (1694–1746) to Immanuel Kant (see pp141–143) have attempted to define taste. Kant and Hume (see pp.24–25) saw it as the ability to enjoy art or nature, to appreciate beauty or excellence. Hume added that it is also a matter of being able to say *why* you enjoy it – which he called "discrimination". A more recent view is that it consists in the ability to recognize special properties, of having what has been called "an aesthetic sense". Having such a sense, and directing it correctly – something often associated with the appreciation of "high" rather than popular culture – may carry with it a certain cachet. Opportunities arise for what might be called "bluffing your way". In *Le Bourgeois Gentilhomme*, the 17th-century French dramatist Molière made fun of the pretensions to superior taste of would-be social climbers.

Hume recognized the possibility of genuine disagreement about taste, identifying two kinds of relativity in such matters, writing in *Of the Standard of Taste* (1757): "The one is the different humours of particular men; the other, the particular manners and opinions of our age and country."

Free expression is highly prized in democratic societies, so voluntary regulation of media industries in relation to decency is often preferred to state censorship. In a number of European countries, this poster elicited so many complaints that it was withdrawn.

Decency

Decency is harder to pin down than its opposite, indecency. Even indecency, however, takes many forms. One of these is obscenity. Strictly, the term obscenity means what is repugnant or disgusting to the senses, and is not necessarily confined to sexual matters – though in modern times it has been used largely in this connection and has been the subject of a number of legal attempts at definition. One of the most famous of these in Britain was the 1868 judgement of Lord Chief Justice Cockburn in the case of *R v Hicklin* that obscenity involves "a tendency … to deprave and corrupt" – a phrase incorporated into the 1959 Obscene Publications Act, which sought to distinguish between art and literature on the one hand and pornography on the other.

Pornography is often understood as the explicit depiction of sex in art or literature in a way that is lacking in artistic merit. Indeed, on this basis, the question of merit becomes the main criterion for distinguishing between art and pornography. In the USA, this was made explicit in the case of *Roth v US* (1957), which resulted in the formulation of the "LAPS" standard: that the work should have "literary, artistic, political or scientific" value. Irrespective of this test, those opposed to pornography say that it is dehumanizing, that it is a type of community pollutant and also that it can provide a stimulus to many socially harmful practices, including rape, murder and child abuse. Those who do not wish to see pornography censored or banned deny that it has these effects – they may even claim that it can have beneficial effects, at least where adults are concerned – but in the main they are more likely to rest their case on the principle of freedom.

> *"Wherever you can ascertain a delicacy of taste, it is sure to meet with approbation; and the best way of ascertaining it is to appeal to those modes and principles, which have been established by the uniform consent and experience of nations and ages."*
>
> David Hume, *Of the Standard of Taste*

Moral philosophers in public life have tended to favour freedom from state interference. The British philosopher Bernard Williams (1929–2003), in a report commissioned by the British government in 1979, recommended a policy that had been successfully applied two decades earlier to the issues of prostitution and homosexuality: restriction without prohibition. This means that obscene or pornographic material should not be banned, but that it should not obtrude on the unintending or youthful eye – in other words, it should be discreetly available to the consenting adult.

Taste and decency, then, while in essence matters of personal judgement, are very much in the public domain. The case for non-interference is based on the libertarian principle of excluding only what harms others, while the case for control can be made on broader grounds of aesthetic taste and social propriety.

Blasphemy and the arts

Blasphemy forms a special case of offence to taste. Originally meaning slander or profane speech, it has come to mean offensive or insulting speech about God. In England, the blasphemy law was for several centuries considered an outdated irrelevance, but new life was breathed into it by the successful private prosecution of a magazine called *Gay News* in 1979 for an offensive depiction of Jesus Christ. The outcome of the case was to turn the concept of blasphemy into a matter of hurt to people's feelings or sensibilities rather than an insult to the divinity. Subsequently, the 1989 *fatwa* (religious decree) issued by the Iranian spiritual leader, Ayatollah Khomeini, against the British author Salman Rushdie following publication of his novel *The Satanic Verses* (1988) for a claimed offence to Islam led to a debate about the limits of legitimate criticism of religion. The debate centred on whether the blasphemy law should be abolished or, on the contrary, extended to apply to religions other than Christianity (see also p.190).

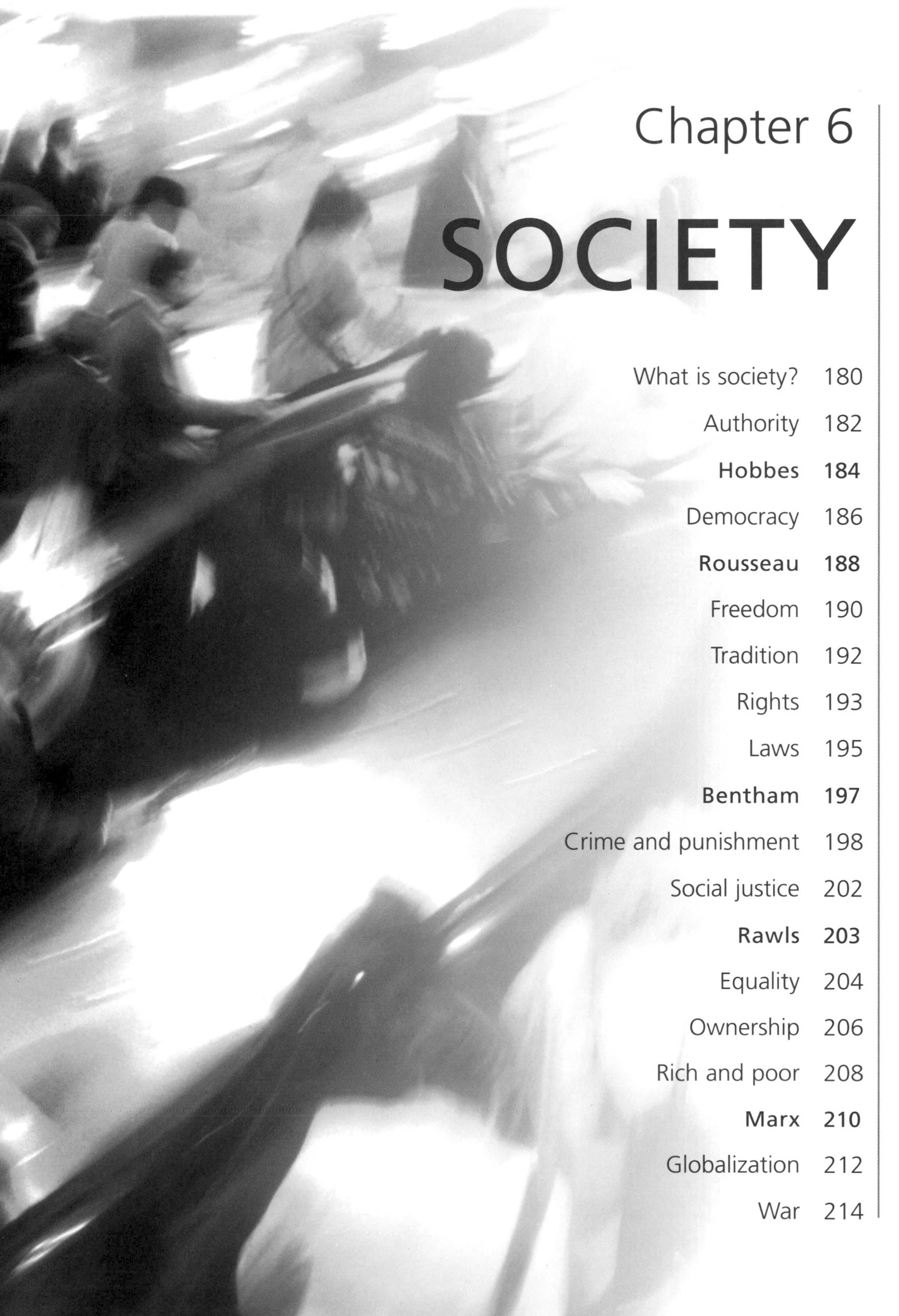

Chapter 6

SOCIETY

What is society?

Individual human beings live together in societies – with rules, hierarchies and power structures. But what makes a group of people into a society? What types of society are there, why do we have them and how do they work?

A human society seems to be more than just a collection of individuals, for a society is structured by complex rules, some enforced by a central authority, others more subtly by expectation and custom. Yet human society is not like a society of ants or bees, in which each member seems predetermined to perform a certain role, apparently for the good of the whole, according to a fixed pattern.

So the metaphysical question of the relation between individual and society is not a straightforward one. The individualist view is that, ultimately, the only things that exist are individual human beings. Society, in this view, is simply a name for a group of human beings who have gathered together. The alternative, holist, view says that there is more to society than this. France, for example, seems not to be reducible simply to a collection of people who live within a certain area. Rather, says the holist, France seems to transcend the individuals who compose it. Karl Marx (see p.210) reminds us that we can barely conceive of individuals outside society because the things that make us distinctively human – language, production, economic cooperation – are social achievements, relying on the interaction of great numbers of people.

But whether we are more sympathetic to the individualist or holist view, each society somehow needs to find a balance between individual goals and interests on the one hand, and the common good on the other. The potential for conflict between these two objectives generates many of the questions of political philosophy. Different traditions of thought within political philosophy conceptualize the moral relation between the individual and the social whole in quite different ways.

Margaret Thatcher, the former British prime minister, famously remarked: "There is no such thing as society. There are individual men and women and there are families." This metaphysical comment was prompted by her moral contention that people are often too quick to give up the duty of looking after themselves, and too ready to ask "society" to bail them out. Self-reliance is advocated in rather extreme form by libertarians, who

Aristotle on man as political animal

A central question for political philosophers has always been how "naturally fitted" human beings are for living in societies. In biological terms we could ask: "are human beings herd animals?" The ancient Greeks made a distinction between nature and convention, allowing them to divide the world into things that exist according to nature and things that exist because of human action. This distinction can be applied to human society itself. Are human societies and states natural or artificial? Have we invented them, or are they an inevitable part of human existence?

Aristotle (see pp.13–15) was in no doubt about this, claiming that "it is evident that the state is a creation of nature, and that man is by nature a political animal" (*Politics*, Book I). In his view, human beings have no real choice but to live in societies, and, furthermore, in societies of a political nature. Anyone who by nature is not fitted to live under a state must be "a wretch or a superhuman", says Aristotle, likening such a "natural outcast" to an isolated piece in a game of draughts. Conceiving of an individual as existing entirely outside of society, therefore, simply makes no sense: such a person simply would not be a human being.

In society, an intricate web of rules, responsibilities and norms discourages individuals from infringing each other's rights.

make a strong distinction between voluntary and coerced behaviour. In this libertarian view, individuals may voluntarily form themselves into whatever type of society they choose. However, the state, which has coercive powers, should act purely as a "nightwatchman", to ensure that people do not infringe each others' rights. In a libertarian world there would be policing and law courts, but no state-funded schools or hospitals or even a central bank.

At the opposite pole is the idea of the state as all-encompassing, with all social life organized, or at least supervised, by the state. Something like this is seen, for example, in some theologically-based states, and in other highly autocratic regimes. Here the point of the state is not so much to protect people from each other, but to make sure that people live the right way. The rights of the individual take second place, where necessary, to the rights of the state.

> *"The multitude of productive forces available to men determines the nature of society; hence the 'history of humanity' must always be studied and treated in relation to the history of industry and exchange."*
>
> Karl Marx and Friedrich Engels, *The German Ideology*

Most political philosophers agree with libertarians that the state should not have the power to intervene to this degree in people's lives. But, contrary to libertarianism, it is usual to expect the state to provide basic conditions for all citizens to enjoy a decent chance of living a worthwhile life. Thus the role of the state is partially enabling: to help people find a place in society. This includes state provision of many services, and, usually, some redistribution of income from rich to poor.

Another question on which contemporary theorists often differ is the extent to which the state should seek to influence the values of its citizens. The liberal view is that the state has no business in declaring any way of life better than any other, provided that no harm is done to third parties. However, "communitarians" argue that there is special value in coexisting as a community and so the state should take special measures to protect the community. These could be, for example, restrictive laws to preserve traditional industries and pastimes, and policies designed to encourage people to work together in local organizations.

Authority

Political authority is the right to command, and to punish those who fail to obey. But how can any individual or group, or the state, come to have such a right over others in society and how do they justify exerting it?

According to the American philosopher Robert Nozick (1938–2002), the fundamental question in political philosophy is: why not anarchy? Why should we have a state at all? As defined by German sociologist Max Weber (1864–1920), the state is an organization that successfully "claims the monopoly of the legitimate use of physical force within a given territory".

If political authority is essentially coercive, it is natural to ask how it could be justified. For if we have the right to autonomy ("self-rule"), it is hard to see what gives the state the right to tell us what to do, or to punish us if we disobey.

The relationship between the individual and the state was debated in the ancient world. In *Crito*, Plato portrays Socrates awaiting execution. Socrates is invited by his friends to flee, but he feels duty bound to accept his punishment, unjust though he believes it to be. He argues that he has made an agreement to obey the laws of Athens, and that it would be wrong of him to break that agreement.

The social contract

The theory of the social contract was developed in the 17th and 18th centuries by thinkers such as Hobbes (see pp.184–185), Locke (see pp.82–83)

Political authority can take many forms, from a tax demand to an intimidating display of physical force, as in this line of riot police facing anti-globalization protesters in 1999. But whichever way authority manifests itself, disobedience is liable to be punished.

> *Individuals have rights, and there are things no person or group may do to them (without violating their rights). So strong and far-reaching are these rights that they raise the question of what, if anything, the state and its officials may do.*
>
> Robert Nozick, *Anarchy, State and Utopia*

and Rousseau (see pp.188–189), and was seen as an elegant way to reconcile individual autonomy with state authority. It held that we each use our autonomy to transfer our rights of self-rule to the state on the understanding that this is best for everyone. In this way we legitimize the authority of the state.

But how is this transfer of right supposed to have taken place? A standard response to this question is to introduce the idea of tacit consent. Purely by residing within the state and receiving the benefits that it provides, we tacitly give our consent to the state. If we don't like it, we can leave.

However, critics argue, leaving is often easier said than done, and so remaining can hardly be construed as freely given consent. As David Hume (see pp.24–25) argued, one may as well suggest that a passenger, carried aboard a ship while unconscious, agrees to stay on board when it is on the high seas, even though he would soon perish if he tried to leave by jumping overboard.

A more recent approach is to appeal to the idea of fairness. Each of us benefits from everyone else's obedience to laws – and so, out of fairness to our fellow citizens, we too have a duty to obey those laws, rather than taking a "free ride" on the obedience of others. Although this reasoning sounds plausible, we may ask whether it is really sufficient to justify the state punishing those who disobey.

Alternatively, it might be argued that the initial assumption that we have a right to autonomy is flawed. From a utilitarian point of view, for example, political morality is based on the principle of maximizing the balance of happiness over unhappiness in society, rather than considering the rights of individuals. On this basis, the only question is whether the state does more to advance human happiness than its absence would, and on this ground its victory seems assured. However, precisely because it ignores rights to autonomy, utilitarianism is more often rejected than accepted. Nevertheless the idea of existing without an enforceable law is not an attractive one. If John Stuart Mill (see pp.139–140) is correct that all that makes life valuable for one person depends on the existence of restraints on the lives of others, then punishing those who try to "ride for free" seems reasonable enough.

Anarchism

Many political philosophers who wrestle with questions about the authority of the state call themselves "philosophical anarchists". This may be something of a surprise to those for whom the term "anarchist" conjures up the image either of a cloaked, bomb-throwing lover of chaos, or a stone-throwing hater of capitalism. Yet the main claim of philosophical anarchists is simply that no theorist has offered a compelling justification of the existence of political authority. Other anarchists go further and argue that we should live without political authority – without states, governments, police, armies or law courts. However, anarchists do not necessarily oppose organization, even complex social organization. Their complaint is with coercion: the fact that the state – immorally in their view – forces people to behave in some ways rather than others, and will punish them for disobeying. Nevertheless, anarchists typically take moral duties very seriously indeed – as they must if they are to maintain their objection to the state on the grounds that it is intrinsically immoral. Indeed, a common anarchist claim is that the state itself is the cause of the problems of crime, selfishness,and anti-social behaviour that supposedly justify the state's existence. The state, then, is held by anarchists to have corrupted us all, and we would be better off without it.

Hobbes

Thomas Hobbes was born in Malmesbury, England, in 1588, and lived to the exceptional age of 91. It is said that his mother went into labour on hearing that the Spanish Armada had set sail to invade England. Thus, Hobbes remarked in his autobiography that his mother "brought twins to birth, myself and fear". Fear, indeed, played a central role both in Hobbes' life and in his philosophy. Greatly disturbed by the unrest that was to lead to the English Civil War, Hobbes was one of the first to flee to France, in 1640, not returning to England until 1651 – a year that saw both the publication of his most influential work, *Leviathan*, and the end of the civil war.

The brutality of the war, Hobbes observed, was a sign of how life would be without government, in

Hobbes and geometry

Hobbes was enormously influenced by Euclid's *Elements* (see illustration), which sets out the principles of geometry. This work impressed upon him the importance of clear definition and rigorous argument (in *Leviathan* Hobbes suggests that most error in philosophy is the consequence of faulty definition). In his *Brief Lives*, John Aubrey (1626–95) reports that, at the age of 40, Hobbes for the first time glanced at a page of Euclid. Seeing a particular proposition, he declared: "By God, this is impossible!" But he then followed the proof back through its steps to the initial axioms (assumptions), which appeared self-evident, and came to understand that, if one accepted Euclid's axioms, this proposition – like all Euclid's propositions – followed through clear logic. This inspired Hobbes to apply a similar method, grounding his political philosophy in general truths about human beings, which in turn were grounded in his metaphysics. He attempted to set out simple definitions, such as the idea that men call "good" what they desire ("Whatsoever is the object of any man's appetite or desire; that is it, which he for his part calls good"; *Leviathan*, Chapter 6), and to argue from these definitions to particular controversial conclusions – above all, for the necessity of an absolute sovereign. Sadly, the demonstrations in Hobbesian political philosophy never seem to have the rigour and force of demonstrations in Euclidean geometry.

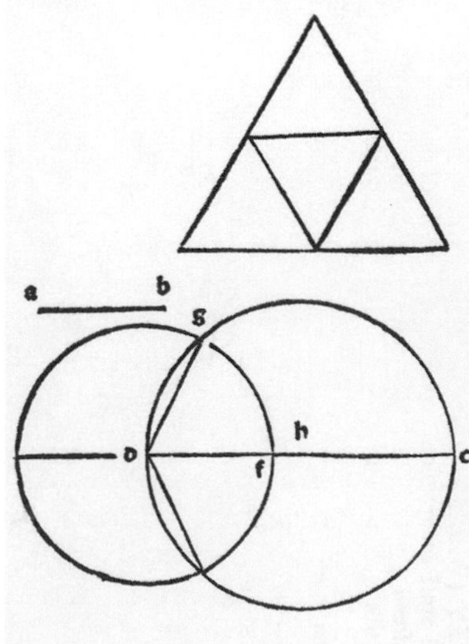

Figura intra figuram dicitur ĩscribi quando ea que inscribitur eius in qua inscribitur. latera vno quoqз suorum angulorum ab interiore parte contingit. ¶ Circumscribi vero figura figure perhibetur quotiēs ea quidē figura eius cui circūscribitur suis lateribus omnibus omnes angulos contingit.

Propositio. .1.

Intra datum circulum date linee recte que diametro minime maior existat equam rectam lineam coaptare. ¶ Sit linea data.a.b.circulusqз datus.c.d.e.cui9 diameter.c.d.qua nō ē maior linea.a.b.volo itra datū circulū coaptare lineā eq̄lē.a.b que si fuerit equalis diametro cōstat ꝓpositū.si aūt minor ex diametro sumat.d.f.sibi eq̄lis ⁊ sup punctū.d.ƒm quātitatē linee.d.f.describat circulus f.e.g.secans datum circulum in punctis.g.⁊.e.ad alterum quorum ducatur linea a puncto.d.vt.d.e.vel.d.g.eritqз vtralibet earum equalis linee.a.b.eo q vtraqз earū est equalis linee.d.f.per diffinitionem circuli:quare habemus ꝓpositū.

the "state of nature". Such a situation, Hobbes claimed, would be calamitous. In the absence of government, every person would naturally be suspicious of every other, destroying any possibility of fruitful cooperation. Hobbes argued that everyone would be equal to the degree that any person could kill any other – at least with sufficient help from others – and so no one would be invulnerable to attack. In such circumstances, individuals would be compelled to attack each other not only in competition for scarce resources, but also in self-defence and even for reputation, to deter others. Only the existence of a government (or, in Hobbes' terms, a sovereign) to pass and enforce laws could bring peace. Without a government there would be no civilization – no agriculture, trade, science or art. Life, he famously remarked, would be a state of war of all against all.

Hobbes is often thought to have assumed that human beings are naturally selfish, and it is true that he bases his political philosophy on his "science of man", in which it is argued that human beings constantly seek "felicity" – the power to satisfy their never-ending desires. However, it may be more accurate to say that he thought it irrational to trust others unless one can be assured that one's trust will not be abused.

To those who question the need for such suspicion and distrust in the state of nature, Hobbes asks them to consider the steps we take to ensure our own security even when living under civil government. We lock our doors, we ride armed, we even lock our chests against members of our household. If this is how we act in the presence of government, it is hard to see how we could reasonably be less suspicious in its absence.

Escaping the state of nature

But we are not, Hobbes argued, doomed to remain in the state of nature. Eventually, reason and fear of death will lead people to formulate laws – "convenient articles of peace" – that guide them out of mutual war. This leads people in the state of nature to give up their natural right to attack others and to defend themselves on condition that everyone else also gives up such rights. By this contract they hand over their rights to a state authority (a government or sovereign), which accordingly acquires power to rule.

> *In the state of nature … the life of man [is] solitary, poor, nasty, brutish, and short.*
>
> Thomas Hobbes, *Leviathan*

Thomas Hobbes 1588–1679

Famous for his apparently pessimistic view of human nature, the English philosopher Thomas Hobbes argued in his great masterpiece *Leviathan* that the only way to avoid the horrors of "war of all against all" is through passive, unquestioning obedience to an absolute sovereign.

The existence of a government or sovereign, then, creates conditions in which we can trust one another, and consequently enjoy all the civilizing benefits of cooperation. Further, Hobbes believed that such a body must have absolute, unlimited power if it is to ensure peace. Many remain unconvinced by Hobbes' defence of the absolute sovereign. One important criticism is that people may have more to fear from a tyrant in power than from their fellow human beings in a state of nature. Another objection is that absolutism is unnecessary, since even a sovereign with more limited powers, bound by a constitution perhaps, could bring an end to the war of all against all.

Hobbes' reply, at least to this second criticism, is simple and direct: the only way of limiting the sovereign's power is with a greater power. The idea of limiting the sovereign's power merely by a constitution makes no sense. Who could enforce it? If there is any such person or group, it must, in effect, have greater power. And the greatest power of all, on this analysis, must be unlimited. According to Hobbes we have a stark choice: absolutism or the war of all against all.

Democracy

If there is anything that seems beyond question in contemporary politics, it is that democracy is a good thing. But opinions vary about the nature of democracy and about why democracy is so valuable to society.

Democracy is most obviously a procedure of decision-making by majority vote. However, democratic societies typically include much more than processes of majority rule. A free press, extensive civil rights and processes of public consultation are just some of the institutions we expect in a democratic society. Furthermore, in modern democracies very few decisions are taken by anything like a majority vote. Rather, we elect the people who will govern us. This system, known as representative democracy, is contrasted with direct democracy in which the people do indeed vote on particular issues and policies. Direct democracy is very rare in contemporary politics, although some theorists regard direct democracy as the only truly authentic form of democracy.

Democracy has not always enjoyed the high esteem it has today. Perhaps its most influential critic was Plato (see pp.76–79). The essentials of Plato's argument, which he developed in his *Republic*, can be stated very simply. Ruling is a skill, and the exercise of any skill is rationally best left to experts. However, in a democracy the people rule, but the people are not expert rulers. Therefore it follows that democracy is irrational.

Athenian democracy

The democracy experienced by Plato and Socrates in ancient Athens was markedly different from the democracies we know today. First, political rights were granted only to male citizens – that is, free-born men of Athenian descent, which excluded slaves, those whose parents were not both citizens and, of course, women. Second, members of the government were not elected but appointed by lottery, for elections were thought to discriminate undemocratically against the unpopular. Finally, all male citizens were entitled to take part in the public debate and decision-making of the assembly, and were in fact encouraged to do so by payment for attendance. Plato worried that the ability to carry the day by means of fine speechmaking may have little to do with the strength of argument presented, and that rhetoric and charisma would dominate reason and wisdom – which were the special skills of the philosophers. Accordingly, he argued that sound government is not possible until the kings become philosophers, or the philosophers kings.

Defending democracy

Essentially, there are two ways of replying to Plato. First, we might confront him on his own ground by arguing that democracy – at least under the right circumstances – can produce very good decisions. Perhaps, for example, if we vote for representatives to make our political decisions rather than voting directly for policies, as happened in the Athenian assembly, we may get more satisfactory results. Alternatively, we might argue that democracy is not to be judged in terms of the quality of the decisions it makes, but on other grounds – perhaps on the basis that it connects individuals to the decisions of society as a whole, promoting feelings of belonging to society. In this second approach, the value of democracy derives from its role as a form of collective self-rule, and as such embodies ideas of human equality, community and free will.

Showing that democracies can make good decisions may seem difficult. Even if our decision is only to elect representatives, how can we be sure we will elect the right ones? But a response can be found in an argument inspired by Rousseau (see pp.188–189) and formulated by the French mathematician, philosopher and statesman

Condorcet (1743–94). Even if no individual is an expert, a majority vote among a large enough group will be virtually certain to be correct – provided that each individual is more likely to be right than wrong. It can therefore be perfectly reasonable to rely on a group even when it would be foolish to rely on any one person within that group. Condorcet worried that an ignorant electorate turns into an excellent argument against democracy (it will be virtually certain to produce the wrong answer). However, we can see that, under the right conditions, with an involved, active and educated electorate, democracy can be effective.

> *Democracy substitutes election by the incompetent many for appointment by the corrupt few.*
>
> George Bernard Shaw, *Man and Superman*

But even if we doubt democracy's ability to make enlightened decisions, it does have one great advantage, as Karl Popper (1902–94) pointed out in his critique of Plato, Hegel and Marx, *The Open Society and Its Enemies* (1945). It is a system that allows the removal of unpopular rulers without overt conflict or bloodshed. The importance of this speaks for itself.

However, can we always trust democracies? What is to stop the majority passing laws that oppress the minority? In fact, modern democracies contain extensive protections for minorities, often in the form of a constitution. So constitutions can be seen as providing a justified limitation to democratic power: individuals have rights, and not even a democratic vote, or a decision by an elected representative, can legitimately override these rights. Viewed in this light, a constitution is not so much a limitation on democracy but an intrinsic part of its functioning.

Effective democratic government relies in part on a fair electoral system. This can be difficult to establish, especially in a state more used to absolute rule. The November 1987 election in Haiti, pictured below, was the first after 30 years of dictatorship.

Rousseau

Jean-Jacques Rousseau was born in the Swiss free city-state of Geneva. His mother died in his infancy, and, deserted by his father when still a child, he was brought up by his mother's family and became apprenticed as an engraver to his uncle. Unhappy with his relations' harsh discipline, Rousseau ran away at the age of 16, and after wandering through France and Italy became established in Paris in the household of Madame de Warens, where he enjoyed a life of study and leisure for some years. Initially a musician, he attempted to find fame and fortune through the invention of a more rational form of musical notation. He failed, but after moving to Paris he became acquainted with the radical intellectual circle of d'Alembert and Diderot and contributed articles on music to the great *Encyclopédie* (see p.97).

Rousseau finally made his name by winning the Dijon Academy Prize in 1750 with his essay *Discourse on the Arts and Sciences*. Contrary to the spirit of the age, Rousseau argued that progress in the arts and sciences had done more to corrupt morality than to purify it. His next important, and much more substantial, work, *Discourse on Inequality* (1753), argues that previous philosophers have been incorrect in their understanding of the "natural state of man". Unlike Hobbes, who postulated a war of all against all (see pp.184–185), Rousseau believed that natural human compassion would lead to a state of relative tranquillity. Rousseau accuses the philosophers of attributing to the "savage" – the human being outside of society – the characteristics of modern man, corrupted and softened by luxury and domestication. Without laws modern man would fall into war, but this is not an account of humans in their natural state. For Rousseau, the life of the savage – unspoilt, living on skills and wits – has a noble quality and much to recommend it.

> *God makes all things good. Man meddles with them and they become evil.*
>
> Jean-Jacques Rousseau, *Emile, Book I*

Jean-Jacques Rousseau 1712–1778

Jean-Jacques Rousseau, a brilliant, troubled thinker, is famous for his depiction of the "noble savage" and his work on the theory of the social contract. He aspired to the creation of a society in which people could enjoy true political freedom.

"Forced freedom"

Rousseau is best known for his later work, *The Social Contract* (1762), which is an attempt to work out how it is possible to find a form of political association in which each person may "unite himself with all [but] still obey himself alone, and remain as free as before". This apparently impossible task is achieved, argues Rousseau, by the "social contract" (see also pp.182–183) in which people hand over their rights to the whole community, and thus also to themselves as part of the community, under the direction of the "general will". The general will, argues Rousseau, is discovered, but not created, by democratic voting among the citizens. It is not obvious how exactly this is to be understood, and a wide range of interpretations has been attempted. Some have read Rousseau as a radical democrat, others as a defender of a semi-tyrannical state, a reading encouraged by his remark that those who refuse to follow the general will should be "forced to be free". Yet it is clear that Rousseau's concern is that individuals should develop their own reason and sense of duty, rather than live in conformity with an externally imposed code. We are free – autonomous – only when we live according to the laws we make for ourselves. In reality, as Rousseau recognizes, this means living as part of a self-governing group.

The bearing of Native North Americans, such as this chief of the Nez Perce tribe, made them a popular subject for 19th-century photographers, and before that for painters. Such impressions of dignity may have inspired Rousseau's idea of there being a noble quality to life in the natural state.

Rousseau's ideal form of political association resembles an idealization of his native city-state of Geneva. In order to be truly free it must be limited in size, composed of people who already have a bond with each other, and without grave disparities of wealth. Unlike other thinkers Rousseau did not argue that such a state, once achieved, could survive in perpetuity, but acknowledged that it would inevitably decay. However it remained, for him, our highest aspiration.

Rousseau was a complex, contentious and even contradictory figure, and nowhere is this more apparent than in his attitude to child rearing. His book *Emile* (1762) is something of a manual of radical parenting, in which he argues, for example, that fathers should educate their own sons. Yet his own five children, borne by his long-term companion Thérèse le Vasseur, were all placed in the hands of a foundling home.

Quarrelsome to the last, and seeing conspiracies against him everywhere, in his later years Rousseau wrote *Confessions* (posthumously published in 1781), a remarkable tale of an extraordinary life, and one of the first candid autobiographies ever written. Rousseau, with surprising lack of foresight but customary fondness for controversy, predicted that no one would attempt the task of honest autobiography again.

Rousseau and the French Revolution

Rousseau and Voltaire (see p.127) are often cited as the thinkers who inspired the French Revolution. Although Rousseau had been dead for more than a decade when the revolution broke out in 1789, it is easy to see a connection between his ideas and the slogan of the revolutionaries: "Liberty, equality, fraternity". Certainly the task of founding a truly free society was one for which Rousseau would have had great sympathy, and the revolutionary Robespierre and the Jacobins had no doubt that they were his followers. But, as ever with Rousseau, the issue is complex. For example, he believed that a free society must incorporate a civic religion, while the revolutionaries were hostile to religion. Their worship of reason owes more to Voltaire than Rousseau, who did not share the view that reason, in the form of the arts and sciences, had led to progress. Rather, he stressed the importance of natural instincts. So even if Rousseau's ideas did influence the revolutionaries, it seems unlikely that such influence was based on a close reading of the texts.

Freedom

In liberal democratic societies freedom is often regarded as being of the highest value. However, the question of what it is to be free has been subjected to much debate: how do we distinguish between being *free*, being *able* and being *allowed* to do something?

What is freedom? Put the other way around, what would make someone unfree? In a simplistic view, anything at all that prevents me from doing something reduces my freedom. However, this argument seems implausible. My lack of stamina prevents me from swimming the English Channel. Yet it seems strange to claim that this makes me unfree. It seems we need a distinction between lack of ability and lack of freedom.

One influential view claims that only other people can make someone unfree. But are all restrictions on freedom the result of actions by others? Could shyness, for example, render me unfree? Certainly it could stop me from doing things I would like to do. Perhaps addiction is an even more plausible example; people may claim to be "slaves" to their addiction. The Latvian-born Oxford philosopher Isaiah Berlin (1909–97) distinguished between negative freedom, which is an absence of external constraints, and positive freedom, which requires rational self-control and mastery over one's own appetites. Berlin warned that positive freedom is a dangerous idea, as it implies that others may have a clearer understanding than you of whether or not you do exercise such self-control, and so may claim that they can rightfully coerce you in the name of freedom. In Berlin's view negative freedom offers better protection from tyranny.

Politically, an important debate concerns the relation between money and freedom. If I cannot afford a ticket to the opera does this mean I am unfree to go, or is this simply a lack of ability, akin to lacking a talent? Some argue that I lack freedom, because if I try to go to the opera without paying I am likely to be ejected. Others see freedom as a matter of permissibility. I am permitted to go to

The Satanic Verses

In 1988, shortly after the publication of the novel *The Satanic Verses* by Anglo-Indian author Salman Rushdie, British Muslims began to protest that the book's content was blasphemous under Islamic law. the book was banned in India, Pakistan and South Africa. The Muslim protests, including riots and book burnings, culminated with a decree (*fatwa*) by Iran's religious leader, Ayatollah Khomeini, proclaiming the book to be a work of blasphemy and offering a reward for the death of Rushdie, who subsequently went into hiding under police protection.

The episode raised fierce debate on freedom of speech and the responsibilities of the writer. Some argued that Rushdie had been deliberately provocative and that a book so deeply offensive to Muslims should not have been published. It was suggested that if the nature and integrity of a serious attempt at art causes offence, that is acceptable, but anything that sets out to provoke is not. There were those who maintained that all speech and writing should be free from censorship, while others argued that causing offence to those who hold sincere religious belief is never acceptable, whatever the motives.

Even if it were desirable, it is hard to see how any law could be enforced that requires courts to police an author's motives and to attempt to decide whether an author is deliberately trying to shock, or whether any such shock is a by-product of a serious attempt to create art. Given this difficulty, we seem to be left with the choice of allowing all blasphemous texts or allowing none (unless we want to give special protection to one particular religion). A liberal society worthy of its name should not find it hard to decide this issue.

the opera – there is no law against it, and I am not banned by the management – but I am currently unable to take advantage of this permission. By this view my freedom to go to the opera remains intact. Money affects ability, not freedom. The importance of this debate is that one side will say that if we are to equalize freedom we must equalize wealth, whereas the other side says that this is to confuse two quite different issues. Perhaps this debate really shows that we operate with more than one concept of freedom: one relating to real possibility, the other to permissibility.

> *Freedom for the pike is death for the minnows.*
>
> R.H. Tawney, *Equality*

Freedom of conscience and expression

Historically, freedom of worship, belief and speech have been among the most prized freedoms, and the establishment of these freedoms is in large part the achievement of movements promoting toleration of diversity. Initially, toleration was a matter of not persecuting those of minority religious belief; in other words, the guarantee of liberty of conscience. More recently the idea of toleration has been extended to toleration of diverse lifestyles, which includes, for example, accepting that people should be free to live openly in homosexual relationships should they so choose.

Nevertheless the idea of toleration has itself come under criticism. Toleration of something can be taken to presuppose an underlying negative attitude towards it; one "puts up with" something of which one basically disapproves. Because of this, those who live according to the values of minority religions or cultures, or follow unusual lifestyles, or hold unpopular views, may say that they do not want merely to be tolerated, but to be accepted. According to this account, tolerance is not enough – even if it is a tremendous advance over intolerance.

From the earliest settlers onward, many people have fled to the United States to escape persecution elsewhere. Symbolizing this idea of freedom from fear is the figure of Liberty, whose statues on both East and West coasts have welcomed millions of immigrants.

Tradition

How important is it that we maintain the traditions of our societies? Defenders of tradition argue that our traditions contain the accumulated wisdom of previous generations. Critics reply that traditions are just as likely to reproduce the prejudices of less enlightened times.

Conservatism is sometimes portrayed as an instinctive aversion to all change, but its underlying philosophy can be far more sophisticated than this. The conservative insight, memorably set out by the Anglo-Irish parliamentarian Edmund Burke (1729–97), is that traditions and institutions take an enormous amount of time and effort to set up, but can very easily be destroyed beyond repair. Consequently the burden of proof should always fall on those who wish to make significant change, and this burden should be a very heavy one. Our traditions, urge conservatives, have evolved and contain the wisdom and values of ages. The tragedy is that often we take these for granted, and only recognize them when they are gone and it is too late to go back. Furthermore, any changes we make are bound to have consequences that we have not anticipated, and these consequences may not always be welcome.

In the 20th century the argument for the importance of tradition was developed by political scientist Michael Oakeshott (1901–90), an opponent of what he termed "rationalism". Oakeshott argued that politics had become dominated by an obsession with "techniques" to solve a series of perceived crises. He re-emphasized the importance of practical knowledge, experience and judgment, which cannot always be summarized into a set of principles. He likens political action to a traditional craft, learnt through apprenticeship. Politics should not be seen as a form of social engineering, needing the application of theoretical principles or the development of novel methods.

Critics will argue that while traditions can carry the wisdom of ages, they are just as likely to contain their prejudices, and John Stuart Mill (see pp.139–140), for example, railed against the tyranny of custom, which he thought stunted individuality. Oakeshott happily concedes that tradition must allow for difference and change. Both thinkers believe that we should not be slaves to tradition, yet if we neglect our traditions entirely we may find ourselves in a world we like even less.

Hunting for sport

Hunting for sport is part of the traditions of many societies. The idea of hunting (and shooting and fishing) for recreation – rather than for food or for pest control, which are often seen as separate cases – repels many people. Surely, they argue, there can be no grounds for killing innocent creatures just for the thrill of it? Defenders of hunting might counter that their sport is a valuable social practice, which preserves important traditions, such as a sense of community, a connection with the past and standards of excellence in animal husbandry associated with "the hunt". These, defenders of hunting will argue, are more important than the lives of the animals killed. However, opponents might argue that the "sense of community" that hunting perpetuates is based on outmoded social hierarchies and habits of deference. In the end any view about the moral permissibility of hunting for sport is, therefore, a view about the moral importance of human traditions.

> “*Society is … a partnership not only between those who are living, but between those who are living, those who are dead, and those who are to be born.*”
>
> Edmund Burke, *Reflections on the Revolution in France*

Rights

Political philosophers have puzzled over the nature of a "right" for centuries. Do our rights depend entirely on the legal system we live under or are there certain "natural", or "human", rights that are common to us all and that transcend the law of the land?

The general idea of a legal right seems straightforward. We know that there are laws that aim to protect us, for example, from assault and fraud. However, this is not the only sense in which we use the idea of a right. The law may not recognize a right that some claim it should, for example the right of a homosexual couple to adopt a child. In such cases it is claimed that there is a moral right that, as yet, is not a legal one. The question of what our rights are is not settled, therefore, simply by looking at the relevant legislation.

The notion of a moral right, sometimes called a "natural right", or, most commonly now, a "human right", is not easy to grasp. Indeed it has been regarded as incoherent. Jeremy Bentham (see p.197), commenting upon the French revolutionary "Declaration of the Rights of Man and Citizen" (1789), which set out what it claimed were the "natural, imprescriptible [inalienable], sacred rights of man", declared that "natural rights is simple nonsense; natural and imprescriptible rights rhetorical nonsense – nonsense upon stilts". Bentham argued that the only rights that make any sense are those given by law, and so a natural right – by definition a right not given by law – is a contradiction in terms.

The French National Assembly's "Declaration of the Rights of Man and Citizen" set out democratic ideals for the masses.

Bentham sets a significant puzzle, even if few in the West today would dismiss the idea of natural, or human, rights so quickly. To make progress the structure of a right needs examination. As clarified by the American legal theorist Wesley Hohfeld (1879–1918), the notion of a right is intimately bound up with that of a duty. If I have a right not to be killed then there must be a corresponding duty on others not to kill me. Sometimes the duty may fall on one particular person, as is common with rights and duties created by contracts and promises, but the human right of one person can mean duties for everyone else. Accordingly many rights theorists have become dismayed about the proliferation of rights claims in the second half of the 20th century, for such "rights inflation" threatens to devalue them all. For example, many philosophers have objected to the inclusion of a right to vacations with pay in the 1948 United Nations' "Universal Declaration of Human Rights" (see box, p.194), because it is not always apparent on whom the corresponding duty falls. It is not clear that employers, or the government, can always afford to meet this duty, especially in poor countries. Perhaps no one has the duty. But what, then, becomes of the right?

The Universal Declaration of Human Rights

In 1945 representatives of 50 countries met to draw up the United Nations Charter. The horrors of the recent world war led the delegates to pay special attention to the idea of human rights. This eventually resulted, in 1948, in a visionary and aspirational "Universal Declaration of Human Rights", incorporating economic and social rights alongside the more obvious political rights. At its heart is the idea that all human beings have the right to be treated with dignity and respect, whatever their sex, race, religion or national or ethnic identity. Although intended as a statement of aspiration rather than a treaty binding on all nations, the Declaration has been adopted, at least in principle, by most countries. Violations, though still common, are treated as morally inexcusable, and international pressure is often brought to bear on "rogue" states in an attempt to bring their practices into line.

This complaint against rights inflation is closely related to a debate between those, such as the libertarian Robert Nozick (1938–2002), who believe that the only genuine human rights are "negative rights" (rights to non-interference), and those, such as followers of John Rawls (see p.203), who believe that there are "positive rights" (rights to assistance). For example, like all rights, my claimed right to life generates duties for others. But what duties, exactly? Certainly the duty of non-interference – the duty not to kill me. But if my life is threatened because I have no food or I am seriously ill, does my right to life mean that others have a duty of assistance, which obliges them to feed me or provide medical aid? Of course, some people do have special duties of this kind, perhaps parents and doctors, but does the duty fall on all?

Any attempt to settle this question requires a deeper analysis of the idea of a right, and in particular, attention to the issue of *why* we may be said to have rights. By one analysis, defended by the Oxford legal theorist Joseph Raz, we have rights in order to protect our vital interests. This is known as the "interest" or "benefit" theory of rights. Certain negative rights are very easily justified in this framework. We have rights against arbitrary arrest, for example, because our vital interests require security, which would be impossible if we were subject to detention merely on the whim of the government or its agents. So to protect our interest in having a fair chance to live the life we want to live, we need certain negative rights of non-interference and indeed some positive rights of assistance. For example, according to this theory, there should be a positive right to emergency medical care.

One important objection to benefit theory is that it appears unable to explain how we can have rights to do things that do not protect our interests. According to the theory, for example, the right to commit suicide seems very hard to justify .

The main competitor to benefit theory is choice theory, defended by, among others, the political philosopher Hillel Steiner. This starts with the claim that there is a range of issues in which my choice, and my choice alone, should determine what should happen. Initially, this sounds very plausible, and certainly solves the "right to suicide" problem. However, the theory has the apparent defect that those incapable of making choices, such as very young children or adults in a persistent vegetative state, have no rights. While some rights theorists accept this as the natural consequence of their view, others consider it a serious enough objection to reject choice theory. After all, do we really want to say that an infant has, strictly speaking, no rights?

Clearly both theories have their advantages and disadvantages. A new generation of theorists is attempting to arrive at a hybrid view that combines the strengths of both theories while avoiding their weaknesses, in which it is argued, for example, that although rights exist to protect our vital interests, one of our interests is freedom of choice. In this view it is possible to argue that those who choose to harm themselves may have the right to do so.

Laws

Most of us accept without question that the government has the right and duty to pass laws to regulate and coordinate our behaviour. But what, precisely, is a law? What makes a law good or bad, and what should we do if we disagree with the law?

Without law, argued John Locke (see pp.82–83), even the best of motives would not stop us from falling into grave disputes. For even if we all want to act well, we may have different ideas of what this means. With a declared law – even if we do not agree with every detail of it – we at least know how to govern our own lives, aware of what we must not do and what may befall us if we step over the mark.

Thomas Hobbes (see pp.184–185) defined law simply as the command of the sovereign. This straightforward view expresses Hobbes' disagreement with Thomas Aquinas (see p.112), who argued that an unjust law is no law at all, and that there are moral constraints to what can even count as law. Whether one has more sympathy with Hobbes or Aquinas, most would agree that there can be good and bad laws. What makes a law good or bad is another question, as is what we should do about it once we have decided that a law is bad.

Laws can be bad in the sense that they are inefficient. But they can, it seems, also be morally bad: perhaps unfair or overly restrictive. Should, then, laws simply attempt to codify the current conventional morality in society? This is the conservative view. Of course morality is never entirely static, but essentially, according to this view, the law is a declaration of society's belief that certain behaviour should not be permitted because it is morally wrong. This contrasts with the liberal view, which argues that the law should not take a moral stance. Rather, it should create a framework in which people can live according to their own ideas of what is valuable, without having a conventional view forced upon them. Of course, even from the liberal standpoint, the law must prohibit actions and

> *"Laws and institutions require to be adapted not to good men, but to bad."*
>
> John Stuart Mill, *The Subjection of Women*

A protester in London defies the law by openly smoking a marijuana cigarette during a demonstration calling for the legalization of cannabis. Liberal theorists argue that an activity that potentially harms only the user should be legal. At the same time, non-smokers are increasingly aware of the dangers of "passive smoking", leading to constraints on tobacco smoking – an activity once unrestricted in many parts of the world.

Civil disobedience

In his famed *Letter from Birmingham Jail* (1963), Reverend Martin Luther King (1929–68) quoted Thomas Aquinas' dictum that "an unjust law is no law at all" to explain his readiness to break the law in his campaign for civil rights for the black minority. Laws requiring segregation degrade both blacks and whites, argued King, and so have no moral authority. Such laws must be openly disobeyed as a way of appealing to the conscience of a community. Non-violent civil disobedience is a form of protest that, while protesting against particular laws, is intended to respect the rule of law in general, since the laws are broken openly and the penalties freely accepted. In King's hands, it proved a very effective tool indeed, even though he did not live to see the completion of the struggle he led.

Martin Luther King was not the first to use this form of protest. Deeply shocked by his experience of discrimination against his fellow Indians in Natal, South Africa, the lawyer Mohandas K. ("Mahatma") Gandhi (1869–1948) instigated a similar campaign in the early twentieth century. He returned to his native India and by 1920 became the effective leader of the Indian nationalists, beginning a mass movement of non-violent civil disobedience against British rule. Independence was eventually achieved in 1947, although Gandhi failed to prevent the partition of the country into India and Pakistan and the accompanying violence between Hindus and Muslims. He made unceasing efforts to reconcile the two sides until he was assassinated by a Hindu fanatic in 1948.

activities that cause, or risk causing, actual harm. But this is the only justification for lawmaking – to prevent people from harming others.

This liberal account of the proper function of law depends, of course, on how we understand the idea of "harm". If we allowed any affront to one's beliefs to count as harm, the liberal theory of law would collapse into incoherence, because there are times when one cannot act at all without offending against someone's moral beliefs. So a more neutral definition of harm is needed if any progress is to be made: perhaps physical harm or harm to material and financial interests is a fair start.

However, we are used to living under laws that cannot be justified solely on this liberal basis that they prevent physical or financial harm to others. We have laws designed to protect people from themselves, for example prohibiting the taking of certain drugs. This is known as paternalism: the law acts as a father might act with regard to his children. We also have laws that do appear to take a moral stand, for example those that prohibit incest. This is known as legal moralism. But how can the liberal justify the banning of drugs if users are only harming themselves? Similarly, why should incest between consenting adults be illegal? And if there is nothing wrong with prostitution (as in the liberal view there should not be), why is living off the earnings of a prostitute illegal? From a fully liberal standpoint such laws are not justified. In order to resolve this apparent anomaly, a consistent liberal will have either to show that drug taking, incest and prostitution *do* harm those who do not take part in them (for example, they could point to the wider social harm caused by organized criminals who fund their activities by drug dealing), or argue that the laws against such practices should be reviewed and reformed as necessary.

Bentham

Coming from a legal family, Jeremy Bentham was destined for a career in law, but convinced his father that he was better suited to the criticism of the law, rather than its practice, and this is how he spent his life.

Bentham's best known work, *An Introduction to the Principles of Morals and Legislation* begins with the controversial claim – albeit one that seemed obvious to Bentham – that "Nature has given us two sovereign masters; pleasure and pain". This gave Bentham both his theory of human psychology – that human beings seek pleasure and try to avoid pain – and his theory of morality, that we should maximize the balance of pleasure over pain. Utilitarianism, therefore, asks us to pursue the course of action that will most tend to promote pleasure. This, in turn, requires us to calculate, or at least estimate, how anyone affected by our decision would be affected by any alternative course, and to include their pleasure or pain in the calculation to arrive at a sum total. Finally, we should follow the course of action which produces the highest total of happiness. This simple idea dominates all Bentham's social thinking, especially in the areas of law, punishment and social reform.

Utilitarianism has been criticized for its insensitivity to the distribution of happiness, because the greatest total of happiness may be achieved by a policy that has terrible consequences for a small minority. In principle we could, for example, sometimes maximize happiness by punishing an innocent person or making someone a slave. Bentham's response would be that the consequences of such action would always be worse in the long run: for example, if we suspected that we lived in a society that sometimes punished the innocent, we might all become anxious and unhappy. Whether or not one finds this a convincing response, Bentham's intention was to present a radical, deeply humane theory, which emphasizes that nothing is good or bad unless it is good or bad for human beings or other sentient creatures. The fact that a certain action is claimed, say, to add to the glory of God, is for Bentham a reason neither for nor against it. Utilitarianism is a rational rather than religious basis for morality.

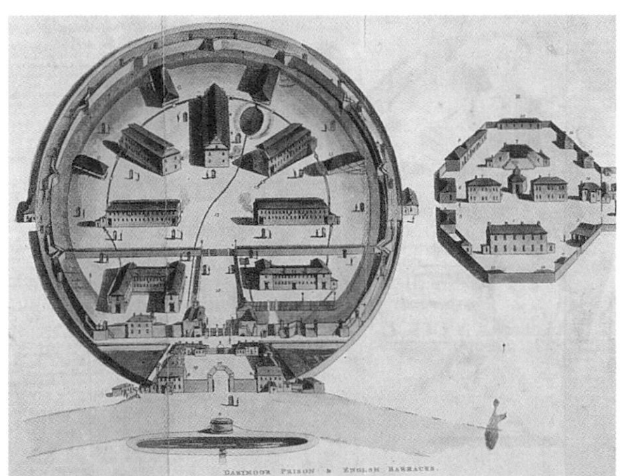

In Bentham's Panopticon prison design, inmates can be kept under constant observation by a limited number of warders.

Bentham's influence continues to be felt today in much of public administration. For example, the practice of calculating the costs and benefits of various policy options has its origins in his work. His theory of punishment, which aims to strike a balance between humaneness and cost-effectiveness, also carries weight. Bentham even produced a design for a prison to reflect his ideas. Known as the Panopticon, from the Greek meaning "all-seeing", the plan allowed the maximum inspection of prisoners with the minimum of staff.

Jeremy Bentham 1748–1832

A prolific writer, Jeremy Bentham produced works on morality, politics, economics and law. He is best known as the founder of utilitarianism, the doctrine that it is the moral duty of individuals and government to bring about in society the greatest balance of happiness – understood as pleasure – over pain.

“To base a justification of punishment on threat is to liken it to the act of a man who lifts his stick to a dog. It is to treat a man like a dog instead of with the freedom and respect due to him as a man.”
Georg Hegel, The Philosophy of Right

Crime and punishment

Most people will accept that every society needs to have laws and some form of sanctions on those who break them. But is breaking a law always a crime, in the sense of rendering one liable for punishment? And what, in any case, justifies punishment?

The concept of crime goes hand in hand with that of law: on the face of it, to commit a crime is to break a law. However, acting in a way that is contrary to the letter of the law is not always regarded as a crime. For criminal responsibility – liability to punishment – requires not just a "guilty act", but normally a "guilty mind" too. A person will often escape criminal responsibility, and hence punishment, if it can be shown either that the act was committed unintentionally or that he or she lacked sufficient rational capacity to understand fully what they were doing. To be criminally responsible, it is not normally necessary to know that one was breaking a law – ignorance of the law is no excuse – but one has to be considered capable of knowing what one was doing; what action one was performing. For this reason children below a certain age, and the insane, normally escape criminal responsibility. Hence the notion of criminal responsibility seems to presuppose a notion of moral responsibility. If one is not morally responsible then often one is not criminally responsible either.

> *...Anyone who maims another shall suffer the same injury in return: fracture for fracture, eye for eye, tooth for tooth; the injury inflicted is the injury to be suffered.*
>
> Leviticus 19–21

Ordinary adults, in exceptional circumstances, may also escape both moral and legal responsibility. In cases of duress, for example, a person may be so overcome by fear, perhaps of torture, that his or her rational capacity is destroyed, resulting in a lack of responsibility for subsequent actions. In addition to cases of duress, provocation leading to a loss of self-control can also function as a partial defence, although rarely a complete one.

Justifying crime

Even those in full rational control of their decision-making faculties can avoid criminal liability in certain circumstances. Sometimes it may seem necessary to break a law in order to comply with some more urgent duty. For example, I might jump a stop light if I am driving a heart attack victim to hospital. In other cases it is simply impossible for individuals to avoid breaking the law, even though they know exactly what they are doing. Some vagrancy laws prohibit people from sleeping in the streets even if they have nowhere else to go. Enforcing such a law can seem unfair, and different courts often take different views about the defence of "necessity".

There are, of course, also cases in which people may have the option of following the law, but doing so would have disastrous consequences, and the most reasonable solution may be to break the law. Consider the mother who can only feed her children by stealing. This, we may be inclined to say, is a morally justified breach of the law, in that it is illegal but excusable. Even so it is likely to lead to some sort of punishment if detected, although possibly of a rather token or lenient nature.

Justifying punishment

It is generally agreed that crime should be punished, but what is the justification for punishment? Philosophers have three main approaches to this issue. Two of these, centring on the ideas of deterrence and reform, look ahead to the consequences of punishment, and ask what good might be done by it. The third looks backward: a crime has been committed and a punishment must be found to fit the crime. This is the retributive theory of punishment.

The point of deterrence, obviously enough, is to deter people from committing criminal actions. Sometimes merely laying down a penalty will have this effect, but often it will not and so criminals must be caught and punished. This, it is hoped, will act to deter others in the future. This is the idea of "making an example" of the guilty.

One difficulty with the deterrence theory is knowing where to stop. That is, it is reasonable to assume that very heavy punishment is likely to be the most effective deterrent. Cutting off the hand of convicted shoplifters would probably reduce the crime rate. Yet many people, criminal and non-criminal alike, would view this as disproportionate, and therefore unjust. So the difficult question for advocates of the deterrence theory is: how should we balance deterrence of criminal actions with just treatment of the offenders? In 18th-century England, attempts to stem the crime rate led to the death penalty being applied to more than 200 offences, including sheep-stealing and "theft on a navigable river". The consequence was that juries often acquitted criminals rather than see them hanged. This led to a situation in which much crime was either punished disproportionately or not punished at all.

Concern for the criminal finds expression in the reform theory, which is based on the humane idea that we should help criminals to overcome their anti-social behaviour – literally teach them a lesson. It is therefore addressed to the criminals themselves, rather than the public at large or indeed the victims of crime. A major difficulty here is finding an effective means of reform. Although a fine or a prison sentence may have the desired deterrent effect, there is certainly no guarantee of this, and the opposite effect – an increased contempt for the law – unfortunately seems just as likely to result. Although claims are often made linking particular forms of punishment to reduced rates of reoffence, there is little clear evidence that any form of punishment really has this effect, since so many other factors may also contribute to an individual's behaviour.

> *To deprive the criminal of the life of which he has proved himself to be unworthy ... is the most appropriate as it is certainly the most impressive mode in which society can attach to so great a crime the penal consequences which for the security of life it is indispensable to annex to it.*
>
> John Stuart Mill, "[1868] Speech in Favour of Capital Punishment"

It is also sometimes objected that reform theory is overly concerned with the plight of the criminal at the expense of society in general and the victim in particular, and forgets that the point of a system of punishment is exactly that – to punish. This issue is at the heart of the theory of retribution. According to this theory, the point of punishment is to restore a moral balance. Justice requires that wrong-doers must suffer. This approach has been out of favour with liberal thinkers for the reason that it seems a primitive, vindictive and emotional response to crime. However, it cannot be denied that victims of crime often do have precisely this response and can think of themselves as doubly injured if justice, in this sense, is not done.

In practice our attitude to punishment probably includes elements of all three theories. The dilemma we may all feel is whether we should "rise above" any feelings of revenge or retribution and restrict ourselves to the task of trying to improve things for the future, or accept that we suffer from a type of moral shallowness if we ignore the basic principle that those who have committed a crime deserve punishment. Indeed, the German philosopher Hegel (see p.30) went so far as to argue that the criminal has a right to be punished, and in a perhaps surprising argument claims that conceiving of punishment in this way shows our respect for the will and humanity of the criminal.

Capital punishment

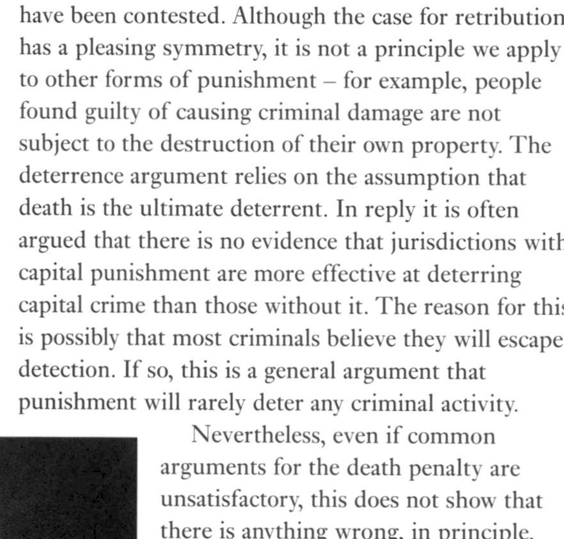

Capital punishment – the death penalty – is currently legal in the majority of US states, in Japan, China and around 80 other countries. But it has been abolished in most European countries and in much of South and Central America. In most places where it is legal, capital punishment is applied only in the case of murder, but practice differs from country to country and it may also be applied to other offences, such as drug dealing.

Can capital punishment be justified? The topic has always engaged strong feelings. The defence of capital punishment relies on arguments based on retribution – that those who take a life deserve to forfeit their own – and deterrence. Reform, obviously enough, does not apply. Both the retribution and deterrence arguments have been contested. Although the case for retribution has a pleasing symmetry, it is not a principle we apply to other forms of punishment – for example, people found guilty of causing criminal damage are not subject to the destruction of their own property. The deterrence argument relies on the assumption that death is the ultimate deterrent. In reply it is often argued that there is no evidence that jurisdictions with capital punishment are more effective at deterring capital crime than those without it. The reason for this is possibly that most criminals believe they will escape detection. If so, this is a general argument that punishment will rarely deter any criminal activity.

Nevertheless, even if common arguments for the death penalty are unsatisfactory, this does not show that there is anything wrong, in principle, with such a punishment. All punishment inflicts a degree of suffering on the convicted criminal. Why should the death penalty be singled out for special attention? Some will say that we have to respect the sanctity of life. However, outside a religious framework it is hard to make sense of this claim.

Perhaps the strongest argument against capital punishment is simply its finality. There is no correcting of mistakes. This was acknowledged by John Stuart Mill (see p.139), who, although celebrated for his liberal views, spoke in defence of capital punishment when a British Member of Parliament. At a time when the alternative to the death sentence was life imprisonment with hard labour, Mill claimed that death was a greater fear, and thus a better deterrent, than hard labour, yet somewhat paradoxically a lesser harm. Mill argued that, irrationally in this case, we fear the lesser harm. Mill conceded that the death penalty should be used only in cases of absolute certainty. Yet critics fairly point out – as indeed Mill himself argues elsewhere – that this is a standard we cannot meet in practical matters, and in murder trials, where passions and emotions run high, mistakes can easily be made.

Social justice

Justice is often understood in legal terms. However, social justice is a moral, not a legal, issue. Put simply, it involves giving each person what he or she is entitled to. Deciding how this entitlement should be calculated remains at the centre of philosophical debate.

Legal justice is a matter both of the correct application of the laws of the land, and the prior derivation and implementation of fair principles of law. Economic or social justice is harder to pin down. The simplest definition is "giving each person their due". But this in turn requires a definition of what people are due, and this is far from simple. Alternatively, justice may be defined as "treating like cases alike". Accordingly, it is unjust to treat people in different ways unless there are relevant differences between them. So, for example, it is generally considered perfectly just to give one person a job rather than another if the first is more talented than the second, but not if the only difference between them is their gender. However, it will not always be as clear as this which differences are relevant.

> *The prevailing belief in 'social justice' is at present probably the gravest threat to most other values of a free civilization.*
>
> Frederick von Hayek, *The Mirage of Social Justice.*

The obscure nature of social justice has led some thinkers, such as Frederick von Hayek (1899–1992), to deny that there is any such thing. Nevertheless, various accounts have been offered. According to one view, social justice requires taking into account all of those affected by a decision, and trying to arrive at a resolution that produces the best accommodation of all interests. This, then, bases justice on the idea of looking at things from the other person's point of view, and is termed "justice as impartiality".

An alternative view is that social justice is more a matter of fair distribution of the burdens and benefits of social cooperation. This conception starts from the premise that if human beings cooperate they can produce much more than if each person lived and worked in isolation. This additional yield is regarded as a "surplus", and justice requires a fair division both of the surplus itself and of the efforts that went to produce it. The idea that those who work should receive fair reward for their efforts is central to this theory, which is commonly known as the theory of "justice as mutual advantage".

But what about those who are unable to work, and thus cannot contribute to the creation of the surplus? Do they have any claim on others for assistance? From the point of view of justice as impartiality we need only ask: "In their position, would we feel that we need the help of others?" From the likely affirmative answer it seems clear that their claim is indeed justified. However, from the position of justice as mutual advantage those who do not contribute have no claim as they play no part in the system of cooperation. Consequently, although we may help those who cannot help themselves out of charity, we have no duty of justice, according to this theory, to do so.

It appears to follow from the theory of justice as impartiality that being born with little talent, or with a disability that makes it impossible to work, should be seen as unjust in itself. However, some have disputed this, arguing that nature itself is neither just nor unjust; these are terms that can only apply to people and the consequences of their actions – it is not the fact of differential talent that is unjust, but how we choose to respond to it. Any injustice derives from the social arrangements that reward different talents with different life prospects.

Rawls

Rawls' masterpiece, *A Theory of Justice* (1971, revised 1999) sets out the principles that he believes should govern society. First, each person should be accorded the most extensive basic liberties compatible with a similar set for all (the "liberty principle"). Second, everyone should have a chance not only to exercise their talents but to acquire such talents in the first place (the "fair opportunity principle"). Third, and most distinctively, Rawls argues that justice requires of us to act according to what he calls the "difference principle": that we should make the worst off as well off as possible.

John Rawls 1921–2002

In the view of many, the Harvard philosopher John Rawls was the greatest political philosopher of the 20th century. His theory of social justice was developed by means of a modified form of social contract theory, from which he derived principles that combine ideas of liberty, equality and economic efficiency.

The liberty principle is not the idea that we should be free to do what we want, irrespective of the effects on others, but rather that each person should have equal and extensive civil rights and liberties such as the freedom of speech. Rawls clarifies his position by arguing that if the principles clash, the liberty principle should be satisfied first, then the fair opportunity principle, and last the difference principle. The only case in which our liberties can legitimately be restricted is in times of grave scarcity. Otherwise basic liberty is more important than economic advantage.

Even if we think that justice requires an equal division of resources, there is a sense in which this is likely to be inefficient. A system with incentives for people to work hard may well create a much larger stock of resources than a system of flat equality. Indeed the surplus created could be redistributed to make everyone better off. In certain circumstances, therefore, even the worst off could benefit from inequality. Hence Rawls derives his simple but much-debated principle that a society is just only if the worst off in that society are better off than they would be under any other arrangement.

Rawls's originality lies not only in his principles of justice, but also in his method for devising them. He proposes a thought experiment in which a collection of people, each representing different social groups, comes together to try to agree on a set of principles to regulate their society. This he calls "the original position". However it is unlikely that such a group would agree to anything, because of the diversity of individual interests and values. Consequently, Rawls suggested, they should each be imagined to be ignorant of their own sex, race, talents, values and so on. Behind this "veil of ignorance" people do not know how the principles would affect them personally. They do know that everyone wants what Rawls calls the "primary goods": liberty, opportunity, income, wealth and "the social bases of self-respect". These, Rawls argues, are goods that will help you whatever your particular ends in life. Ignorance, under these circumstances, generates impartiality, and so the parties in "the original position" choose in everyone's interests. Rawls argues that it is this impartiality that will lead people to choose his principles of justice, for they are designed to support the position of everyone, refusing to sacrifice any group in society for the sake of any other.

> "*Rights secured by justice are not subject to political bargaining or the calculus of social interests.*"
>
> John Rawls, *A Theory of Justice*

Equality

Most countries today make an explicit and legally binding commitment to the equality of all their citizens. But the idea of equality comes in many different forms. Political equality and economic equality may be two quite different things.

Whether one believes that equality among human beings is an achievable, or even a desirable, aspiration depends to a large extent on how one understands equality. Some believe that in order for two people to be considered equal they have to possess an identical set of attributes. As this is not the case even for the most closely related individuals, they argue, it is nonsense to think that human beings in general are born equal. However, critics of this viewpoint maintain that the claim to the right to be treated as an equal is not premised on claims about factual equality – identity of attributes. Consequently, demonstrating the existence of factual inequalities does nothing to undermine the case for moral and political equality.

Perhaps the clearest notion of equality is equality before the law. This is the principle that the law should apply equally to all, irrespective of social status, gender, race, wealth, birth or other privileges. Although often taken for granted in theory, whether it applies in practice is quite another matter. Socio-legal studies often suggest that members of some groups are more likely to be found guilty of crimes than another, or that they are more likely

This painting by John Trumbull shows the signing of the United States Declaration of Independence in 1776. Perhaps the most influential statement in the Declaration is that "all men are created equal" – not in terms of their abilities but in terms of their rights.

to be brought to trial if arrested. Nevertheless, few people would seriously defend the idea of inequality before the law, however imperfectly equality is realized in practice.

Closely related to equality before the law is political equality: equal rights to vote, stand for office and so on. Again there is wide agreement that all citizens are equally entitled to such rights, but what makes one a citizen is a more difficult question. Is residence enough, or can there be resident non-citizens – perhaps "guest workers" – who enjoy a reduced set of political rights? Even among citizens discriminations may be made; for example, the US Constitution states that only "natural born" US citizens are permitted to run for president. Nevertheless the general idea of equal political rights for citizens is widely accepted.

More controversial is the idea of equality of opportunity. In its simplest form, this involves non-discrimination, particularly in employment, both in initial appointment and in terms and conditions. For example, in the United Kingdom until 1975 it was common to advertise jobs with two rates of pay, with a lower rate for women. Clearly this violated any ideal of equality of opportunity. However not all cases are so clear. If a job requires physical strength, does equality require that men and women both take the same qualifying test? Or does it require different tests to take into account the fact that women typically are not as strong as men? The answer may depend on the context: for example, if a certain level of physical strength is indispensable to the safe or competent performance of a task, it would seem irresponsible to do anything other than apply exactly the same test.

This idea of equality of opportunity is essentially that of meritocracy, whereby a job, or a university place, should go to the best qualified person irrespective of their gender, or ethnic background, or the school they went to or their family connections. However, it ignores the fact that the ability to acquire talents and qualifications varies considerably, especially given people's different family backgrounds, which provide widely differing levels of financial and emotional support. Does true equality of opportunity, therefore, require remedial education and training to give everyone an equal chance of acquiring talents? And if the family really is a barrier to equal opportunity, does the demand for the latter mean that we should even consider the abolition of the family? Few would wish to go so far, yet it seems to be one possible consequence of an unstinting pursuit of equality.

Economic equality

Perhaps just as controversial is the idea of economic equality. This idea comes in several forms. One is the theory that all people should receive equal resources: essentially, equal income and wealth. Another theory, found in Marxism, is that people should have an equal opportunity to meet their needs. A third, somewhat different, idea is that all should have an equal chance of achieving happiness, or a fulfilling life, and that economies should be structured to achieve this goal. Economic equality, then, is a matter of using the economy to achieve an ideal of equality. Strict equality of economic goods (equal distribution of money and other wealth) is only one version of such a theory.

There is much philosophical dispute as to which theory best fulfils the idea of economic equality. However, some philosophers have argued that the broad political aim of equality does not require equality of any particular thing. Rather it should aim at the avoidance of poverty and a secure framework in which people may determine the contours of their own lives on the basis of their own choices. And, indeed, in Western societies the elimination of poverty has more often been the goal of economic policy than the achievement of some form of economic equality. But it remains a matter of deep dispute whether this reflects a morally justified realism on the part of governments, or a cowardly deference to existing entrenched privilege.

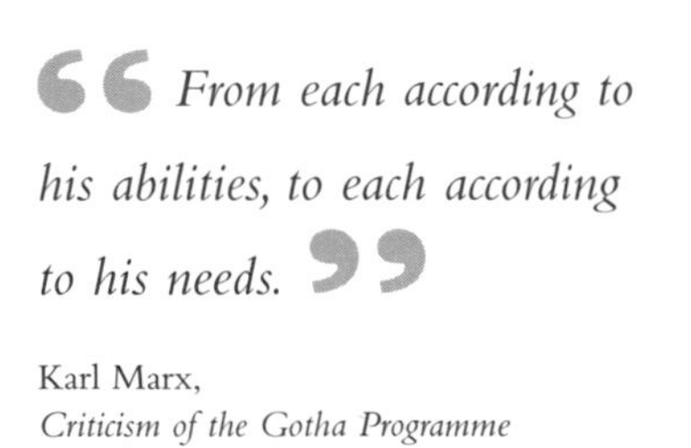

"From each according to his abilities, to each according to his needs."

Karl Marx,
Criticism of the Gotha Programme

Ownership

The right of individual ownership is essentially the right of exclusive use. To deny this right is to advocate systems of common property, such as communism. Hence the question of the justification of individual property rights is of fundamental moral and political significance.

Private property is not so much a thing as a cluster of rights between a person and a thing. These can include the right to possess; to enjoy; to exclude others; to destroy; to sell; to rent out; and perhaps other rights too. These rights can be separated. Feudal serfs, for example, had the right to occupy and cultivate their land, but not to sell it. But the central philosophical question is how anyone can come to hold any of these rights.

> *"The fruits of the earth belong to everyone; the earth itself to no one."*
>
> Jean-Jacques Rousseau, *Discourse on Inequality*

Every material object and all land now in private hands was either once unowned or is derived from something once unowned. Property requires initial appropriation: there has to be a first owner. When an object is unowned anyone may exercise certain rights over it: they may walk on it, touch it and so on. Yet once it becomes someone's property no one may perform such actions without the permission of the new owner. The act of appropriation, then, not only generates new rights, but also cancels existing rights of everyone else. How can this happen? Some say that it cannot, and so advocate communist systems of property.

John Locke (see pp.82–83) provided a philosophical defence of individual property rights that remains at the forefront of debate even today. He was writing at a time when the monarch was theoretically regarded as having the right to tax or dispossess individuals at will: the legacy of the feudal theory of property. However, Locke argued that those who labour have a natural right to the fruits of their labour. In extending this reasoning to the ownership of land, he argues that each person owns himself and his labour. Just as one has a right

Hegel: Property as self-expression

Many defences of ownership are based, ultimately, on need. Locke argued that we must make objects our private property if we are to survive. For to survive we must consume and therefore destroy objects, and what right can we have to do this if we do not own them? The German idealist philosopher G.W.F. Hegel (see p.30) saw things very differently, however. Property, he argued, is a form of self-expression. It is the externalization of the will into an object that has no will of its own. To appropriate an object is to give it a purpose; it becomes an extension of the self of the property owner.

This gives a pleasing rationale to why it is one comes to own what one has made or modified: there is a sense in which you have put yourself into it. Not your labour, as Locke would have it, but your will. You have modified it in accordance with your intentions, and so it seems fitting that it should become the property of you, rather than of someone else or of no one. There is also something appealing in the argument that property can be a form of self-expression; but the question remains of whether this argument can be extended to justify property rights as we know them, which include the right to sell, bequeath and dispose of property as we wish. For can the purchaser of property also be said to be expressing his or her will through ownership? Perhaps, but surely not in the same way that its original owner was.

Formerly known as Ayers Rock, Uluru in Australia's Northern Territories officially reverted to an indigenous name in 1985 when the Australian government recognized the group ownership rights of the local Aboriginal peoples.

to whatever one owns, one has a right to anything that is inextricably mixed with what one owns, as long as that thing was not previously owned by anyone else. In labouring on land, Locke suggests, one inextricably combines one's labour with that land and thereby comes to own it. He adds two further conditions for such appropriation to be legitimate. First, what one takes into ownership must not be wasted, and, second, one must leave "enough and as good for others". Plausible though Locke's argument may seem, its main flaw is that he does not explain why labouring is not a way of losing your labour rather than gaining that on which one labours. More generally, though, while it is common to believe that people are entitled to whatever they work on or make, it is hard to develop this into a moral justification of private property rights, particularly permanent rights that may be bequeathed and inherited – the type of property rights we commonly recognize today.

But what if we denied individual rights of ownership? We would be committed to some form of communism. Yet human experience of communism, at least in its Marxist-Leninist form, has been dismal. It is a commonplace to say that communism has not worked. This observation then becomes an argument for the alternative to communism: a system of private property rights.

This argument justifies ownership rights in terms of their beneficial effects. The idea that property can be justified because it is a beneficial human convention, rather than a matter of natural right, was defended by David Hume (see pp.24–25). Contemporary followers of Hume argue that private property, coupled with a free market (perhaps modified to allow governments to supply public facilities such as roads and emergency services, and limited support for the poor) does more to advance human well-being than any alternative system, such as the common property of communist utopia. Typically the argument emphasizes the incentives provided by property rights and the possibility of profits. According to this view, how exactly the initial appropriation takes place becomes less important. The vital issue is to get land and other property into private hands so that it can be used effectively. It is, of course, an empirical claim that private ownership has such advantages, and it may be that this argument also justifies reserving areas of common property. It must also of necessity grant governments a significant role in precisely determining what a right in property entails. So while this argument will not yield absolute property rights, it does provide a foundation for individual rights to both the ownership of land and of goods (see also box, opposite).

Rich and poor

One of the most startling aspects of the modern world is the coexistence of extremes of wealth and poverty. According to the UN, the assets of the world's three richest people are greater than the combined GNP of 600 million people in the world's poorest countries.

It has become a commonplace that there are almost unimaginable disparities in wealth between the richest people in the richest countries and the poorest of the poor countries. However, the first question to ask is what it means to be rich or poor. For obvious reasons much more attention has been given to defining poverty than to defining wealth, but neither is a simple matter.

One common way to define poverty is to set a "poverty line", defined as a certain level of income: any individual or family receiving an income below this line is then said to be poor. But where do we draw this line? Sometimes it is set it in relative terms, for example at half of the median income in a society. One criticism of this approach is that people may drop below the poverty line even when their income is rising, if it is rising less quickly than is average for their society. For this reason some theorists prefer an absolute measure. But no one income figure can represent an absolute poverty line, for what you can buy depends on local prices and other factors, which may vary from society to society. For example, whether one spends income on buying a car may depend on the

The Indian city of Mumbai (formerly Bombay) provides a stark contrast between rich and poor. Although Mumbai boasts some of the most valuable real estate in the world, more than half of the city's inhabitants live in slums or, literally, on the street.

Poverty relief and dependence

The argument that society has a duty to care for those who cannot take care of themselves is widespread. At the same time many people implicitly or explicitly make a distinction between the "deserving poor" – who, through no fault of their own, cannot work – and the "undeserving poor" – who, it is believed, choose not to work. The latter, it is claimed, do not deserve support. Societies observe this distinction more or less strictly, but they all face the issue of how to balance a concern for the needs of the poor against the cost of providing for everyone who makes a claim. Sometimes this may seem an impossible dilemma: generous support for the poor is alleged to encourage a culture of dependency in which people rely on the state rather than on their own efforts. Yet it has been counter-argued that voluntary unemployment is caused not by the attractiveness of unemployment benefit, but by the poor pay and conditions of available jobs. In this view, few people are happy to depend on others, and most would rather support themselves and their families through their own efforts. The truth is probably that no single argument explains all voluntarily unemployment. All societies face the dilemma of, on the one hand, not encouraging people to rely on welfare benefits, while on the other hand treating those who receive them in a humane and dignified manner.

adequacy of local public transport. Again, what one perceives as necessary for a respectable life varies greatly from society to society.

Consequently, measures of absolute poverty must focus on what one can do with one's income. A simplistic account defines poverty in terms of one's ability to purchase a "basket of goods", where the "basket" will include such things as adequate accommodation, a nutritious diet and so on. More sophisticated measures concentrate entirely on what one can achieve, rather than simply purchase. The Nobel Prize-winning economist and philosopher Amatrya Sen has proposed the idea of "basic capability for functioning", and a similar idea has recently been adopted by the United Nations in its annual Human Development Report. This uses what it calls the "human poverty index" and, for developing countries, concentrates on life expectancy, adult literacy and certain economic provisioning (including access to health services, safe water and infant nutrition), rather than any absolute or relative income figure. This gives a much more realistic account of what it is to fail to meet a threshold of basic requirements.

> *The power of population is indefinitely greater than the power in the earth to produce subsistence for man.*
>
> Thomas Malthus, *An Essay on the Principle of Population*

Sharing the wealth

It seems beyond dispute that much of the worst of the world's poverty could be eliminated through a relatively modest transfer of resources from the wealthiest countries to the poorest. Millions of lives could be saved, and hundreds of millions of them improved, with little effect on the living standards enjoyed by the wealthy. As the contemporary philosopher Peter Singer has argued, it seems that there is a compelling moral case to make such transfers – it is little more than the duty of common decency. Yet it is curious that even those who accept this argument, whether as private citizens or politicians, do so little to put it into effect. If we could relieve the great suffering of those near to us at minimal cost we would regard it as monstrous if we failed to act. Yet as the distance increases we seem to expect less and less of ourselves. Perhaps distant suffering is less vivid, or we doubt that our efforts will be effective when we cannot intervene in person. Perhaps there is also a thought, expressed well by the English economist Thomas Malthus (1766–1834), that as long as population continues to increase, which it almost inevitably will, large-scale misery is unavoidable. Nevertheless, our failure to act is troubling, and it may well turn out to be one of the great moral failings of the present age.

Marx

Marx was born in the German city of Trier and initially studied law, turning to philosophy to write a doctoral thesis comparing Democritus and Epicurus. Increasingly involved in the philosophical and political controversies of his day, Marx was greatly influenced by a group of radical young thinkers known as the Young Hegelians. Marx defined his position partly in reaction both to the work of Hegel himself (see p.30) and to the Young Hegelian Ludwig Feuerbach (1804–72), who had attempted a materialist transformation of Hegel's idealism. Owing to his involvement in politics, Marx was unable to secure an academic post, and turned to journalism. However, his writing remained too radical for the authorities, and the journals he wrote for were closed down and Marx himself was exiled. Living in Paris in the early 1840s, he wrote a remarkable series of texts that show him at his most philosophical. He returned to Germany in 1848 – the year he and Friedrich Engels published the *Communist Manifesto* (see box) – to take part in the attempted revolutions that erupted that year across the region. Exiled again following their failure, Marx moved to London. From this point on he focused on the economic analysis of capitalism – the form of economy in which production is aimed at profit – and his theory of historical materialism, which sees history as driven by economic interests. Together these studies gave rise to the prediction that capitalism would eventually break down and, through revolutionary action, be replaced by communism.

Karl Marx 1818–1883

The influence of Karl Marx on 20th-century history is beyond measure. At one time close to half the population of the world lived under systems of government claiming to be founded on his ideas.

As Marx struggled to raise his family in London, Engels was living and working in Manchester, becoming sufficiently affluent to send money to Marx to relieve the worst of his poverty. Marx's life was divided between his devotion to his economic and political studies and the basic need to feed his family, while at the same time engaging in exhausting disputes with other socialist activists and theorists. Marx's great masterpiece, *Das Kapital* (*Capital*) volume 1, was published in 1867; volumes 2 and 3 were published posthumously in 1885 and 1894 respectively, having been edited by the elderly Engels (who was also busy with his own writings) from a mass of material left by Marx (see box). In *Das Kapital*, Marx argues that labour is the source of all value, and that capitalist profit is the result of the economic exploitation of the worker, by means of the "extraction of surplus value" – value created by the worker beyond that necessary to pay him or her a subsistence wage.

> “*The philosophers have only interpreted the world; the point is to change it.*”
>
> Karl Marx, *Theses on Feuerbach*

Marx's early philosophical works focus on the concept of alienation, which for Marx is not primarily a subjective state of mind, but an objective fact. According to Marx, for as long as capitalism lasts the majority of people will be unable to live lives properly worthy of a human being. This is one way in which human existence becomes alienated from the human "essence", our individual or social nature. Alienation is best understood in the context of Marx's discussion of religion, which he famously called "the opiate of the people". Feuerbach argued that God had not created man in his own image. Rather, human beings had invented a God in human image, and it is for this reason alone that humans resemble God. We have imagined the best of our features (our power, our knowledge, our benevolence), raised these features in thought to an infinite level, and then attributed them to a non-existent being. In this way, rather than enjoying the human characteristics that make up our essence, we worship this essence in the form of a distant and non-existent God. This, then, is religious alienation, and it is a barrier to living a truly human life.

Marx accepted this analysis but argued that Feuerbach had not looked deeply enough into *why* human beings acted this way. Feuerbach presents religious alienation as essentially an intellectual mistake. For Marx there must be a deeper cause, and this he finds in our economic life. Human beings, he says, are essentially productive creatures, capable of enormously creative and elaborate forms of production, in an immense network of mutual reliance. Hence we are also communal beings. However, under capitalism most of us produce in a stilted, one-sided manner that does not engage our creative powers. Perhaps even worse, we are screened off from each other and relate only through economic exchange. Hence we cannot enjoy our essence on earth, and this explains why we turn to a fictional heaven.

In Marx's view, only under communism – with common ownership of property and production – can we recapture the human essence and live a life fitting for human beings. This will involve making full use of each individual's productive capabilities and seeing other human beings as fellow members of a human community with valid needs, rather than merely as potential sources of profit. Marx is clear, however, that communism cannot be achieved merely by the force of reason or argument. First, communism presupposes a level of material wealth and production that cannot exist except as a successor to capitalism. So the historical mission of capitalism is to raise the level of productivity to the point at which communism is possible. Second, the capitalist ruling class has a powerful interest in maintaining capitalism and so will resist any attempt to change the nature of economic life. Therefore capitalism will give way to communism only as a result of a revolution by the workers – aided by intellectual revolutionary theorists such as Marx himself and his followers.

Marx and Engels

In the 1840s, Marx and Friedrich Engels (1820–95) began a collaboration that would last until Marx's death in 1883 and produced, most famously, the jointly authored *Communist Manifesto* (1848). Marx was, by mutual acknowledgment, the intellectual driving force, but Engels was an impressive writer and thinker in his own right, as well as a provider of moral and financial support to Marx. Engels edited Marx's work after his death, and controversy still rages over how faithful he was to Marx's intentions and the degree to which he distorted Marx's message. For example, it is clear from Engels' own writings that he thought that running a centrally planned communist economy would be a rather simple affair. This greatly influenced the development of "Marxist" states such as the Soviet Union. However, Marx was much more circumspect about the precise nature of communism, arguing that from the standpoint of the capitalist era it was impossible to say anything in detail about the future economic organization of communism. Engels filled the resulting theoretical vacuum with his own somewhat more dogmatic pronouncements. Nevertheless, without Engels' support, and his energy in preserving Marx's legacy after his death, few people might have been aware of Marx's work, and the history of the 20th century could have been unimaginably different.

Globalization

There is much heated debate today about globalization. To some, it is a positive force, bringing freedoms and opportunities to the peoples of underdeveloped countries. To others, globalization is simply a way for the richer nations to profit from the poorer ones.

Theories of globalization are a response to the undeniable fact of marked social and economic change throughout the globe, as a consequence of improved communications and the freer movement of people, goods and capital beyond traditional national borders. Some welcome the opportunities this brings, while others see it as a threat to established ways of life, and to the economic prosperity and even political independence of poorer nations.

Those who view globalization in negative terms point to a tendency towards the global domination of the poor by the rich. One factor contributing to this trend is homogenization. As communications improve and goods are distributed more widely, countries have come to resemble each other more and more in their material culture; or, more precisely, as stressed by the French philosopher Jean Baudrillard, they have tended to adopt the material culture of the United States, with the same shops, the same television programmes and, increasingly, the same commercial values.

The rise of the multinationals

This erosion of distinctive local and national characteristics is also a consequence of a more fundamental economic change: the growing global domination of a relatively small number of large multinational firms, which have the financial resources to enter almost any local economy worldwide. Smaller indigenous businesses find it very difficult or impossible to compete with the multinational giants, which soon reach a position of

Self-help through free trade?

Why are rich countries rich and poor countries poor? It is tempting to think that this must relate to the possession of natural resources, or the damaging effects of colonization. Yet there are rich countries without natural resources and former colonies with dynamic, wealth-generating economies. Lacking a simple cause, historical developments have resulted in a pattern of global trade that means the rich thrive and the poor stay poor. As wealthier countries have built up productive manufacturing and service bases, they export finished goods to poorer countries that often cannot compete in such markets and must continue to rely on precarious primary production, carried out by low-skilled workers under harsh conditions. Whether or not such trading conditions are unjust in themselves, they are certainly unequal in their effects.

The question of global free trade between relatively strong, wealthy economies and weak, poor ones is rarely a merely economic one; considerations of justice are also central. It is claimed by some that richer countries deliberately perpetuate their own interests and relative advantage by imposing asymmetrical terms of trade, insisting on protectionist tariffs to shield domestic industries against new competition from developing nations that could – in a truly free market – produce more cheaply because of their lower labour costs. Under present conditions, profits from wealthier countries are effectively recycled by governments to developing countries in the form of aid, which does nothing to address an underlying pattern of trade that impedes not only the economic development of the poorest nations but erodes their self-reliance. While it is possible that genuine global free trade may help poor countries, at present the less than transparent system of import tariffs and domestic subsidies means that such a claim remains untested.

Multinationals are quick to seize an opportunity: this mural in Poland would have been unimaginable under communism.

market dominance, and return their profits to shareholders who are predominantly in North America, western Europe and Japan. This process is said by critics of globalization to reinforce and accelerate global income differentials. But perhaps most worryingly, it is claimed that large multinationals can become the dominant interests in economically weak countries in which they operate. As the local economy becomes increasingly dependent on large corporations, it becomes difficult to hold these corporations fully to account, because although their presence causes problems, their absence would be economically devastating. In extreme cases a small and relatively poor country could effectively be held hostage by multinationals, which may be tempted to relax or disregard local safety and environmental regulations, and may use their political and financial influence to extend their operations beyond their existing legal remits. Clearly this raises vital questions of local political autonomy and the fair division of the benefits and burdens of enterprise.

Those who see globalization in more positive terms tend to downplay these changes, and argue that multinationals are often able to influence, for example, human rights policy in host countries, and may also be better employers than local industries, offering higher wages and longer paid leave. Defenders of globalization emphasize the benefits of worldwide political and economic integration, and the free movement of people, capital and goods. This leads to increased choice and, it is claimed, improved life prospects for all. However, critics see this as a self-serving argument, designed to justify the enrichment of a tiny minority at the expense of the peoples of less developed nations.

Restricting free trade and the free movement of capital and investment in favour of protecting local industries against competition might be one solution to the perceived problems of globalization. However, it is not a straightforward answer. Such protectionism will certainly be to the advantage of local industries and their employees in the less-developed world. But on the other hand, these populations are consumers as well as producers, and restricting global free trade will restrict their access to a wider range of goods that may be lower priced or of higher quality, or both. It might be argued that it is unjust to impose such restrictions on developing populations. Interestingly, those on both sides of the debate claim to be arguing in favour of the well-being of poorer economies. On the surface, at least, the dispute concerns only the best means of improving their lot.

> “ *Commerce is the grand panacea which … will serve to inoculate with the healthy and saving taste for civilization all the nations of the world.* ”
>
> Richard Cobden, *England, Ireland, America*

War

War has caused some of the greatest suffering known in human history. Even so, many philosophers have argued that there may be times when a nation can morally justify going to war – or indeed when it cannot justify not going to war.

When is it right to go to war? And what limits are there on action in pursuit of victory? Of the many moral questions about war these are the ones most discussed by philosophers. In an effort to answer these questions, Augustine (see pp. 116–117) and Thomas Aquinas (see p.112) both developed ideas of the "just war", the first condition of which is that there must be a "just cause".

One obvious example of a just cause is the right of self-defence, and this may involve not just an effort to repel invaders but also an attack on the territory of the invading power. Furthermore, if a country has a treaty with another to provide mutual support in case of invasion or attack, obligations under such a treaty may sometimes require it to join in a war, however reluctantly. We are already on more difficult ground here, for one could ask whether any country might legitimately enter such an agreement with another. Can it be morally right to commit one country to war against another that has not wronged it?

Another contentious area is whether an appeal to self-defence can ever be made to justify a "pre-emptive strike" against a country that is presumed to have hostile intentions, in order to destroy its military capability. If we accept that a right to self-defence exists, then it seems plausible that, at least in some cases, it can justify pre-emptive action. However, without unequivocal evidence that the country against which such a strike is launched is actively planning an attack or invasion, appeals to the principle will be very dubious.

Perhaps the most difficult question is whether one country may legitimately invade another simply in order to remove its leadership, when there is no threat to other countries. If the target country is a democracy, with a system that allows the people to remove their leaders if they wish, then it is hard to see how an invasion could ever be justified. The moral situation may be different if the regime is autocratic, brutal and oppressive. If there is clear evidence that the majority of the population would welcome such intervention, and that peaceful measures either are not available or have failed, then it seems possible that military intervention by a foreign power can be justified, or even morally required. The situation can be compared to that of assisting a stranger who is being attacked by another. But finding compelling evidence to support the "rescue" of an entire nation is fraught with difficulty – how can people be induced to express their opposition to a regime that brutally suppresses dissent? A failed attempt at "regime

Liberal democracy and peace

The eminent US political scientist Michael Doyle observed in 1983 that although liberal democracies have often gone to war, there has never been a war between two well-established liberal democracies. In this context a liberal democracy is defined as a country that has some sort of representative democracy, constitutional protection of rights and liberties and private property. Why should countries like these not wage war against one another? Perhaps the culture of tolerance and compromise in a liberal democracy means that there is a general will to resolve disputes by negotiation rather than by brute force. However, there is no universally accepted explanation and, accordingly, it is not obvious what attitude will prevail in the future. With the establishment of more and more democracies in the world, we do not know whether this will lead to an increasingly peaceful world or simply to an eventual empirical refutation of the theory of the liberal peace.

Even with the latest missile-guidance systems, the bombardment of Baghdad in 2003 killed many civilians. The Thomas Aquinas doctrine of "double effect" legitimizes deaths such as these, because despite having been foreseen, they were not intended.

change" – to use the term coined in relation to the US-led invasion of Iraq in 2003 – can make things far worse for a population than they were before. So the cases to which such conditions apply may be very rare.

Even if one has a just cause for war, it does not follow that everything is permitted in pursuit of that cause. According to just war theory, one's actions in a war must be proportionate to its aims. Since the Second World War, acts that violate this proportionality principle have been punished as war crimes. Examples of war crimes include deliberately targeting non-combatants, especially women and children, and the severe mistreatment of prisoners of war.

While it is generally accepted that it is wrong to target civilians, there are cases in which meeting legitimate military aims will inevitably, or very probably, lead to the deaths of some civilians, for example those living near a strategic target. Does this mean that it is wrong to attack such a target? Here some have appealed to the doctrine of "double effect", first formulated by Thomas Aquinas: as long as civilian deaths are not intended, and one's military aims are legitimate, it is excusable to act in a way that will predictably lead to such deaths as a side-effect. However, this is a very controversial claim, for surely such unintended side-effects could be catastrophic, and it is hard to accept that blame is avoided if these known effects, though not intended, were foreseen. Indeed the distinction between what is intended and what is simply foreseen, particularly in the mind of a person who orders a bombing raid or pulls a trigger, can be hard if not impossible to draw.

> *We do not seek peace in order to be at war, but we go to war that we may have peace. Be peaceful, therefore, in warring, so that you may vanquish those whom you war against, and bring them to the prosperity of peace.*
>
> Augustine, cited by Thomas Aquinas in *Summa Theologica*

Bibliography

GENERAL WORKS

Blackburn, S. *Think*. Oxford: Oxford University Press, 1999.

Blackburn, S. *Being Good*. Oxford: Oxford University Press, 2003.

Nagel, T. *What Does It All Mean?* Oxford: Oxford University Press, 1989.

Russell, B. *The Problems of Philosophy*. Oxford: Oxford University Press, 1980.

Scruton, R. *Modern Philosophy: An Introduction and Survey*. London: Sinclair Stevenson, 1994; New York: Allen Lane, 1995.

WORLD

Barnes, J. *Aristotle: A Very Short Introduction*. Oxford: Oxford University Press, 2000.

Berkeley, G. *Principles of Human Knowledge and Three Dialogues*. Edited by Robinson, H. Oxford: Oxford University Press, 1999.

Blackburn, S. and Simmons, K. (Eds.) *Truth*. Oxford: Oxford University Press, 1999.

Ernest, S. and Tooley, M. (Eds.) *Causation*. Oxford: Oxford University Press, 1993.

Hart, W.D. (Ed.) *The Philosophy of Mathematics*. Oxford: Oxford University Press, 1996.

Hume, D. *Enquiries Concerning Human Understanding and Concerning the Principles of Morals* [1751]. (3rd edition.) Selby-Bigge, L.A. and Nidditch, P.H. (Eds.) Oxford: Oxford University Press, 1975.

Le Poidevin, R. *Travels in Four Dimensions: The Enigmas of Space and Time*. Oxford: Oxford University Press, 2003.

Leibniz, G.W. *Philosophical Texts*. Translated and edited by Francks, R. and Woolhouse, R.S. Oxford: Oxford University Press, 1998.

Lowe, E.J. *A Survey of Metaphysics*. Oxford: Oxford University Press 2000.

Moore, A.W. *The Infinite*. (2nd edition.) London: Routledge, 2001.

Moran, D. *An Introduction to Phenomenology*. London: Routledge, 2000.

Penrose, R. *The Emperor's New Mind*. Oxford: Oxford University Press, 1999.

Singer, P. *Hegel: A Very Short Introduction*. Oxford: Oxford University Press, 2001.

MIND AND BODY

Chalmers, D.J. (Ed.) *Philosophy of Mind: Classic and Contemporary Readings*. New York: Oxford University Press, 2002.

Davidson, D. "Thought and Talk" in *Mind and Language* by Guttenplan, S. (Ed.) Oxford: Clarendon Press, 1975.

Dennett, D.C. *Elbow Room: The Varieties of Free Will Worth Wanting*. Cambridge, Massachusetts: MIT Press, 1984.

Descartes, R. *Meditations on First Philosophy* (1641), in *Descartes: Selected Philosophical Writings* (pp. 74–122). Cottingham, J., Fodor. J.A. *The Language of Thought*. Sussex: Harvester Press, 1976.

Foucault, M. *Madness and Civilization: A History of Insanity in the Age of Reason*. Translated by Howard, R. New York: Pantheon, 1965.

Frege, G. *On Sense and Reference* [1892] in *Translations from the Philosophical Writings of Gottlob Frege* (pp. 56-78). Geach, P. and Black, M. (Eds.). Oxford: Basil Blackwell, 1960.

Grice, H.P. "Meaning" in *Philosophical Review*, 66, (1957), pp.377–388.

Hume, D. *A Treatise of Human Nature* [1740] Selby-Bigge, L.A. and Nidditch, P.H. (Eds.). Oxford: Oxford University Press, 1978.

Jackson, F. "Epiphenomenal Qualia" in *Philosophical Quarterly*, 32, (1982), pp.127–136.

James, W. "What is an Emotion?" (1884) reprinted in *Mind*, 9, pp.188–205.

Locke, J. *An Essay Concerning Human Understanding* [1690].

Lycan, W. C. *Philosophy of Language: A Contemporary Introduction*. London: Routledge, 1999.

Martinich, A.P. (Ed.) *The Philosophy of Language*. New York: Oxford University Press, 1996.

Nidditch, P.H. (Ed.) Oxford: Clarendon Press, 1989.

Nagel, T. "What is it Like to be a Bat?" in *Philosophical Review*, 4, (1974), pp.435–450.

Parfit, D. *Reasons and Persons*. Oxford: Oxford University Press, 1984.

Putnam, H. "The Meaning of 'Meaning'" in *Language, Mind, and Knowledge* (pp. 131-193). Gunderson, S.K. (Ed.). Minneapolis: University of Minnesota Press, 1975.

Searle, J.R. "Minds, Brains and Programs" in *Behavioral and Brain Sciences*, 3, (1980), pp.417–57.

Smart, J.J.C. (1959). "Sensations and Brain Processes" in *Philosophical Review*, 68, (1959), pp.141–156.

Solomon, R. "Emotions and Choice" in *Explaining the Emotions*. A. Rorty (Ed.). Berkeley: University of California Press, 1980.

Spinoza, B. *Ethics* [1677]. Parkinson, G.H.R. (Ed.). Oxford: Oxford University Press, 2000.

Stoothoff, R. & D. Murdoch, D. (Eds.) Cambridge: Cambridge University Press, 1988.

Wakefield, J.C. "The Concept of Mental Disorder: On the Boundary between Biological and Social Values" in *American Psychologist*, 47, (1992), pp.373–388.

Wittgenstein, L. *Philosophical Investigations*. New York: Macmillan, 1953.

KNOWLEDGE

Chernaik, C. *Minimal Rationality*. Cambridge, Massachusetts: MIT Press, 1989.

Dancy, J. *An Introduction to Contemporary Epistemology*. Oxford: Blackwell, 1985.

Gibson, R. *The Philosophy of W.V. Quine*. Gainesville, Florida: University Presses of Florida, 1984.

Greco, G. and Sosa, E. (Eds.) *The Blackwell Guide to Epistemology*. Oxford: Blackwell, 1999.

Harman, G. *Reasoning, Meaning, and Mind*. Oxford: Oxford University Press, 1999.

Howson, C. and Urbach, P. *Scientific Reasoning: The Bayesian Approach*. La Salle, Illinois: Open Court, 1989.

Kitcher, P. *The Advancement of Science*. New York and Oxford: Oxford University Press, 1993.

Lowe, E.J. *Locke on Human Understanding*. London: Routledge, 1995.

Millar, A. *Reasons and Experience*. Oxford: Oxford University Press, 1991.

Morton, A. *A Guide through the Theory of Knowledge*. (Third edition.) Oxford: Blackwell, 2002.

Quine, W.V. and Ullian, J. *The Web of Belief*. New York: Random House, 1978.

Rowe, C. *Plato*. London: Palgrave MacMillan, 1984.

Schwartz, R. *Vision*. Oxford: Blackwell, 1994.

Shope, R.K. *The Analysis of Knowing*. Princeton, New Jersey: Princeton University Press, 1983.

Skyrms, B. *Choice and Chance*. (3rd edition.) Belmont, California: Wadsworth, 1986.

Stein, E. *Without Good Reason*. New York: Oxford University Press, 1996.

Unger, P. *Ignorance: a case for scepticism*. Oxford: Oxford University Press, 1975.

Zagzebski, L. *Virtues of the Mind*. Cambridge: Cambridge University Press, 1996.

FAITH

Anselm, *Proslogion* [1077] excerpted in Cottingham, J. (Ed.) *Western Philosophy*. Part 5. Oxford: Blackwell, 1996.

Aquinas, T. *Selected Writings*. McInery, R. (Ed.) Harmondsworth: Penguin, 1998.

Augustine of Hippo. *Confessions*. Translated by Pusey, E.B. London: Dent, 1953.

Cottingham, J. *On the Meaning of Life*. London: Routledge, 2003.

Davies, B. *Philosophy of Religion: a guide and anthology*. Oxford: Oxford University Press, 2000.

Hick, J. *Evil and the God of Love*. London: Macmillan, 1977.

Hume, D. *Dialogues Concerning Natural Religion* [written *c*.1755, published 1779]. New York: Haffner, 1966.

Kierkegaard, S. *Concluding Unscientific Postscript* [1846]. Translated by Swensen, D.F. Princeton, New Jersey: Princeton University Press, 1941.

Le Poidevin, R. *Arguing for Atheism*. London: Routledge, 1996.

Mackie, J.L. *The Miracle of Theism*. Oxford: Oxford University Press, 1982.

Paley, W. *Natural Theology* [1802] in Rowe and Wainwright, 1973.

Palmer, M. *The Question of God*. London: Routledge, 2001.

Pascal, B. *Pensées* [c. 1660]. Krailsheimer, A.J. (Ed.) Harmondsworth: Penguin, 1966.

Peterson, M., et. al. *Reason and Religious Belief.* Oxford: Oxford University Press, 1998.

Plantinga, A. and Walterstoff, N. *Faith and Rationality*. Illinois: University of Notre Dame Press, 1983.

Quinn, P.L. and Taliaferro, C. *A Companion to the Philosophy of Religion*. Oxford: Blackwell, 1997.

Rowe, W. and Wainwright, W. *Philosophy of Religion: Selected Readings*. New York: Harcourt Brace Jovanovich, 1973.

Smart, J.J.C. and Haldane, J. *Atheism and Theism*. Oxford: Blackwell, 1996.

Taliaferro, C. *Contemporary Philosophy of Religion*. Oxford: Blackwell, 1998.

Voltaire. *Philosophical Dictionary* [1764]. Harmondsworth: Penguin, 1972.

Voltaire. *Candide* [1759]. Harmondsworth: Penguin, 1979.

Wittgenstein, L. *Culture and Value*. Oxford: Blackwell, 1980.

ETHICS AND AESTHETICS

Aristotle. *Ethics*. Translated by Thomson, J.A.K. Harmondsworth: Penguin, 1976.

Almond, B. *Exploring Ethics: a traveller's tale*. Oxford: Blackwell, 1998.

Bentham, J. *Introduction to Principles of Moral and Legislation* [1789]. London: Athlone Press, 1970.

Dworkin, R. *Life's Dominion: an argument about abortion and euthanasia*. London: HarperCollins, 1995.

Finnis, J. *Natural Law and Natural Rights*. Oxford, Clarendon Press, 1980.

Hare, R.M. *Moral Thinking: its levels, methods and point*. Oxford: Oxford University Press, 1981.

Hume, D. *Enquiries Concerning Human Understanding and Concerning the Principles of Morals* [1751]. (3rd edition.) Selby-Bigge, L.A. and Nidditch, P.H. (Eds.) Oxford: Oxford University Press, 1975.

Kant, I. *The Moral Law* [originally *Groundwork of the Metaphysic of Morals*] H. Paton, H. (Ed.) London: Hutchinson, 1948.

MacIntyre, A. *A Short History of Ethics*. New York: Macmillan, 1966.

MacIntyre, A. *After Virtue*. London: Duckworth, 1981.

Mill, J.S. *On Liberty and Other Essays*. Gray, J. (Ed.) Oxford: Oxford University Press, 1991.

Nietzsche, F. *On the Genealogy of Morals* [1887]. Translated by Kaufman, W. and Hollingdale, R.J. New York: Vintage Books, 1969.

Nietzsche, F. *Beyond Good and Evil*. Translated by Hollingdale, R.J. Harmondsworth: Penguin, 1971.

Norman, R. *The Moral Philosophers: an introduction to ethics*. Oxford: Oxford University Press, 1983.

Nussbaum, M. *The Fragility of Goodness: luck and ethics in Greek Tragedy and Philosophy*. Cambridge: Cambridge University Press, 1986.

Plato. *Republic*. Translated by Lee, D. (2nd edition.) Harmondsworth: Penguin, 1974.

Rawls, J. *A Theory of Justice*. Oxford: Oxford University Press, 1971.

Sartre. J.-P. *Existentialism is a Humanism*. Translated by Mairet, P. London: Methuen, 1948.

Singer, P. *Animal Liberation*. (2nd edition.) New York: Random House, 1990.

Singer, P. *Practical Ethics*. (2nd edition.) Cambridge: Cambridge University Press, 1993.

Smart, J.J.C. and Williams, B. *Utilitarianism: for and against*. Cambridge, Cambridge University Press, 1973.

Walzer, M. *Just and Unjust Wars*. Harmondsworth: Penguin, 1987.

Williams, B. *Ethics and the Limits of Philosophy*. Cambridge, Massachusetts: Harvard University Press, 1985.

SOCIETY

Aristotle. *The Politics*. Everson, S. (Ed.) Cambridge: Cambridge University Press, 1996.

Bentham, J. *Introduction to the Principles of Morals and Legislation*. London: Methuen, 1982.

Berlin, I. *Liberty*. (2nd edition.) Oxford: Oxford University Press, 2002.

Burke, E. *Reflections on the Revolution in France* [1790]. London: Penguin, 1968.

Cohen, G.A. *Self-Ownership, Freedom, and Equality*. Cambridge: Cambridge University Press, 1995.

Dworkin, R. *Sovereign Virtue*. Cambridge Massachussets: Harvard University Press, 2000.

Hampsher-Monk, I. *A History of Modern Political Thought*. Oxford: Blackwell, 1992.

Hayek, F. von. *Law, Legislation and Liberty*. London: Routledge and Kegan Paul, 1982.

Hegel, G.W.F. *The Philosophy of Right*. Knox, T.M. (Ed.) Oxford: Clarendon Press, 1952.

Hobbes, T. *Leviathan* [date]. MacPherson, C.B. (Ed.) London: Penguin, 1968.

Hume, D. *A Treatise of Human Nature* [Book III, 1740]. (2nd edition.) Selby-Bigge, L.A. and Nidditch, P.H. (Eds.). Oxford: Oxford University Press, 1978.

Kymlicka, W. *Contemporary Political Philosophy: An Introduction*. Oxford: Oxford University Press, 1990.

Locke, J. *Two Treatises of Government* [1690]. Laslett, P. (Ed.) Cambridge: Cambridge University Press, 1988.

Marx, K. *Selected Works*. McLellan, D. (Ed.) (2nd edition.) Oxford: Oxford University Press, 2000.

Mill, J.S. *Utilitarianism and Other Writings*. Warnock, M. (Ed.) Glasgow: Collins, 1962.

Nozick, R. *Anarchy, State, and Utopia*. Oxford: Blackwell, 1974.

Rawls, J. A Theory of Justice. (Revised edition.) Oxford: Oxford University Press, 1999.

Rosen, M. and Wolff, J. (Eds.) *Political Thought*. Oxford: Oxford University Press, 1999.

Rousseau, J-J. *The Social Contract and Discourses* [1762]. Cole, G.D.H., Brumfitt, J.H., and Hall, J.C. (Eds.) London: Everyman, 1973.

Wolff, J. *An Introduction to Political Philosophy*. Oxford: Oxford University Press, 1996.

Index

Note: Page references to main text are in plain type, those to box text are in **bold**, and those to captions in *italics.*

A

B

C

D

Text Acknowledgments

The authors and publishers would like to thank the following for permission to reproduce their copyright material. Every care has been taken to trace copyright owners, but if we have omitted anyone we apologize and will, if informed, make corrections in any future edition.

Page 17: from "An argument for the Identity Theory" by David K. Lewis in *Journal of Philosophy* 63 (1966) 17–25, p.22; **22** from "On the notion of cause" in *Mysticism and Logic* by Bertrand Russell, Routledge, London, 1925; **32** from "The Origin of the Work of Art"in *Martin Heidegger: Basic Writings* (translated by David Farrell Krell), Routledge, London, 1977; **46** from *Philosophy and Scientific Realism* by J.J.C. Smart, Routledge, London, 1963; **52** from *The Language of Thought* by Jerry Fodor, 1976, reprinted by permission of Pearson Education Inc., Addison Wesley Longman, Glenview, Illinois; **54** from *Not Passion's Slave: Emotions and Choice* by Robert Solomon, Oxford University Press (OUP) Inc., New York, 2003; **59** from *Tractatus Logico-Philosophicus* by Ludwig Wittgenstein, Routledge, London, 1955; **60** from *Philosopical Investigations* by Ludwig Wittgenstein, Routledge, London, 1967; **64** from "Freedom and Necessity" in *Philosophical Essays* by A.J. Ayer, Macmillan, London, 1954; **69** from *The Myth of Mental Illness* by Thomas Szasz, HarperCollins, New York, 1974; **89** Reprinted by permission of the publisher from 'Two Dogmas of Empiricism" in *From a Logical Point of View: Nine Logico-Philosophical Essays* by Willard V. Quine, Cambridge, Massachusetts: Harvard University Press, Copyright © 1953, 1961, 1980 by the President and Fellows of Harvard College, renewed 1989 by W.V. Quine; **95** from *The Problems of Philosophy* by Bertrand Russell by permission of Oxford University Press, Oxford, 1912; **98** from *The Logic of Scientific Discovery by Karl Popper* [trustees]; **101** from *Autobiography* by Bertrand Russell, Routledge, London, 1967; **124** from *Encountering Evil: Live Options in Theodicy* by John H. Hick (ed. Stephen T. Davis), T & T Clark International, a Continuum imprint, 2002; **127** from *Candide* by Voltaire (translated by Roger Pearson), by permission of Oxford University Press, Oxford, 1998; **156** from *Existentialism and Humanism* by Jean-Paul Sartre (translated by Philip Mairet), Methuen, London, 1948; **159** from *The Sovereignty of Good* by Iris Murdoch, Routledge, London, 1970; **162** from *The Life of Reason* by George Santayana, by permission of Constable and Robinson, 1954; **164** from *Reproducing the Future* by Marilyn Strathern, by kind permission of the author; **168** from *The Question Concerning Technology* by Martin Heidegger, HarperCollins, New York, 1977; **169** from *A Sand County Almanac* by Aldo Leopold, OUP Inc., New York, 1949; **170** from *The Question Concerning Technology* by Martin Heidegger, HarperCollins, New York, 1977; **183** from *Anarchy, State and Utopia* by Robert Nozick, Blackwell, Oxford, 1982; **187** from *Man and Superman* by George Bernard Shaw, Society of Authors, London, on behalf of the Bernard Shaw Estate; **191** from *Equality* by R.H. Tawney, courtesy Pickering & Chatto, London, 1931; **203** Reprinted by permission of the publisher from *A Theory of Justice* by John Rawls, Cambridge, Massachusetts: The Belknap Press of Harvard University Press, Copyright © 1971, 1999 by the President and Fellows of Harvard College.

Picture Credits

The publishers would like to thank the following people and photographic libraries for permission to reproduce their material. Every care has been taken to trace copyright holders. However, if we have omitted anyone we apologize for this and will, if informed, make corrections in any future edition.

AA = Art Archive, London; AKG = AKG images, London; BAL = Bridgeman Art Library, London; SPL = Science Photo Library, London

1 BAL/Vatican Museums and Galleries, Vatican City; **2–3** Corbis/Roger Ressmeyer; **7** AA/Anagni Cathedral/Dagli Orti; **8–9** Corbis/Scott T Smith; **11** Corbis/Darrell Gulin; **13** BAL/Kunsthistorisches Museum, Vienna, Austria; **14** AKG/ Sammlungen des Stiftes, Klosterneuburg, Austria/Eric Lessing; **16t** SPL/Laguna Design; **16b** Corbis/Roger Ressmeyer; **18** AA/Musée des Beaux Arts Rouen/Dagli Orti; **19** Mary Evans Picture Library/ Captain Provand & Indra Shiva/ Harry Price Collection; **21** Corbis/Jose Fuste Raga; **23** BAL/ Wingfield Sporting Gallery, London; **24** BAL/National Gallery of Scotland, Edinburgh; **27** Getty/Image Bank/ Grant Faint; **29** BAL/Lauros/ Giraudon/Bibliothèque Nationale, Paris, France; **30** BAL/ Nationalgalerie, Berlin; **32** BAL/Private Collection/© ADAGP, Paris and DACS London 2004; **33** Corbis/Hulton-Deutsch Collection; **35** Getty/Stone/Matthias Clamer; **36** Corbis/Helen Norman; **37** National Maritime Museum, London; **38** BAL/ Niedersachsisches Landesmuseum, Hanover; **39** Corbis/ Clouds Hill Imaging Ltd; **40–41** SPL/Eckhard Slawik; **42–43** Corbis/ Massimo Mastrorillo; **45** SPL/Scott Camazine; **47** BAL/Yale Center for British Art, Paul Mellon Collection, USA; **48** Corbis/ Michael Nicholson; **49** AKG; **51** Corbis/ Randy Wells; **52** Steve Pyke; **53** NHPA/Stephen Dalton; **54** Corbis/José F Poblete; **57** Magnum/Cornell Capa; **59** AKG; **61** Corbis/Museum Narodowe, Poznan/Ali Meyer; **62** Eye Ubiquitous/Hutchison/ Jeremy Horner; **64** AKG/Austrian National Library, Vienna; **65** Robert Harding.com/Walter Rawlings; **66** AKG; **67** AA/Musée Fabre Montpellier/Dagli Orti; **68** Kobal Collection/20th Century Fox; **70** SPL/Dr Linda Stannard, UCT; **72–73** Corbis/Massimo Listri; **74** Corbis/Farrell Grehan; **76** AA/Museo Capitolino Rome/ Dagli Orti; **77** Corbis/Mimmo Jodice; **79** Corbis/Russell Underwood; **80** Photonica/Masato Kameya; **81** Photonica/ Masao Oto; **82t** Corbis/Michael Nicholson; **82b** Corbis/ Peter M Fisher; **85** Moviestore/Warner Bros; **86** Corbis/ Galen Rowell; **88** Corbis/ Bettmann; **89** Bernard Quine; **90** Corbis/Charles O'Rear; **94** Corbis/ David Keaton; **96** Corbis/ Bettmann; **97** Corbis/Archivo Iconografico, S.A; **98** SPL/ David Parker; **99** Corbis/Christie's Images, London; **100** Getty/Stone/Eddie Soloway; **101** Corbis/ Matthias Kulka; **103** BAL/Giraudon/Musée d'Orsay, Paris, France; **105** Corbis; **106–107** Getty/Image Bank/Michael Orton; **109** BAL/ British Library, London; **110** Corbis/John Miele; **111** Image DJ; **112** BAL/Museo di San Marco dell'Angelico, Florence; **113** AA/ Museo di Castelvecchio Verona/A Dagli Orti; **115** Corbis/Hulton-Deutsch Collection; **116t** AA/ Santa Maria delle Carceri Abbey Carceri/Dagli Orti; **116b** BAL/Giraudon/Bibliotheque Sainte-Genevieve, Paris; **118** Rex Features/SIPA; **119** AA/Château de Blois/Dagli Orti; **121** BAL/Giraudon/Private Collection; **122** Corbis/Sygma/ Fabian Cevallos; **124** Corbis/Jason Hawkes; **126** Corbis/Tom Wagner/SABA; **127** Corbis/Archivo Iconografico, SA; **128** Corbis/Bettmann; **129** AA/Galleria degli Uffizi Florence/ Dagli Orti; **130** Corbis/Annie Griffiths Belt; **131** AA/ Archaeological Museum Naples/Dagli Orti; **132–133** Corbis/ Gregor Schmid; **135** Getty/Image Bank/Jean de Boisberranger; **136** Corbis/Mug Shots; **138** Corbis/Archivo Iconografico, SA; **139** BAL/The Illustrated London News Picture Library, London; **140** Zefa/G Baden; **141** Corbis/Bettmann; **142** Corbis/Clouds Hill Imaging Ltd/David Spears; **143** BAL/ Trustees of the Watts Gallery, Compton, Surrey; **145** Corbis/ Wally McNamee; **146** Corbis/David Lees; **149** Corbis/Ray Juno; **151** Rex Features/ Universal; **152** BAL/Simon Carter Gallery, Woodbridge, Suffolk,; **153** Corbis/Bettmann; **154** Corbis/Sygma; **155** Magnum/Bruno Barbey; **156** Magnum/ Henri Cartier-Bresson; **157** Magnum/Guy Le Querrec; **159** BAL/Musée Condé, Chantilly; **160** BAL/Brooklyn Museum of Art, New York, USA; **162** BAL/Osterreichische Galerie, Vienna; **165** SPL/ZEPHYR; **167** Corbis/Bob Krist; **169** Corbis/Lester Lefkowitz; **170** Corbis/Yann Arthus-Bertrand; **172** Getty Images/Anthony Harvey; **173** Corbis/Hulton-Deutsch Collection; **175** Corbis/Gianni Dagli Orti; **176** Rex Features; **178–179** Corbis/Tom & Dee Ann McCarthy; **181** Corbis/Alan Schein Photography; **182** Corbis/Christopher J Morris; **184** Corbis/ Bettmann; **185** Corbis/Michael Nicholson; **187** Corbis/Paul A Souders; **188** Corbis/Archivo Iconografico, SA; **189** Corbis/ Christie's Images; **191** Corbis/Paul A Souders; **193** BAL/ Giraudon/Musées de la Ville de Paris, Musée Carnavalet, Paris; **195** Corbis/Gideon Mendel; **196** Magnum/Bruce Davidson; **197t** Mary Evans Picture Library; **197b** Mary Evans Picture Library; **198** Corbis/Terry W Eggers; **201** Corbis/Tom Wright; **203** Steve Pyke; **204** Corbis/Bettmann; **207** Corbis/Charles & Josette Lenars; **208** Corbis/Viviane Moos; **210** AA/Karl Marx Museum Trier /Dagli Orti; **213** Corbis/Steve Raymer; **215** Getty/Mirrorpix

---

Captions for illustrations on pages 1–3:
Page 1: Detail (of Plato and Aristotle) from the *School of Athens* by Raphael. Plato (left) points upwards with one hand and holds his book *Timaeus* in the other; Aristotle (right) holds a copy of his *Ethics*.
Pages 2–3: Supernova 1987A, in the large Magellanic Cloud near the Tarantula Nebula.